China's Belt and Road Power Transition

SUNY series, James N. Rosenau series in Global Politics

———————

David C. Earnest, editor

China's Belt and Road Power Transition
Preparations and Blowbacks

CHIEN-PENG CHUNG

Published by State University of New York Press, Albany

© 2025 State University of New York

All rights reserved

Printed in the United States of America

No part of this book may be used or reproduced in any manner whatsoever without written permission. No part of this book may be stored in a retrieval system or transmitted in any form or by any means including electronic, electrostatic, magnetic tape, mechanical, photocopying, recording, or otherwise without the prior permission in writing of the publisher.

Links to third-party websites are provided as a convenience and for informational purposes only. They do not constitute an endorsement or an approval of any of the products, services, or opinions of the organization, companies, or individuals. SUNY Press bears no responsibility for the accuracy, legality, or content of a URL, the external website, or for that of subsequent websites.

For information, contact State University of New York Press, Albany, NY
www.sunypress.edu

Library of Congress Cataloging-in-Publication Data

Name: Chung, Chien-Peng, author.
Title: China's Belt and Road power transition : preparations and blowbacks / Chien-peng (C.P.) Chung.
Description: Albany : State University of New York Press, [2025]. | Series: SUNY series, James N. Rosenau series in global politics | Includes bibliographical references and index.
Identifiers: LCCN 2024028665 | ISBN 9798855800920 (hardcover : alk. paper) | ISBN 9798855800944 (ebook)
Subjects: LCSH: Yi dai yi lu (Initiative : China) | China—Foreign economic relations. | China—Economic policy—2000– | International economic relations. | Geopolitics—Economic aspects—China.
Classification: LCC HF1604 .C49335 2025 | DDC 337.51—dc23/eng/20240923
LC record available at https://lccn.loc.gov/2024028665

I dedicate this book with profound gratitude to the late professors
Scott Eddie and David Martin Jones,
and other teachers and academic friends who have
over the years helped me in my career in one way or another.
You will never know how much I owe you.

Contents

List of Abbreviations		ix
Preface		xi
Introduction: The Greatest Roadshow on Earth		1
Chapter 1	Introducing China's Belt-and-Road Initiative	17
Chapter 2	The Silk Road Economic Belt: Bringing Together China's Eurasian Forums	43
Chapter 3	Reimagining the 21st Century Maritime Silk Road	71
Chapter 4	China's "Health Silk Road" Diplomacy	117
Chapter 5	China's Evolving Belt-and-Road Initiative	131
Chapter 6	Blowback to the Belt-and-Road Initiative Power Transition	153
Conclusion		163
Notes		169
References		171
Index		213

List of Abbreviations

21st Century Maritime Silk Road (MSR)

artificial intelligence (AI)

Asian Infrastructure Investment Bank (AIIB)

Association of Southeast Asian Nations (ASEAN)

Bangladesh-China-India-Myanmar (BCIM)

Belt-and-Road Initiative (BRI)

China-ASEAN Free Trade Area (CAFTA)

Comprehensive and Progressive Trans-Pacific Partnership (CPTPP)

Conference on Interaction and Confidence Building in Asia (CICA)

China–Pakistan Economic Corridor (CPEC)

Chinese Communist Party (CCP)

East Asia Summit (EAS)

exclusive economic zone (EEZ)

Export-Import Bank of China (Exim Bank)

fifth-generation (5G)

global financial crisis (GFC)

information and communications technology (ICT)

information technology (IT)

x | List of Abbreviations

nongovernmental organization (NGO)

People's Liberation Army (PLA)

People's Liberation Army Navy (PLAN)

People's Republic of China (PRC)

Regional Comprehensive Economic Partnership (RCEP)

Silk Road Economic Belt (SREB)

Trans-Pacific Partnership (TPP)

United Arab Emirates (UAE)

World Trade Organization (WTO)

Preface

The Belt-and-Road Initiative (BRI) serves as the most important instrument for China to create an alternative global economic and geopolitical order to the one currently dominated by the United States, and the successful execution of this global infrastructure development strategy would position China to succeed the US as the prime mover of world events in a "power transition." With the BRI, China is trying to guarantee itself a central role in the international supply chain, advance Chinese priorities and alignment in targeted countries according to its long-term strategic interests, and redefine existing rules of international economics and politics for global governance. By creating a new Sino-centric network of economic, financial, political, and strategic relations worldwide, the Chinese Communist Party leadership under Xi Jinping has made the BRI the primary medium for China to build enough worldwide influence among foreign countries and regional organizations to challenge the US for the top position in the international hierarchy of states. However, the BRI is itself the culmination of a sequence of economic and geostrategic events and chain reactions that dates back to the start of the global financial crisis and resultant great recession beginning in 2008.

Formulated in 2013 as part of China's "national rejuvenation" of the golden age of the ancient Silk Road, the BRI consisted primarily of a land-based Silk Road Economic Belt (SREB) and an oceangoing Maritime Silk Road (MSR). While the SREB links Central Asia, Russia, and Europe by land with China's western hinterland across Eurasia, the MSR connects China's coast with Southeast Asia, South Asia, East Africa, and the Mediterranean Sea. Bridging the SREB and MSR is the China–Pakistan Economic Corridor, which extends from China's northwestern Xinjiang region to the port of Gwadar on Pakistan's Indian Ocean coast. The BRI's financing arm is the China-backed Asian Infrastructure Investment Bank, but its projects are also heavily funded by loans from Chinese state-owned policy banks such as the China Development Bank and China Export-Import Bank. The BRI's geographical scale has since expanded to include more than 140 countries, incorporating many in Africa, the Middle East, South Pacific, and Latin America. The ambitions of the Xi leadership have seen the BRI further extended with the introduction of a Health Silk Road (for the provision and joint development of medical supplies and COVID-19 vaccines), Digital Silk Road (for connecting the world's internet through fiber-optic cables and upgrading big data technology for monitoring people), and a Polar Silk Road (for developing arctic shipping routes and offshore arctic fossil fuel and mineral mining). Although the BRI is multilateral in form, "Belt-and-Road" agreements are negotiated bilaterally between China and the countries concerned, which usually work in Beijing's favor as the stronger economic party.

The Chinese leadership believes that the funds, construction projects, and promises offered by the BRI will generate widespread beliefs in the inexorability, legitimacy, and therefore acceptability of a Chinese international order, at least among the elites of recipient states, especially if the rule of law, public accountability, awarding contracts without competitive bidding, and control of corruption are not insisted upon as conditionalities for Chinese loans or investments. Given time, a steady purpose, and consistent efforts, Beijing could, by means of the BRI, reorient global trade networks, set technical standards that would disadvantage non-Chinese companies, increase its political influence over countries by providing an authoritarian state-capitalist development model as an alternative to Western liberal democratic capitalism, and acquire power projection capabilities for its military through high-technology imports. However, India, Australia, and Japan have stayed away from the initiative, and the US has as well, since the Trump presidency and several large Western economies have been raising barriers to trade, investment, and technology transfer with China that had provided the funds and know-how for Chinese companies to invest in their many large projects abroad. China's COVID-19 lockdowns, its friendship with Russia in the war with Ukraine, and Xi's desire to assert comprehensive control over his country's economy have been driving foreign investors away from China. Some foreign governments have restricted or banned Chinese 5G (fifth-generation) infrastructure and equipment for fear that the Chinese government could gather intelligence and information from them.

China leaves many of its BRI partners open to massive debt and unfavorable domestic popular responses, which would ultimately hurt the pockets of the Chinese companies involved and the reputation of the Chinese government. The BRI is also up against new rival investment development schemes such as the US' Build Back Better World and the G7's Partnership for Global Infrastructure and Investment. As a strategic pushback, warships from Western countries have been sailing through the contested China Seas. China under Xi, in weaving together a BRI for the purpose of creating and augmenting a bloc of states aligned or beholden to it, might have overplayed its hand and invited a Western backlash. The power transition theory in international relations is littered with examples of unsuccessful challenges against the predominant state for world leadership, and this could be one of them.

Introduction

The Greatest Roadshow on Earth

In an interview, Lee Kuan Yew, the first prime minister of Singapore, was reported as saying, "It is China's intention to be the greatest power in the world. . . . At the core of (Chinese) mind-set is their world before colonization and the exploitation and humiliation that brought. . . . The Chinese . . . want a revived China, (and) their great advantage is . . . their economic influence" (Allison, Blackwell, and Wyne 2013, xxvii, 3, 14–16). If indeed the goal is to revive China to the time before "colonization" when it was arguably the greatest power on earth, then the worldwide influence of the Belt-and-Road Initiative (BRI) could be the path to achieving this. The BRI certainly has the potential to serve as a vehicle for the leadership of the People's Republic of China (PRC) and its ruling Chinese Communist Party (CCP) to create a new alternative global economic and geopolitical order to the one currently dominated by the US and the West. With the execution of the BRI, the Chinese leadership is placing China in good stead to succeed the US as the prime mover of world events. Failing that, it would still confer upon China an effective veto on US international actions such that the US will have to take China's views and interests into account when making its decisions. In other words, China is getting itself ready for a power transition, which is a theoretical proposition that portends a dissatisfied challenger preparing to overtake a declining satisfied hegemon, as it rises to near parity in economic, military, and technological strength to the hegemon, through peaceful means or otherwise, thus enabling the challenger to become the new preeminent world power (Organski and Kugler, 1980). Indeed, the US National Security Strategy report, released on October 12, 2022, by President Biden's administration, recognizes that the PRC is the

2 | China's Belt and Road Power Transition

US' only competitor with both the intent to reshape the international order and the economic, diplomatic, military, and technological power to do it (NSS 2022, 23). In December 2023 Nicholas Burns, the US ambassador to China, referred to China as his country's "systemic rival" (Delaney 2023). This book will argue that the BRI is the primary medium for China to build enough worldwide influence among foreign countries and regional organizations to replace the US in the top position of the international hierarchy of states and preeminent writer of their rules of interaction.

Purpose of the Study

This study makes two important contributions to the existing body of research on China's foreign economic relations: (1) it provides a comprehensive treatment of not just world geographical continent and maritime regions but also functional aspects of the BRI endeavor such as the Health Silk Road, Digital Silk Road, and Polar Silk Road, and (2) it explores in detail Beijing's motives, policy goals, and strategies to put in motion a "power transition" by demonstrating that the BRI is more than just a good idea or a worldwide infrastructure development endeavor for China and the targeted countries; it is a means to reorganize the international political, economic, and security order currently led by the US. At the very least, with the BRI as a breakout measure, China's leader Xi Jinping is indicating to his own compatriots and the world that he does not want his actions or that of his country's to be constrained.

In China's own neighborhood of Asia, according to a 2023 survey by Australia's Lowy Institute, the US in is the number one position, ahead of China in position number two (80.7 percent vs. 72.5 percent), in terms of comprehensive power, defined as the capacity of a state to direct or influence the behavior of other states, non-state actors, and the course of international events, which comprises eight measurements: economic capability, military capability, resilience, future resources, economic relationships, defense networks, diplomatic influence, and cultural influence. The only measure that the US lags behind China is economic relationships (63.7 percent vs. 98.3 percent), with China trailing far behind the US in terms of defense networks (23.7 percent vs. 84.6 percent), although the gaps are much less in other measurements. This measurement of economic relationships is an indicator of the success, at least partially, of China's BRI.

Power transition theory provides a compelling argument on what drives leaders to achieve preeminence for their states. The power transition framework differentiates between "powerful and satisfied" and "powerful and dissatisfied" states. The satisfied states are those that designed the "rules of the game" after the last major war, while dissatisfied states are newcomers and "challengers" that "seek to upset the existing international order and establish a new order in its place" (Organski 1968, 361, 366). The argument goes that once a more or less symmetric power relationship is reached between the dominant power and the rising dissatisfied challenger, a hegemonic war may occur. However, it is not an inevitable consequence of increasing capabilities, for the significant "motivation driving decisions for war is relative satisfaction with the global or regional hierarchy" (Abdollohian et al. 2000, 9).

The concept of a power transition holds value by calling attention to both the hierarchy of capabilities and the hierarchy of prestige, which is a synonym for status or reputation. Status consists of collective beliefs about a state's standing in the international community, based on attributes such as "military power, economic development, cultural achievements, diplomatic skill, and technological innovation," and is recognized by voluntary deference from others (Larson and Shevchenko 2019, 3). Status is important because high-status states enjoy certain rights and responsibilities that low-status states respect. According to Larson and Shevchenko, "Great power status carries with it the expectation that the state will be consulted on important issues" (233–34), and they maintain that it is the pursuit of status, more than wealth or power, that drives the foreign policy choices of China and Russia (14–16). However, Murray emphasizes that a state cannot "simply assert its social status . . . only when recognized does it assume the authority it needs to secure the identity it seeks" (46).

Several power transition theorists have identified status inconsistency as a major source of dissatisfaction in times of power transition (for an overview, see Maoz 2010, 225). As one state's position in the power hierarchy does not necessarily correspond to its position in the prestige hierarchy, it is this notion of a mismatch between power and prestige that is at the core of power transition. As the rising power increases its power, it generates a mismatch because the prestige hierarchy still favors the dominant power, but the possibilities are also growing for the rising power to institutionalize its leadership status. It is when the rising power views the international order as prohibitive to the realization of its status aspiration that it becomes dissatisfied. Michelle Murray (2019) contends that the failure to recognize a rising power's status claims is the primary cause of spiraling competition and conflict during power transitions (14–17). When an established power denies a rising power the status that it believes it deserves, this is "experienced by the rising power as disrespect," which then responds to perceived humiliation by engaging in "forceful contestation with the established power" (73–74). However, by "compelling the recognition" it desires, the rising power may cause the dominant power to take actions to prevent the challenger's ascent (Onea 2014). Policies of "status accommodation" may ameliorate or avoid conflict, but states at the top of status hierarchies are often reluctant to sacrifice their privileged positions (Larson, Welch, and Shevchenko 2019, 250; Murray 2019, 202).

China's Xi leadership promotes the BRI not just to strengthen China's comprehensive power but also to increase its prestige in the international order. As both power and prestige expand to raise China's influence on the world stage, this could in turn bolster Xi's domestic political standing to keep the party and country under his firm control. This study argues that pushing the BRI as a global infrastructure development strategy to guarantee China a central role in the international supply chain would create a Sino-centric network of economic, financial, political, and strategic relations with foreign countries that would enable China to accumulate enough influence worldwide to challenge the US for the top position in the international hierarchy of states. In need of economic and technological development funds, the Global South and poorer countries of Europe have been a natural constituency for efforts to promote Chinese global leadership, but the COVID-19 pandemic not only disrupted global supply chains but also put many BRI-related infrastructure projects on hold. With China's pessimistic post-COVID economic recovery, lending for the BRI has tightened, as rising government debt from 2.1 percent of GDP in 2013 to 6.1 percent in 2021 has hindered China's ability to finance large-scale infrastructure projects under the BRI (Wu 2023). Furthermore, with China's ongoing technology conflict with the US and the West, and a full-scale war between Russia and Ukraine, this study contends that the BRI as Beijing's primary power transition instrument has been experiencing unintended adverse results and a serious, if not fatal, blowback.

Motives of the Belt-and-Road Initiative

If the BRI is the pathway to global dominance for China, then the convoy in front, led by the US, must give way. However, the current power distribution is such that China cannot yet rise to world leadership status by itself, as much as PRC president-cum-CCP secretary general Xi Jinping would like that as his political and foreign policy legacy. China's leadership has to increase its hard power capacities first by creating a new Sino-centric network of economic, financial, political, and security relations worldwide through a strategy of coordinating blueprints with economic, financial, technological, maritime, and military dimensions. It should be pointed out that although the theory asserts that power transition increases the likelihood of conflict or war between great powers, it is not inevitable (Organski 1968) if they can successfully divide division of spheres of interest or influence. In any case, it behooves a rising power with a large territorial and demographic size not just to be as powerful as it can be but also to have many friends and allies to recognize it as their leader and contribute to its economic growth through trade, investment, provision of raw materials. It also needs allies to help confront or outflank the resident preeminent world power whose dominance of world affairs is not to the challenger's liking, or to prevent a preemptive attack by the hegemon to destroy the putative challenger.[1]

Accordingly, the BRI is Beijing's most important geopolitical and economic instrument to advance the internationalization of Chinese priorities and to redefine existing rules of international economics and politics for global governance. As such, although the BRI cannot be just a commercial program, economic power and growth must be its motivator since the primary driving force of power transition is differential material growth rates among great powers. Hence, the BRI is first and foremost an economic concern. By launching the BRI, China is trying to guarantee itself a central role in international goods, services, and raw material transactions. Since then, the geographic scale of China's BRI has expanded far beyond its original Eurasian and Asian Maritime Silk Road connections to include more than 140 countries in Africa, the Middle East, and Latin America. At the same time, the BRI's ambitions have also been extended with the introduction of a Digital Silk Road (for connecting the world's internet through fiber-optic cables and upgrading technology for monitoring human movements), a Polar Silk Road (for developing arctic shipping routes and offshore arctic fossil fuel and mineral mining), and a Health Silk Road (for the provision and joint development of medical supplies and vaccines).

The BRI is marketed as a global finance and investment dispensation exercise by China, but it is much more than an international development strategy. The initiative is where the official promotion of Chinese national pride under Xi's "new era" couples with the belief that globalization or cross-border movement of factors of production with no or minimum impediment will lead to overall gains for countries and individuals. This marriage of nationalism and globalism is not coincidental, for the ruling Chinese Communist regime has done well under both since the end of the Cold War. Unfortunately for China, globalism has been on the retreat since the beginning of the US-China trade and technology dispute, the worldwide spread of COVID-19, China's friendship with Russia in the Russo-Ukrainian war, and Xi's desire to assert comprehensive control over his country's economy, all of which have been driving away foreign investors. Contrary to expectations, inflationary pressures in the US have not led to any significant measures to drop or lower tariffs against Chinese imports, while the global economic contraction has accelerated the reckoning by some developing countries with BRI-related debts.

Still, China's strategic thinking is oriented toward long-term and intergenerational perspectives. Given time, a steady purpose, and consistent effort, by means of the BRI, Beijing could reorient global trade networks, set technical standards that would disadvantage non-Chinese companies, increase its political influence over countries, and acquire power projection capabilities for its military through civilian-military dual-use high-technology imports. The Achilles' heel in this vast enterprise, which requires funds and know-how from Chinese companies to invest in its many large projects, is that the US and several large Western economies have been raising barriers to trade, investment, and technology transfer with China, from which China has been profiting.

The US, Japan, and some Western countries may look askance at the perceived autocratic, nationalistic, or self-aggrandizing nature of China's Xi leadership. Do countries involved in the BRI view the initiative as a positive Chinese program that brings significant benefits, either political or economic? This query is misplaced. The pertinent question to ask is rather, Has the governing regime of the recipient country used the BRI's funds, projects, and promises to advance its own domestic agenda of staying in power? If so, and the Chinese leadership must be cognizant of this, then BRI-related processes will generate shared beliefs in the inexorability, legitimacy, and therefore acceptability of a Chinese international order, at least among the elites of recipient states, especially if the rule of law and control of corruption are not conditions for Chinese loans or investments. However, by not emphasizing the need for improved governance structures, such as public accountability and control of corruption, China condemns many of its partners to massive debt and economic failure, which would in turn hurt the pockets of Chinese companies and lead to unfavorable responses from their domestic publics, impairing the reputation of the Chinese government.

Structure of the Belt-and-Road Initiative

The BRI, initially translated as "One Belt, One Road" and also known as *yidai yilu* in Chinese, is an international development strategy and framework proposed by the PRC and consists primarily of two components: the land-based Silk Road Economic Belt (SREB) and the oceangoing Maritime Silk Road (MSR), with spurs and branches. The SREB and MSR were announced respectively by PRC president Xi Jinping in September and October 2013, while on official visits to Kazakhstan and Indonesia. Apparently, China's national leadership under Xi considers the ancient Silk Road trade routes connecting Asia, Europe, and Africa as a foundation of the development of many great civilizations, China among them. As such, invoking the term *Silk Road* would highlight or emphasize their commercial and cultural links, although today solar panels and smartphones have replaced silk as traded commodities and trains and airplanes have superseded camels as carriers. China's overseeing body for the BRI, in charge of guiding and coordinating work related to the initiative, is the Office of the Leading Group on Promoting the Implementation of Belt and Road Initiatives, established in 2014 under the PRC State Council's National Development and Reform Commission, and headed first by Vice Premier Zhang Gaoli and subsequently by Vice Premier Han Zheng (Zhang 2019, 333–34).

Ostensibly, the BRI is an ambitious project launched by President Xi in late 2013 to build connectivity with over 60 (and eventually 130) countries and 4.4 billion people across the continents of Asia, Africa, and Europe, principally through programs of infrastructure construction (Verlare and van der Putten 2015, 1–7). The BRI provided a good opportunity for China—then flush with cash after some three and a half decades as the world's factory but facing rising domestic labor cost, a sluggish economy, industrial overcapacity, and economic protectionism in Western countries—to integrate its existing bilateral and multilateral engagements with foreign countries into a broader framework of international trade, financial, investment, infrastructure, and policy cooperation. While the SREB links Central Asia, Russia, and Europe by land with China's western hinterland across Eurasia, the MSR connects China's coast with Southeast Asia, South Asia, East Africa, and the Mediterranean Sea. Bridging the SREB and MSR is the China–Pakistan Economic Corridor (CPEC), which extends from the city of Kashgar (Kashi) in China's northwestern Xinjiang (Uyghur) Autonomous Region to the port of Gwadar on Pakistan's Indian Ocean seaboard.

8 | China's Belt and Road Power Transition

The BRI's financing arm for its projects is the Asian Infrastructure Investment Bank (AIIB). The AIIB, founded with the signing of a memorandum of understanding by China on October 24, 2014, with the participation of 56 other countries and an authorized capital of $100 billion (AIIB 2015),[2] is a development bank dedicated to projects that are part of the initiative. On January 16, 2016, the AIIB officially opened for business, focusing on five major aspects: policy coordination, facilities connectivity, unimpeded trade, financial integration, and cultural exchange (NDRC 2015). The Silk Road Fund is another medium-to-long-term investment fund, announced by Xi at the Asia-Pacific Economic Cooperation Summit held in Beijing in November 2014, to provide financial support to implement China's BRI in infrastructure, energy and resources, industrials, and financial services. The fund was later established as a Chinese sovereign wealth fund for supporting private businesses investing in BRI projects. Its committed funding was originally $40 billion, with an initial tranche of $15 billion (RMB 100 billion) added on at the first BRI summit, organized by China in May 2017, of which $10 billion was contributed by four Chinese shareholders: State Administration of Foreign Exchange, China Investment Corporation, Export-Import Bank of China, and China Development Bank (CDF 2019). Participating developing nations and international organizations are eligible to apply for the RMB 100 billion fund to finance their projects (*New Indian Express* 2017). Both the AIIB and SRB are headquartered in Beijing and chaired by Chinese nationals. At the Conference on Interaction and Confidence Building Measures in Asia (which may be considered the security arm of the BRI), held in Shanghai in May 2014 and initiated by China, the PRC leadership urged Asian countries themselves to play a major stabilizing role in fostering security in the Asia region.

The first official paper on the BRI was jointly released by China's National Development and Reform Commission, Ministry of Foreign Affairs, and Ministry of Commerce in March 2015 as the "Vision and Actions on Jointly Building Silk Road Economic Belt and 21st-Century Maritime Silk Road." It could be inferred from the paper that the BRI, branded to appeal to participating countries' infrastructure construction ventures while promoting industrial cooperation and commercial exchange, offers a source of long-term development investment or assistance not offered by Western governments, although BRI credit facilities are generally tied to the purchase of Chinese goods and services. It should be made clear at the onset that the focus of the BRI is investment. It is not an overseas aid program, and even if aid is involved, it is principally project-based development aid rather than general, sectoral, welfare, or emergency assistance, which is not really within the BRI's ambit. China's development aid packages that are part of the BRI include military assistance and peacekeeping, subsidized loans for joint ventures, and cooperative ventures in building infrastructure. Other non-BRI aspects of human resource development, capacity building, and technical cooperation would tend to be financed by concessional loans or interest-free loans, scholarships and training programs, and, in exceptional cases, debt cancellations and grants.

BRI infrastructure projects are generally financed with concessional loans from Chinese state-owned policy banks such as the China Development Bank or China Export-Import Bank (Exim Bank), but China does not make a clear distinction between commercial arrangements and development aid, as aid or grants may be employed to "sweeten" commercial deals for Chinese state and non-state enterprises to enter the targeted countries for developing infrastructure, encouraging trade, and engaging in poverty reduction projects under the BRI. Still, budget allocation for external assistance, so to speak, covers (1) costs of turnkey projects, civilian and military goods, and cash; (2) expenses for trainees from recipient countries and salaries of experts sent to recipient countries; (3) interest subsidies for concessional loans made by the Chinese government or Chinese state-owned banks; (4) rebates for some specific expenses for Chinese firms involved in joint investment and cooperation projects; and (5) fees and administrative expenses for firms implementing aid projects (Brautigam 2011, 755–56). It is believed that in drafting programs and financing plans in a target country, after receiving State Council approval, the PRC's Ministry of Commerce will coordinate policies and implement strategies with the Ministry of Finance, Ministry of Foreign Affairs, and the China Exim Bank before funding is disbursed from Exim Bank and other state-owned financial institutions. What then is the exact role of the AIIB? Simply put, the AIIB functions for China as a "white glove" to diminish Western dominance in international finance and lending by making commercial development loans that are neither strategic nor bilateral to entice major developing countries like India or advanced industrialized countries to get involved with the BRI.

China considers the BRI a commitment to developing countries or countries in need of assistance for infrastructure construction as a sign of responsibility, but also as a long-term foreign policy or strategic outreach, of a potential global power. BRI projects are attractive for various reasons: China provides the financing and its project costs often appear low up front, some infrastructure projects occur in places with difficult economic conditions that have struggled to get financing, and Beijing does not require conditions of public accountability or transparency for investments that European or US investors typically do. However, Chinese financing often occurs under opaque conditions or through contracts with few or no competitive bidding, and it tends to target specific industries or sectors (e.g., energy and transport) that favor Chinese state-owned enterprises, matter to local and regional elites (Conley et al. 2020, 10), and are concomitant with China's national interests as defined by its political elite. Indeed, nearly half of BRI loans are made "off the books" and not reported to the World Bank or the International Monetary Fund (*Liberty Times* 2022). Although the BRI appears to be multilateral, it is primarily a platform for China to make multiple bilateral arrangements, particularly pertaining to trade and investments. As such, whether for state or non-state projects, the BRI typically involves China employing its diplomats and state-backed industrialists to advance personal ties and implement deals with formal institutions or local enterprises in its BRI partner states.

One may ask at this juncture why a broad, multinational scheme such as the BRI is necessary to advance China's commercial ties and infrastructure investment cooperation, considering that China has been doing perfectly well in these aspects for decades before the initiative. This is because the BRI is far from being just a large-scale overseas economic venture coordinated and monitored by the Chinese government. The BRI should be interpreted as a concrete, external expression and power projection of Xi Jinping's guiding philosophy of realizing the "China dream" and his galvanization of national pride through the promise of the "great rejuvenation" of the Chinese nation, floated almost immediately after he assumed the supremely powerful position of general secretary of the CCP in November 2012 (Wu and Yan 2012). National rejuvenation can be interpreted as the revival of the golden age, as during the times of the ancient Silk Road when China was arguably the most wealthy, advanced, and powerful nation on earth, to be realized again under Xi's leadership of the CCP by a modern economy and strong military. If the forward dimension of Xi's dream is an imagined future where China will have displaced the US and resumed its rightful place at the center of the world (Friedberg 2022, 80), the subsequently launched BRI would herald his vision and legacy on a global scale. The BRI has also been seen by Chinese diplomats and scholars to promote Xi's enunciated "community of common destiny" by heralding a "new global and economic order" of "shared interests" and "mutual trust" (Mardell 2017). Praises and expressions of gratitude for the BRI would raise China's national standing in the eyes of its own citizens and thus affirm the legitimacy of the ruling CCP.

Pointedly, to demonstrate that the BRI is Xi's personal initiative and a project solely owned by China, the initiative was announced by the president-cum-general secretary during his official visits to Astana, Kazakhstan, and Jakarta, Indonesia, and not at a meeting of an international or regional forum of states such as the Shanghai Cooperation Organization or ASEAN plus China Dialogue Partnership mechanism, although China is a pivotal member of both. In October 2017, the CCP incorporated the development of the BRI into its party constitution by writing into it "the principle of achieving shared growth through discussion and collaboration, and pursuing the Belt and Road Initiative" (Xinhua 2017b). Unsurprisingly then, access to BRI funding from Chinese policy banks normally correlates with the recipient country's support for priority Chinese policy positions on unification with Taiwan, South China Sea territorial disputes, and China's human rights stance in Xinjiang, among others.

To promote the BRI, the PRC government has organized official Belt-and-Road forums in Beijing and invited government leaders to participate. The first forum was held May 14 to 15, 2017, and attended by 29 heads of state or government; the second forum was held April 25 to 28, 2019, and attended by 37 heads of state or government; and the third forum was held on June 23, 2021. After the outbreak of the worldwide COVID-19 pandemic in early 2020, some BRI projects have been delayed or scaled back because of shortages of workers and raw material after some governments imposed travel restrictions and border controls to contain the pandemic. Significantly, major economies such as the US, Japan, and India have yet to join the BRI, citing a lack of transparency in China's international lending practices, while in Australia only the state of Victoria joined, although this deal was eventually canceled by the Australian federal government in April 2021.

As of March 2021, 139 countries have joined the BRI by signing a memorandum of understanding with China: 39 countries in sub-Saharan Africa, 34 in Europe and Central Asia, 25 in East Asia and the Pacific, 18 in Latin America and the Caribbean, 17 in the Middle East and North Africa, and 6 in South Asia. These countries, plus China, account for 40 percent of global GDP and 63 percent of the world's population (Sacks 2021). The total volume of trade in goods between China and BRI countries increased from around $1 trillion in 2013 to $1.34 trillion in 2019, and

12 | China's Belt and Road Power Transition

the share of BRI countries in China's total trade reached almost 30 percent in 2019 (Xiao 2020).

While emphasizing the benefits of the BRI for developing countries, Beijing has enlisted countries of all income levels to endorse the initiative: 26 low-income countries and 39 lower-middle-income countries have joined the initiative, accounting for just under half of all the participants, while 41 upper-middle-income countries, as well as 33 high-income countries, have signed on, accounting for over half of the BRI participants (Sacks 2021). This is an indication by itself that the BRI is more, perhaps much more, than just economics.

Motivations, especially ambitious ones, often require the means to execute them. Chinese investments in the BRI from December 2013 to December 2020 amounted to about $770 billion pledged or invested, or exceeding $925 billion if construction contracts are included (Xiao 2020). Almost 85 percent of the investments took place in Asia, the Middle East and North Africa, and sub-Saharan Africa, with 2020 registering the lowest increase from the previous year at $47 billion (Green Belt and Road Initiative Center 2021) due to the coronavirus. Decades of economic growth and the control of 30 percent of all assets in China, including 50 percent of the worth of all companies, give the Chinese government the means to pursue ambitious economic policies abroad (Chowdhury 2021, 10). Answering infrastructure needs in developing countries may garner China significant political gains by demonstrating its financial largess, whereby Chinese companies, many if not most of them state-owned, will then manage these infrastructure projects, giving them some degree of influence over the use of critical infrastructure (ChinaPower 2020). By early 2022, the BRI included 2,631 projects worldwide, either promised or in operation, with a combined value of $3.7 trillion, according to the research group Refinitiv's BRI database (Dodwell 2022).

A major accusation leveled against the BRI has been Beijing's engagement in so-called debt trap diplomacy, whereby China actively seeks to push countries into debt with unsustainable loans in order to extract geopolitical concessions or strategic advantages (Chellaney 2017). If the borrowing country cannot repay its loans, Chinese banks would be able to use their status as preferential creditors, backed by their government, to obtain operation rights or other favorable conditions (*Liberty Times* 2022). Whether or not this charge is credible, mounting concerns over debt risks and loan opacity in both recipient countries and China have led to significantly reduced lending. Since 2020, there have been signs that Beijing may be changing its strategy for marketing the BRI through a "second track dialogue mechanism," by building cooperation with foreign "political parties, parliaments, think tanks, local authorities, NGOs (non-government organizations), industrial and commercial associations, media, and universities," to "facilitate China's economic reforms and opening up" (Arase 2021). However, the operationalization of such a new mechanism, let alone its result, is not yet evident.

As this book argues, through the BRI, China will be able to exploit its financial largesse and technological proficiency to influence partner countries to align with its own political and foreign policy interests. The BRI is valuable as a foreign policy tool for China to showcase its one-party authoritarian state-capitalist development model on a global scale, by transferring capital, technology, and advice to needy countries in exchange for raw materials, markets, and purchases, while extending its geopolitical influence and security interests. China has signed over 100 agricultural cooperation agreements with BRI countries, principally across Africa and South America, covering agricultural trade, agricultural investment and technology transfer, investment in infrastructure, and policy coordination (Dace, Singh, and Hooper 2022). This gives China added leverage on the prices and quantities of world food supplies. In making trade and investment decisions, China's avowed opposition to any form of political conditionality or privileges inspires development cooperation, with developing countries particularly. By eschewing interference in the domestic affairs of target countries, such as calling for a particular system of governance or institutional reforms, China demonstrates that it is attentive to something—sovereignty—that many countries are sensitive about. Although direct linkage is hard to prove, dispensing funds for investment is believed to be an important way for China to garner votes in the United Nations and its agencies and support for Beijing's sovereignty claim over Taiwan. By touting its cooperativeness and responsibility as an international state actor, China, through the BRI, is positioning itself not only as the leader of the non-Western, anti-imperialist, and postcolonial Global South by virtue of being a successful, large developing country but increasingly as a worthy alternative to US dominance of the world political-economic order and its brand of liberal democratic capitalism, toward which the CCP, with its desire for monopoly on power and total control over society, has always been anathema.

In terms of international relations theory, the BRI may be said to operate on the basis of complex interdependence. Complex interdependence is the result of a realization by individual nation-states that although they pursue their interests through realist power politics, or realpolitik, their fortunes are inextricably connected with other nation-states in the global political-economic system (Keohane and Nye 1977). Interdependence, mutual reliance, and collaborative efforts between state and non-state actors across countries could be economically rewarding, where each actor is able to maximize gains, all the more so if channeled through international and regional institutions (Keohane 1984). However, and this is important to remember, interdependence need not be equal or symmetrical. Both zero-sum and non–zero-sum (positive sum) could exist with complex interdependence, but countries can benefit to different degrees through cooperation, even under conditions of asymmetrical power relationships. Although win-win mutual gains need not imply that they would be equal or a 50/50 split at all times, the interdependent view maintains that interactions would be beneficial as long as there are absolute gains to both parties, at least in the monetary sense, irrespective of what the relative gains are (Keohane 1984). This, at least implicitly, is the foundation upon which China's arguments for promoting South-South cooperation (among developing countries) or a scheme such as the BRI rests. Hence complex interdependence, or the belief fostered by China that mutual gain is possible, is the glue that holds together the BRI, making it attractive for potential partners to join and possible for Beijing to prepare for a power transition.

Although Xi Jinping is universally credited for initializing the BRI, it must be recognized that the enterprise did not just pop out of the individual or collective mind of the Chinese leader or leadership in 2013, but rather has decades-long antecedents. In 2001, a then-fresh strategy of "going out," which encouraged Chinese domestic enterprises to participate in cross-border foreign investment with neighboring countries, was adopted in China's 10th Five-Year Plan for National Economic and Social Development (2001–2005). Before the end of the year, China was admitted to the World Trade Organization (WTO). Since then, the outward foreign direct investment (FDI) of China has been increasing rapidly. However, as this book posits, the formulation of the BRI itself is the culmination of economic and geostrategic events and chain reactions, essentially tit-for-tat posturing between China and the US, that dates back to the start of the global financial crisis and resultant great recession starting in 2008.

A Brief Review of Literature

Since the BRI was announced in 2013, quite a few studies have been made of the subject. Although many of these works and reports on the BRI are already cited in the manuscript, some recent publications may be of interest to highlight and review current debates and approaches. A review of noteworthy and recently published literature related to the BRI may be categorized on a continuum from the general, where the framing is global and the BRI is not the main focus, to the descriptive, concentrated on world regions and BRI projects in individual countries. Unlike this book, none of these works explicitly adopts power transition theory, or any other international relations theory, as an explanatory framework to understand the connection between the geopolitics of power transition on a global scale and the BRI as a grand strategy devised by China.

On a general level of analysis, Keohane and Nye's classic *Power and Interdependence* (4th ed., 2011) does not deal with the BRI but illustrates both the opportunities for cooperation and realist constraints that present themselves to China's leaders as their country continues its ascent as a global power. Michael Pillsbury's *Hundred Year Marathon* (2016) likewise does not deal with the BRI but analyzes the teachings of traditional Chinese statecraft that underpin China's strategies to replace America as the world's dominant power by 2049, the 100th-year anniversary of the founding of the PRC. Luke Patey's *How China Loses: The Pushback against Chinese Global Ambitions* (2020) frames his discussion of the global backlash against China's assertive economic, diplomatic, and military assertiveness as a feature of US-China structural competition, in which some BRI projects are used as illustrations.

With works discussing the BRI as part of Chinese statecraft, Tom Miller's *China's Asian Dream* (2017) is an early work on the BRI, which argues that under Xi Jinping's leadership, China is pursuing a dream to restore its historical position as the dominant power in Asia by employing its economic strengths for strategic ends, establishing new regional financial institutions, and funding and building highways, railways, ports, and power lines across Central Asia and through the South China Sea and Indian Ocean. Julien Chaisse and Jędrzej Górski's *The Belt and Road Initiative: Law, Economics, and Politics* (2018) is an edited volume with chapters by different non-American authors discussing how the BRI fits into China's new world order as a Chinese geopolitical strategy and how different aspects of the BRI impact specific world regions or states. Eyck Freymann's *One Belt One Road* (2020) is a powerful critique of the BRI as primarily a campaign to restore an ancient model in which foreign emissaries paid tribute to the Chinese sovereign, offering gifts in exchange for trading privileges in China and political patronage. Jonathan E. Hillman's *The Emperor's New Roads: China and the Project of the Century* (2020) offers a highly descriptive but rather

16 | China's Belt and Road Power Transition

unflattering study of several BRI projects based on extensive interviews to reveal how this grand vision, which has generated both loans and resistance, is unfolding. Jerry M. Rosenberg's *The Belt and Road Initiative: The Threat of an Economic Cold War with China* (2022) is yet another critical study on the BRI from an economic perspective but includes a section on alternative schemes proposed by the US and the EU to counter the BRI.

Examining BRI projects on the basis of world regions and individual countries, Bruno Maçães's *Belt and Road: A Chinese World Order* (2019) examines the BRI as a global economic integration scheme by focusing on Eurasia. Richard T. Griffiths's *The Maritime Silk Road: China's Belt and Road at Sea* (2020) concentrates on China's maritime commercial activities, shipping concerns, and perceptions of a "China threat," which he critiques. Strategic and economic rivalry between the US and China in Southeast Asia, the pivotal starting point of the BRI's Maritime Silk Road, is explored in David Shambaugh's *Where Great Powers Meet: America and China in Southeast Asia* (2021). China's power projection and extension of influence in the Southeast Asian region is treated in Murray Hiebert's *Under Beijing's Shadow: Southeast Asia's China Challenge* (2020) and Sebastian Strangio's *In the Dragon's Shadow: Southeast Asia in the Chinese Century* (2020). David Lampton, Selina Ho, and Cheng-chwee Kuik's *Rivers of Iron: Railroads and Chinese Power in Southeast Asia* (2020) is more narrowly focused on China's railway construction in Southeast Asia as part of the BRI and local reactions to these projects. Gerald Chan's *China's Digital Silk Road* (2022) focuses specifically and optimistically on the subject at hand, but it is becoming dated by fast-moving events in the technological "war" or rivalry between the US and China.

Publications on the BRI put out by presses in China sometimes offer country and project statistics, which unfortunately often cannot be independently verified. Hu Zhengyuan's *The Strategy of "One Belt One Road"* (Chinese Communist Party Central Party School, 2017) offers a dated but rare discussion of China's strategic intents with the BRI among high-level CCP cadres, albeit replete with fulsome praises for the contribution of the Chinese government to global infrastructure development. In contrast, articles on the BRI from major newspapers, magazines, and research institutes from Japan, India, the US, and UK, given as references in this book, tend to emphasize the dangers of debt traps in developing countries that are recipients of Chinese BRI funding and construction.

Chapter 1

Introducing China's Belt-and-Road Initiative

Where It All Began: The 2008–09 Global Financial Crisis

Contrary to popular belief, the antecedence of the BRI as a springboard for China's world leadership is not found in Xi Jinping's accession to power in 2012 but years before, when his predecessor Hu Jintao was still in charge. China's success in hosting the Summer Olympics in Beijing in August 2008 coincided with the collapse of major US financial institutions hit by a subprime mortgage crisis, which led to the worst recession in almost 80 years in the US and Europe. Witnessing the advent of what would later be termed the global financial crisis (GFC) and great recession, China's erstwhile prime minister Wen Jiabao (2009) was quick to assert that the origins of the crisis were not just Western but specifically rooted in the failure of American economic regulation and the "blind pursuit of profit." Many Chinese people, from the top leadership to the commonest citizen, became by and large convinced that the US and Western world was in irreversible decline and the unchallengeable number one superpower slot occupied by the US since the collapse of the Soviet Union and end of the Cold War would soon be filled by China. With the US and European governments taking desperately huge expansionary monetary measures to save their economies, and US president Barack Obama inviting China to be a member of the G20 intergovernmental forum to address issues related to the world economy and international financial stability, there would be little over the next few years to dissuade the Chinese from this intoxicating but ultimately wrongheaded belief.

18 | China's Belt and Road Power Transition

Declining demand for Chinese commodities in the recession-hit West turned a 21.9 percent year-on-year growth in Chinese world exports in October 2008 into a 2.2 percent reduction in November, followed by 11 months of continuous and cumulative 16 percent decline, although the percentage of the overall Chinese workforce affected was relatively small (Breslin 2012, 4). Still, the PRC central government announced a RMB 4 trillion stimulus package on November 9, 2009, at the time just under $590 billion at the current exchange rate, and China's local governments also announced their own stimulus plans that collectively amounted to RMB 18 trillion (Yu 2009, 10), focusing on infrastructure development. As legal restrictions prevented local governments from formally raising loans for such purposes, they did so indirectly via locally owned companies known as local investment platform companies (LIPCs or *difang rongzi pingtai gongsi*) (Breslin 2012, 5). By the end of 2009, new bank loans created in China had reached more than double the government-announced stimulus package at RMB 9.6 trillion, with a further RMB 7.96 trillion in new loans in 2010 (Osborn 2011).

Although the 2009 first quarter GDP growth rate of 6.1 percent was the lowest recorded in China over the past 29 years, still, with the growth rate first recovering and then rising each quarter, exceeding 10 percent in the fourth quarter of the year, the much-touted target of 8 percent annual growth was ultimately achieved (and surpassed) (Breslin 2012, 6). Since then, the idea that liberalizing "open-door" reforms, which began in 1978, had made China vulnerable to external economic forces and shocks has become a common theme in the emerging literature on the evolution of new (economic) security issues in Chinese international relations thinking (Yeung 2008). Furthermore, China's exports had expanded so fast, and their volume had become so large, that trade with advanced industrial nations was approaching saturation (Friedberg 2022, 102). With foreign investors and producers in China still sourcing the majority of their components from overseas, neither the tax intake nor the industry upgrades had been anywhere near as large as the leadership expected (Breslin 2012, 7). Domestic consumption was playing too small a role in generating growth, with figures for 2007 showing domestic consumption accounting for about 36 percent of overall GDP and exports and fixed assets investments dominating Chinese growth (8). The attempt to move from a growth to development paradigm was partly undermined by policy responses to the drop in exports in early 2008, as the crisis led the pendulum swing back to promoting growth through bank loans and stimulus packages. The amount of money that China poured into the domestic economy in 2009 to stimulate growth resulted in excess investment, overcapacity, and possible national debt problems. Ultimately, both investment and debts would be purposely exported by China to foreign countries on board the BRI.

The GFC did not mark the start of the rise of China's power, but it certainly accelerated perception of its rise, not least among the Chinese people themselves, not just in the economic realm but also in the technology and military spheres. Qian Gang (2010) has traced the phenomenal upsurge of what he calls "the discourse of greatness" in 2008 and 2009, reflecting a growing national pride in China's apparent increase in global economic power vis-à-vis the existing (crisis-hit) powers. Having originated on New York City's Wall Street, the GFC led Chinese commentators to believe that, although the US economy would eventually recover, in the coming years global economic leadership would become more diffused and less reliant on the US dollar. Consequently, as Wang Jisi (2011, 68) puts it, "Based on the country's enhanced position, China's international behavior has become increasingly assertive." This assertiveness extended to general economic affairs, already China's strong suit, with calls from the governor of the People's Bank of China, the PRC's central bank, for a new "super-sovereign reserve currency" to replace the dollar (Zhou 2009). China already had the world's largest stock of foreign currency reserves before 2008 and emerged from the crisis and recession with the three biggest banks in the world measured by market capitalization (Wines and Wong 2009), as the world's biggest exporter, and as the world's second biggest economy.

The CCP leadership had by then realized that to move up and close the technological gap with the West, China would have to reduce its reliance on foreign technological imports and instead develop its own technologies and set the standards for its own uses through, perhaps paradoxically, the absorption and assimilation of imported technology (State Council 2006, 3). To acquire hard-to-get sensitive technology from around the world, particularly in the areas of energy generation, energy saving, electric cars, information technology, biotechnology, and precision instruments, China launched the Thousand Talents Program in 2008 under the leadership of the CCP Organization Department with the goal of recruiting 2,000 foreign professionals over a 5-to-10-year period (Zweig and Kang 2020, 3–4), initially focused on ethnic Chinese scientists and technology experts with PhDs working at Western universities and research institutes (Ren and

Liu 2019, 2314–17). These diasporic Chinese experts were encouraged to establish high-technology enterprises in China, which often incorporated foreign owners of intellectual property as partners, to co-opt and channel advanced overseas technologies (2314–17). The talent recruitment program has since been expanded to target foreign experts "with full professorships or the equivalent in prestigious foreign universities and R&D institutes, or with senior titles from well-known international companies or financial institutes . . . to work in China on a full-time basis . . . and receive a one-time start-up payment of roughly $158,000 (RMB 1 million) in addition to salary based on previous levels and other significant benefits" (US Senate 2018). This Thousand Talents Program would become the basis of Xi's Made in China 2025 initiative to turn his country into a premier industrial and technological power by 2025. Both programs would eventually fall under the suspicion of the US government for intellectual property theft, espionage by Chinese government agents, and forced technological transfers.

The GFC also accelerated a shift in Chinese military strategy from blunting American power through sea denial, by preventing the US military from traversing, controlling, or intervening in waters near China, to a new focus on building security order through sea control, which sought the capability to hold distant islands, safeguard sea lines, intervene in neighboring countries, and provide public security goods, as demonstrated by increased investments in aircraft carriers, capable surface vessels, amphibious warfare, marines, and overseas bases (Doshi 2021). In addition, China has been developing long-range strike aircrafts, ballistic missiles that target aircraft carriers, supersonic precision-guided cruise missiles, anti-satellite missiles, and electromagnetic pulse weapons capable of knocking out the enemy's electronic systems (Pillsbury 2016, 149–55). This reflects a Chinese perception that the US and Western militaries have been irrevocably weakened by financial contraction resulting from the GFC and great recession, leading to the belief that the Chinese military could afford to be more assertive, not only in protecting China's sea lines of communications, especially its petroleum lifelines, but also in pursuing its maritime sovereignty claims.

By the beginning of the second decade of the 21st century, China's leaders were acutely observing the global alignment of forces to shape an international situation in its favor. As Lee Kwan Yew was reported as saying, China might want to share this century with the US as coequals, but certainly not as its subordinate (Pillsbury 2016, 200). Henceforth, China would pursue gains by creating a world political-economic and geostrategic environment whereby countries would engage China on friendly terms largely in accord with its wishes as the only prudent course of action, given Beijing's increased capability to inflict financial and economic punishment or confer reward.

Maritime Disputes in the China Seas: Chinese Assertiveness and American Reactions

By 2010, China had become the second biggest economy in the world, and the China-ASEAN Free Trade Area (CAFTA), initiated by China, had come into operation. China was already the biggest trading partner of the Association of Southeast Asian Nations (ASEAN) as a whole,[1] and it was likely that CAFTA would turn Southeast Asia into China's economic hinterland. Around the same time, China was also becoming more assertive in its approach to maritime territory, pouring concrete around the islands, reefs, shoals, and other outcrops in waters that it controls, on which it has constructed military installations and telecommunications facilities as well as accommodation for its army and navy. In May 2009, China submitted a map to the United Nations Commission on the Limits of the Continental Shelf that included a "nine-dash line" marking China's "indisputable sovereignty over the islands in the South China Sea and adjacent waters" (Miller 2017, 206). In March 2010, PRC officials were reported to have told two visiting senior US White House officials that China would not tolerate any interference in the South China Sea, which it considered to be part of its core interest (Wong 2010). In September 2010, in the East China Sea, near the Diaoyu/Senkaku rocks disputed by China and Japan, a Chinese trawler collided with a Japanese coast guard vessel and was detained by Japanese authorities. Although the boat's crew and captain were eventually released, it was only after China had suspended rare earth exports to Japan and detained several Japanese citizens in China for spying. Such behavior by China threatened to undermine its carefully cultivated image of a benevolent rising power and opened the way for US intervention.

For some 20 years prior to 2010, the PRC was the darling among its Asian neighbors, strengthening economic linkages with them and advocating a policy of noninterference in internal affairs, contrasting with the apparent bellicose and interventionist US foreign policy after September 11, 2001, in Afghanistan and Iraq. However, China's assertiveness over its maritime territorial claims has encouraged many Asian nations to reassess their choices between China and a more distant and relatively benign US. According to

22 | China's Belt and Road Power Transition

Captain James Fanell, deputy chief of staff for Intelligence and Information Operations of the US Pacific Fleet, in 2007 the US had trouble getting port calls for its ships or landing permission for its aircrafts in East Asia, but by 2013 more nations there wanted US ship visits than could be accommodated by Washington's naval budget (Robson 2013).

Although China has resolved many disputed parts of its immense land border, important maritime sections remain unsettled. China and Japan claim sovereignty over the Diaoyu/Senkaku Islands in the East China Sea, China and Vietnam claim sovereignty over the Paracel (*Xisha*) Islands, and China, Vietnam, the Philippines, Brunei, and Malaysia all claim sovereignty over the Spratly (*Nansha*) Islands. The Paracel and Spratly Island groups lie in the South China Sea, as does Scarborough Shoal, disputed between China and the Philippines. Huge deposits of oil and natural gas are believed to lie beneath the seabed of the East and South China Seas and the area contains some of the world's busiest shipping lanes, through which the bulk of China's oil imports and raw materials pass. Whether fair or otherwise, being the largest country making the most extensive claims in the South China Sea, China is the most obvious target of the other claimants, which are, to a certain extent, supported by the US. The US has never tendered any sovereignty claims over these islands or waters and indeed does not have any grounds to forward such claims. However, the US is involved because two of China's disputes are with countries to which it has defense treaty commitments: Japan and the Philippines.

Constitutionally, China's maritime territorial claims are based on the law on the territorial waters and their contiguous areas adopted by the standing committee of the PRC's legislature, the National People's Congress, on February 25, 1992. This law does not specify China's exact maritime territorial extent, but it does assert the country's sovereignty over the Diaoyu/Senkaku, Paracel, and Spratly Islands. For the Diaoyu claims, China uses the principle of natural prolongation of its land territory, arguing that the Diaoyu outcrops are the natural extension of the Chinese continental shelf out to the East China Sea and thus are under the jurisdiction of China. For the Paracel and Spratly claims, the PRC authorities rely on a map showing a U-shaped "nine-dash line" enclosing most of the South China Sea inherited from the previous Republic of China regime, which was submitted to the UN in May 2009. China also uses the arguments of discovery and historical rights to bolster its sovereignty claims to the territories that it disputes in the East and South China Seas.

What accounts for China's territorial assertiveness at this particular time? The reasons behind China's push cannot be known for certain due to its closed political system, but they can be reasonably surmised. The Chinese People's Liberation Army (PLA) had by then been rapidly expanding and modernizing its navy and air force for 20 years in the post-Cold War era. It is possible that some in China believed that the GFC in 2008 signaled the decline of the US and the time was ripe to become more assertive. Or it could have been China's need to find resources to fuel its rapid economic growth. Given this uncertainty, the reinvigoration of US influence, a sort of pivoting back to East and Southeast Asia, was something to which the elites of Japan and Southeast Asian states, keen to balance and hedge against China's increasing domination of the region, became quite receptive. This in turn spurred the Chinese government to try and break out of this perceived encirclement and containment effort engineered by the US and its allies, with the BRI as its principal means.

China versus the United States in the Diaoyu/Senkaku Islands Dispute

Regarding the Diaoyu/Senkaku Islands, which are really just rocks as they lack freshwater resources to support a resident population, Japan bases its Senkaku claim on discovery, and China claims that the Diaoyus were illegally seized by Japan following China's defeat in the 1895 Sino-Japanese War. Following Japan's surrender in 1945 after World War II, the Senkakus became part of the Ryukyu (Okinawa) Archipelago administered by the US and returned to Japan pursuant to the 1971 Okinawa Reversion Treaty. As China has never accepted that the Diaoyus are part of Okinawa nor recognized Japanese possession over them, it would not acknowledge that the postwar US-Japan Treaty of Mutual Cooperation and Security apply on the Diaoyus. The US position on the treaty is exactly the opposite.

After the discovery of oil in the seabed of the East China Sea near the vicinity of Diaoyu/Senkaku in the late 1960s, claims over the rocks were contested verbally. In February 1996, Japan declared a 200-nautical-mile exclusive economic zone (EEZ), permitted by the 1982 United Nations Convention on the Law of the Sea, which would place the disputed isles and considerable fisheries and hydrocarbon resources in and under the East China Sea within the claimed EEZ of Japan as measured from the Okinawa Islands. To assert physical claim over the Senkakus for Japan, a Japanese right-wing group landed on one of the islands in 1996 to erect a lighthouse, which resulted in the drowning of a Chinese Hong Kong activist as he tried to swim to the island from his boat in protest. This incident led to huge demonstrations in Chinatowns all over the world, and the Chinese government felt compelled to denounce Japan's territorial and EEZ claims in the East China Sea. The position of the US government at that time was that claimants should resolve the dispute "in a peaceful manner through direct negotiations" and that the US had no intention of serving as a mediator. (Jiji Press 1996)

After the Chinese trawler incident in 2010, the Obama administration said it would not take sides in Tokyo's territorial disputes but would honor US security commitments to Japan, and implored both China and Japan to solve the dispute peacefully (Labott 2010). Representing the US as a dialogue partner of ASEAN during the group's annual summit in Hanoi, Vietnam, in October 2010, Hillary Clinton, secretary of state, said the US was willing to serve as mediator in the disagreement (Labott 2010). Nothing came of Clinton's offer, but it demonstrated that the US believed that, unlike 14 years before, the Chinese military already had the wherewithal and confidence to initiate a conflict with Japan over the dispute, and in the process drag the US into a war.

As the dispute escalated between China and Japan in light of the move by the Japanese government to "nationalize" the Senkakus in August 2012, with China's dispatch of civilian ships and surveillance aircrafts in the vicinity, then–US defense secretary Leon Panetta urged China to participate in multilateral efforts to resolve its territorial disputes (Barnes and Spegele 2012). The response from newly minted PRC-cum-CCP-leader Xi Jinping was that the US should stay out of the dispute (Ferguson 2012). Clearly concerned about Xi's response, Obama, in late October 2012, dispatched a top-level bipartisan mission to Beijing and Tokyo made up of four senior members of the US foreign policy establishment: Stephen Hadley, James Steinberg, Joseph Nye, and Richard Armitage, respectively national security adviser during President George W. Bush's second term, deputy secretary of state in the Bill Clinton administration, Clinton's secretary of defense, and deputy secretary of state during Bush's first term. The main purpose of the trip was for the US delegation to make clear to the Chinese leadership and reassure the Japanese government that a Chinese attack on the disputed islands would trigger the US' security obligations to Japan under their mutual alliance (Rachman 2013).

The 2013 National Defense Authorization Act was passed by the US Senate in December 2012 with the statement that "while the United States takes no position on the ultimate sovereignty of the Senkaku Islands, the United States acknowledges the administration of Japan over the Senkaku Islands. The unilateral actions of a third party will not affect United States acknowledgment of the administration of Japan over the Senkaku Islands" (Johnston 2012). Prior to leaving office in January 2013, Secretary Clinton reiterated that the Obama administration opposed "any unilateral actions that would seek to undermine Japanese administration of the islands" (Perlez 2013), and her successor John Kerry reconfirmed that the US' security treaty with Japan covers the Senkaku Islands (*Economist* 2013).

Japanese prime minister Shinzo Abe then threatened that Japan would use force if China tried to land troops on the Senkakus, to which China's Ministry of Defense responded that if Japan were to shoot down unmanned Chinese drones operating close to the Diaoyus, it would be considered an act of war (Valencia 2014). In June 2013 in Sunnylands, California, President Obama urged President Xi during their first summit meeting to "de-escalate" the Diaoyu/Senkaku dispute and deal with Japan through diplomatic channels (Spetalnick 2013). Xi replied that the Pacific Ocean is large enough to accommodate two great powers (Stevens 2013), hinting that China would not accept the status quo of the US remaining the world's only preeminent power. Xi's formulation of the BRI around this time, and his disinterest in inviting either Japan or the US into his scheme, reflected this way of thinking. China soon declared an air defense identification zone (ADIZ) that overlaps significantly with Japan's existing ADIZ above the East China Sea and Diaoyu/Senkaku, although neither China nor Japan has so far tried to enforce their ADIZ regulations against the other.

Obama declared on his visit to Tokyo in April 2014 that the disputed isles were covered by Article Five of the US-Japan Treaty of Mutual Cooperation and Security (*Economist* 2014), which states that if territories under Japanese administration were to come under armed attack, the US would assist Japan militarily. While not surprising, this was the first time a sitting US president made explicit the commitment to come to the Japan's defense of the Senkakus in the event of a third-party attack. Obama's position has given rise to the dominant Chinese view that the US supports Japan in order to deter China from actions to settle the dispute unilaterally. It could well be argued that a major purpose of the BRI, which China began promoting heavily around this time, is to isolate the US-Japan relationship.

China versus the United States in the South China Sea Islands Dispute

With regard to the South China Sea, the US State Department has always maintained that it "takes no position on the legal merits of the competing claims to sovereignty over the various islands, reefs, atolls and cays" (Yu 2003). As such, although South Vietnam was an ally of the US, Washington did nothing when in January 1974 China's PLA Navy seized all the islands in the Paracel group controlled by Saigon. Likewise, when a confrontation occurred between the Chinese and Vietnamese over Fiery Cross Reef (Yong Shu Jiao) in 1988, during which the PRC sank three Vietnamese vessels, killing 72 people, the US made no official comments. Even while Brunei, Malaysia, the Philippines, and Vietnam declared their respective 200-nautical-mile EEZs over parts of the South China Sea, all Southeast Asian countries to various degrees continued to downplay fears of what China's military activities in the South China Sea implied for their need to accommodate its burgeoning interests.

Although the US viewed with concern the 1995 discovery of Chinese construction on Mischief Reef, off the Philippines' Island of Palawan and claimed by Manila, the US' primary interest was freedom of navigation, that is, keeping the sea lanes open for international maritime traffic. The US wanted the Philippines and its ASEAN partners to raise the issue of China's construction in the South China Sea at the annual meeting of the ASEAN Regional Forum (ARF), established by the ASEAN in 1994 for the foreign ministers of ASEAN states to discuss security matters. One consequence of the Mischief Reef discovery was that disputing states found themselves in a race to bolster their claims to sovereignty of occupying outcrops through establishing physical presence or erecting markers. A near collision on March 8, 2009, when several Chinese vessels attempted to block the USNS *Impeccable* in an EEZ claimed by both China and Vietnam, raised the hopes of Vietnam's foreign and defense establishments for keener US attention on the South China Sea to inhibit China's inclination to press its territorial claims (Oxford Analytica 2009). Despite the vast chasm of political ideology that separates capitalist US from socialist Vietnam, Secretary Clinton and Robert Gates, the secretary of defense, accepted invitations from the Vietnamese government and paid respective visits to Hanoi in 2010 to show support for Vietnam in its territorial disputes with China. Although Vietnam had committed to not forming a military alliance or operating a military base with any country, it opened its Cam Ranh Bay naval base to visits by foreign navies in 2009, and in August 2010, US warships docked at Cam Ranh for their first joint naval exercise.

For the US, which was beginning to see China's assertiveness as a strive for regional hegemony in East and Southeast Asia, opportunities for its own intervention were aided by comments made by Chinese ministerial officials to their US counterparts in March 2010 that they saw the South China Sea as part of China's "core interests," on par with Taiwan and Tibet, in which foreign interference would not be tolerated (*Economist* 2010a). This was not well taken by the US. On July 23, 2010, Secretary Clinton told the ARF meeting in Hanoi that her country had a national interest in the security of sea lanes of communication in the South China Sea and freedom of navigation; hoped to see peaceful, multilateral negotiations among disputants to the South China Sea outcrops; was willing to mediate a solution to the dispute; and supported "a collaborative diplomatic process by all claimants for resolving the territorial disputes without coercion" (*Economist* 2010b; Ren and Liu 2013). The implication was, of course, that China was attempting acts of coercion to settle the South China Sea islands disputes in its favor. Two days later, Chinese foreign minister Yang Jiechi struck back and warned the US against inflaming tensions by internationalizing what Beijing has always insisted are bilateral matters to be settled by individual claimants (*Economist* 2010a).

While China wants to negotiate disputes over the South China Sea and its outcrops through bilateral talks involving only the disputants, ASEAN prefers to present a united front, and the US tends to agree. In July 2011, during the ARF meeting in Bali, Indonesia, and at separate meetings with her ASEAN counterparts, Secretary Clinton reiterated US interests in the South China Sea and called on the disputants to back up their claims with legal evidence, ensuring conformity with the United Nations Convention on the Law of the Sea (*Taipei Times* 2012). To ward off further pressure to conduct negotiations on the dispute, China agreed, just before the ARF meeting, to write new guidelines that could eventually lead to a binding code of conduct on the South China Sea.

The subject of the South China Sea dispute was brought up again, this time at the East Asia Summit (EAS) in Bali in November 2011,[2] by none other than the US president himself. Obama was in Australia and Southeast Asia to promote his Pivot to Asia initiative. After repeating that the US was not taking sides in the dispute, Obama declared, "We have a powerful stake in maritime security in general, and in the resolution of the South China Sea disputes specifically, as a resident Pacific power and guarantor of

28 | China's Belt and Road Power Transition

security in the Asia Pacific region" (Ren and Liu 2013). Whether Obama had made an effort before the meeting to forge an anti-China alliance with Southeast Asian countries on the dispute is unclear, but the leaders of Singapore, the Philippines, and Vietnam also addressed the need to discuss the issue multilaterally (Ren and Liu 2013). With US support, ASEAN insisted that the South China Sea dispute be placed on the agenda of the following 2012 EAS in Manila, Philippines, but this move was successfully opposed by China (Nye 2011).

In mid-2012, a tense standoff between warships and fishing boats of China and the Philippines occurred at Scarborough Shoal near Palawan Island of the Philippines, which was then occupied by the Chinese after the Filipino warships withdrew. While the Obama administration again offered to play the role of regional peacemaker, the US contested the Chinese presence by sending the navy to assert its right of navigation (Colby and Ratner 2014). The Chinese government then announced that it was combining the Paracels (Xisha), Spratlys (Nansha), and Macclesfield Bank (Zhongsha) into a prefectural-level Sansha City (Three-sha City) and garrisoning it (*Wall Street Journal* 2012).

After China's Sansha City announcement, Secretary Clinton reiterated at the ARF meeting of July 2012 in Phnom Penh, Cambodia, that "the United States has no territorial claims in the South China Sea, and we do not take sides in disputes about territorial or maritime boundaries; but we do have a fundamental interest in freedom of navigation, maintenance of peace and stability, respect for international law, and unimpeded lawful commerce; and we believe the nations of the region should work collaboratively and diplomatically to resolve disputes without coercion, without intimidation, without threats, and certainly without the use of force" (US Department of State 2012). Although left unmentioned, it was clear which country Clinton's remarks on "coercion," "intimidation," "threats," and "use of force" were directed against. She also urged ASEAN countries to "speak with one voice on the South China Sea" (*Bangkok Post* 2012). The US also strongly supported the drafting of a code of conduct that would lessen the risk of conflict in the South China Sea by covering issues such as the terms of engagement when naval vessels meet in disputed waters to avoid armed confrontations.

By the time of the ARF meeting in August 2014, held in Naypyidaw, Myanmar, it was clear to the participants that they could not expect a halt on China's reclamation work, building efforts, or military construction on the disputed reefs, islands, and other outcrops in the South China Sea could, as they were already a fait accompli. Nonetheless, Secretary Kerry floated a proposal that called on all states to refrain from taking "provocative actions" in the South China Sea. However, aside from the Philippines, this proposal found little support from China or other ASEAN member states (Auslin 2014). Chinese foreign minister Wang Yi, who also attended the meeting, rebuffed the reclamation freeze proposal as counterproductive, saying that it would only fan the flames by emboldening countries like the Philippines and Vietnam to take a hardline stance against China (Beattie 2014). The US then conducted a military exercise with Japan in the South China Sea in October 2014. Seeking to isolate the US diplomatically, Wang also urged Asian nations to come together to solve their own problems without outside interference (Auslin 2014). China calculated that the less Washington was able to influence events in the disputed waters, the more likely Asia's capitals would be to deal with Beijing directly, and one-on-one, in accordance with China's preference. This would give China tremendous advantage on account of its size, wealth, and strength. Involving Asian countries in the BRI, which was already in full swing by then, could only serve to focus their leaders' minds on these attributes. China's leaders were very aware that its advantages vis-à-vis other countries would be further cemented if it could provide more trade and investment opportunities to them through the BRI.

Why Is the US Concerned about China Seas Activities?

By the start of the 2010s, China's rising economic and military capabilities were beginning to make the US concerned for its predominant position in the world, or at least the Western Pacific. The Chinese government had amassed large holdings of US government debts, and Americans had made huge investments in China. As such, China already had considerable sway over US economic calculations. China's control, whether de facto or de jure, of the South and East China Seas, and acquiescence of Southeast and East Asian countries to that control, would mark the beginnings of a Chinese Monroe Doctrine, which would allow China to rule this salient maritime connection between the Indian and Pacific Oceans. Although China is not yet able to challenge the US' role as superpower, China has sufficient missile and anti-warship capabilities in the South and East China Seas to make US intervention there very costly. China is becoming powerful enough that the superpower cannot simply do what it wants in Asia. It is to forestall any move by the Chinese to veto US action that explains America's desire to check China's power and influence in the East and Southeast Asian region, beginning with Obama's "pivot" or "rebalance."

The United States' Pivot, or Rebalance, to Asia: Provoking the BRI

It was China's assertiveness starting around 2010 in the China Seas that triggered many Asian states to grow sharply concerned about Beijing's intentions and ask Washington to increase its attention to and presence in the region. To keep in view China's territorial sovereignty disputes, as well as the changing strategic balance, in East Asia and the Western Pacific, the Obama administration geared up for a pivot of American global strategy toward the region. This was the message delivered by Obama to the federal parliament of Australia in Canberra, where he singled out cooperation in the South China Sea as a challenge. This announcement would be followed by attendance at the EAS and ASEAN meetings in Bali, Indonesia, in November 2011. Obama's was the first US administration to elevate Asia as a primary strategic priority, as by 2012 China and Japan had become the US' second- and third-largest trade partners. As president, Obama visited Asian countries annually, and his first secretary of state, Hillary Clinton, took her first official trip abroad to Asia and returned a dozen times over the following four years. The Pivot to Asia was meant to demonstrate America's commitment to maintaining US interest and influence in the Asia-Pacific, even while recovering from the GFC at home, and get in a position of readiness to face a fast-rising China. Years of American disengagement from ASEAN countries during the previous George W. Bush presidency, and its obsession with fighting terrorists and state building in Afghanistan and Iraq, had allowed China to take leading roles in regional economic and security dialogue, with various degrees of formality, involving states in Northeast Asia, Southeast Asia, Central Asia, South Asia, Australasia, and the South Pacific. To stay engaged in Asia, both to take advantage of China's economic growth and multilateral forums and to express concern about its military expansion, the US hoped to take part in any sustained regional architecture that would consider its membership.

In a November 2011 article in the *Foreign Policy* journal entitled "America's Pacific Century," Secretary Clinton outlined six elements of Obama's Asia-Pacific strategy, of which four—engaging regional multilateral institutions, expanding trade and investment, forging a broad-based military presence, and deepening working relationships with emerging powers including China—directly or indirectly involved US efforts to cultivate regional multilateral arrangements. These arrangements included the system of "spokes-and-hub" bilateral military alliances between the US and its allies, Trans-Pacific Partnership, ARF, EAS, and ASEAN Defense Ministerial Meeting Plus. It was deemed important for the US to stay actively engaged in Asia for its own interests. With both the US and Europe then struggling with weak economic circumstances, Washington hoped to open new markets in Asia for US goods and services to lower domestic jobless rates (Richburg 2021). As Obama administration officials believed, a more pronounced US security presence in Asia would be an insurance policy for a stronger trade position in the region (Carter 2013), and a more prominent economic role would provide a sounder argument for maintaining a forward military position in the Asia-Pacific.

As much as the Pivot was about redirecting US forces and attention from elsewhere in the world to the Asia-Pacific, it was also about the US rebalancing within the Asia-Pacific to reflect Southeast Asia's emerging prominence and importance, particularly with CAFTA in 2010, as the 600 million Southeast Asians were by then already producing more than $2 trillion in goods and services annually (Tang 2013). China certainly took advantage of the US' preoccupation with security issues at home and wars in Iraq and Afghanistan during the George W. Bush presidency to expand its power in Southeast Asia through trade, investment, and tourism. To the extent that the US was worried about the increasing discrepancy between the military capabilities of China and ASEAN, Southeast Asian countries also had concerns, shared by the US, that ASEAN would become overly dependent on China if the group were to draw closer to its economic orbit (Oxford Analytica 2012). As such, constraining China's actions through engaging Southeast Asian countries and Asia-Pacific allies of the US seemed to have been the focus, if not the raison d'état, of the Pivot. As such, it has also been termed the "rebalance" to Asia.

Political scientist Robert Gilpin has argued that as a rising state's relative power increases, it will attempt to change the norms and rules governing the international economic and military system, the division of spheres of influence, and the distribution of territory, while the dominant power then attempts to adjust its policies to accommodate this rise and maintain its favored status quo. If this is so, the Pivot could be interpreted as an apparent strategy of denial, by the US, of China's moves to limit what the US considers its accustomed roles, power, and influence in the Asia-Pacific region, and as a clear attempt by the US to cope with a rising China within the current international system.

32 | China's Belt and Road Power Transition

WHAT THE PIVOT ENTAILS

Centering Southeast Asia

In recognizing the centrality of ASEAN for the Pivot strategy, Obama signed onto ASEAN's Treaty of Amity and Cooperation (which stipulates that its signatories must resolve disputes with one another peacefully without the use or threat of force), held annual ASEAN-US meetings while he was president, and appointed the first US resident ambassador to ASEAN. Obama and secretaries of his cabinet also broke with past practices by meeting with members of Myanmar's military junta, in hopes of improving relations with that country.

Repositioning Military Forces

The Pivot proposed redeploying US military forces then stationed in Europe, Iraq, and Afghanistan. The US Navy would release unmanned aerial vehicles from Afghanistan and maritime patrol aircrafts from the Middle East, more guided missile destroyers would be moved to the Western Pacific, and a high-altitude ballistic missile defense system would be deployed in the US Pacific territory of Guam (Lyle 2013). According to Tom Donilon, Obama's first national security advisor, the US Pacific Command would reinforce its operational capabilities on submarines, fifth-generation fighter jets such as the F-22 and F-35, and reconnaissance platforms (2013). Obama's first defense secretary, Leon Panetta, said that the US would gradually reposition 60 percent of its warships to Asia by 2020, up from the current 50 percent, as part of the new military strategy centered on Asia (Chow 2012). There were already occasional warship deployments to Singapore, marines stationed in the northern Australian city Darwin, and military trainings with India, Malaysia, Vietnam, Thailand, and Cambodia as well as plans to increase both the number and scale of these training exercises. China considered all this as unnecessary meddling by an external actor in its own backyard, which had to be countered.

Strengthening Alliances and Encouraging Intra-Asian Security Networks

As a foreign policy behavior, the Pivot was a US hedge on China's peaceful integration into the international system by first and foremost strengthening military cooperation with Japan and South Korea. Japanese prime minister Shinzo Abe was a staunch advocate of the US-Japan Security Treaty (Fukushima 2012). The first ever US-Japan-South Korea joint naval exercise was held in waters off the Korean peninsula in June 2012. Although the five US bilateral alliances with Japan, South Korea, Australia, Thailand, and the Philippines have remained the bedrock of US defense policy in the Asia-Pacific region, Panetta's trips to Vietnam and India in 2012 underscored the importance of searching for new strategic partners, as Vietnam and India have maritime and land border disputes with China, respectively. After US officials visited Cambodia in 2010, a staunch friend of China that past US administrations have all but ignored, maneuvers between the Cambodian military and US Marines followed. The US also tried to introduce the Terminal High Altitude Area Defense missile system to South Korea over China's vehement objections. By involving India in triangular (US-Japan-India, US-Australia-India) military exercises, the Pivot also attempted to link the Pacific and Indian Oceans in new operational paradigms (Oxford Analytica 2012). These military exercises would become the basis of the Indo-Pacific Strategy of the succeeding Trump administration. Tightening intra-Asian security relations, such as those between India and Vietnam, Japan and the Philippines, or Japan, Australia, and South Korea, have in the 2010s created new regional strategic realities that the US believed it could take advantage of. The Indian navy has been training Vietnamese submariners, Tokyo has sold patrol crafts to Manila, and Japan entered into its first post–World War II security alliance since the US-Japan Security Treaty with Australia in 2007 (Lobe 2013). The Chinese leadership saw these moves that were either led or encouraged by the US as a budding American containment effort directed against China, and China made the necessary preparations to frustrate it, including going out to seek foreign friends and allies.

Trans-Pacific Partnership

Aside from focusing on Southeast Asia, repositioning military forces from elsewhere to Southeast Asia, and strengthening regional alliances and encouraging intra-Asian security networks, the architectural pièce de résistance of the Pivot was the promotion of free trade talks called the Trans-Pacific Partnership (TPP) in November 2011. The TPP, with 11 negotiating countries, would represent an annual trading relationship totaling $1.4 billion (Lyle 2013). In spite of US backing, however, as the TPP required extensive liberalization in trades, services, investments, rules regarding trade and investment, and government procurements, talks on market access progressed slowly. Beijing, which was not invited to join the TPP, perceived the proposed free trade partnership as a political move to create a US-dominated economic counterweight to rival CAFTA. The US already had free trade agreements with three TPP parties: Australia, South Korea, and Singapore. As such, the focus of the US seemed to be on recruiting participants rather than concluding negotiations (Chin 2012). Perhaps the TPP was really for the US to demonstrate its commitment and engagement in Asia, and not so much to provide concrete trade and investment benefits for American companies. This could be the reason why the TPP was not given "fast-track" status by Congress under the Obama administration, which would have enabled it to be voted on without changes to its provisions, and why President Trump pulled the US out of the negotiations on his first day in office. In this sense, China's BRI may be considered a visionary response to counteract both the TPP, at least in the trade and investment realm, and probably also the intra-Asian security networks created by the US.

ASEAN Regional Forum

Consisting of 27 member states, the ASEAN Regional Forum (ARF) is the Asia-Pacific region's main multilateral arrangement for the promotion of international security and a venue for the US to institutionalize its stay and sway in East Asia and the Western Pacific. It has also created an opportunity for Vietnam and the Philippines to get Washington to support their claims over the disputed Spratly Islands, as both countries have conducted military exercises with the US Navy in the South China Sea. Although Secretary Clinton attached symbolic significance to attending ARF meetings, which to some extent succeeded in reversing the perception of neglect under the George W. Bush administration, by using the ARF to help nations organize against China in talks over contested islands in the South China Sea, the US has been seen by some observers as being too involved in the region's territorial disputes (Allam 2013). Repeated US offers to China and ASEAN disputants to act as a mediator based on "international law" was not appreciated by China, as China does not consider itself to be a threat against freedom of navigation and is adamant about not involving non-claimants to help resolve a matter over which it says it has indisputable sovereignty.

East Asia Summit

Obama became the first US president to sign the ASEAN Treaty of Amity and Cooperation in 2009, a necessary step in paving the way for his own attendance at the EAS two years later when ASEAN invited the US to participate as a full member state, together with Russia. Secretary Clinton had insisted that China's maritime disputes with its neighbors be on the agenda of the 2012 EAS in Manila, but her move was opposed by China (Nye 2015). Leaders of EAS member states have used the forum to discuss regional, nontraditional security concerns over the spread of pandemic diseases, terrorism, piracy, energy, food security, natural disasters, and environmental degradation. Notwithstanding the occasional attendance of its presidents or secretaries of state, the US has always considered the EAS as little more than a talk-shop, even more so than the ARF. However, as long as Chinese leaders are making an effort to attend these meetings, even if it is just to "give face" to ASEAN as the host, it would be in the interest of the US to do so.

ASEAN Defense Ministers' Meeting Plus

In October 2010, the first ASEAN Defense Ministers' Meeting to include defense ministers from ASEAN's dialogue partners was attended by Obama's secretary of defense, Robert Gates. The forum provided the US an opportunity to refocus its attention from bilateral defense cooperation to multilateral engagement, particularly with ASEAN. US secretaries of defense have since dialogued with their ASEAN counterparts on the sidelines of these meetings. At the second meeting, in August 2013, after conducting disaster relief and emergency response exercises, and with the South China Sea in mind, member countries decided to establish practical measures to reduce vulnerability and incidents at sea due to miscalculation (Mindef 2013). It was at this meeting that Gate's successor, Robert Hagel, invited all defense ministers of ASEAN to a meeting in Hawaii, which took place in 2014.

THE PIVOT AS COPING MECHANISM AGAINST CHINA'S RISE

Gilpin has argued that as a rising state's relative power increases, the dominant power attempts to adjust its policies to accommodate this rise to peacefully maintain the system that exists in its favor (Gilpin 1983). At least until the end of the Obama presidency, China has been pursuing a strategy of peaceful development while gradually shaping the international system to its advantage by carefully avoiding any direct confrontation with, or challenge from, the US to avoid any act of counterbalancing (Copeland 2000; Schweller and Pu 2011; Wang 2010, 555).[3] The US under the Obama administration seemed less interested in seeking outright (and costly) containment of China than in molding the environment in which China's rise would take place by affecting its strategic options and calculations. Indeed, the US foreign policy establishment would, since the mid-2000s, like China to be a "responsible stakeholder," but within the international system led by America. If, as argued by Keohane, a state would be concerned with relative gains only if there was significant expectation of resulting damage to itself (Keohane 1993), then it is obvious that the Pivot should be read as a series of actions by the US to widen or at least maintain the power gap between itself and China, a gap that, from the US' perspective, had been uncomfortably narrowed by China in recent decades. As such, under the Pivot, repositioning the military, strengthening alliances, negotiating free trade partnerships, and participating in structured multilateral arrangements of states in the Asia-Pacific region seemed to be important means for the US to defend and advance its own interests by frustrating or undermining that of its opponent, while at the same time minimizing disruption to the international system.

Obama had emphasized that reduction in US defense spending, as mandated by Congress, would not come at the expense of the Asia-Pacific region, but budget cuts had already slowed troop redeployments from elsewhere by the end of his first term in office (Stearns 2013). If the drastic cuts, which began with the Sequester in 2013, were extended for a decade, there would have to be a 10 percent cut in US defense spending (Carter 2013). Furthermore, the US military is likely to shrink to fewer than 520,000 ground troops eventually, meaning that it would be cheaper to move troops and their families back to the US and rotate smaller units abroad for short deployments and training exercises, in line with Obama's plan for rotating 2,500 US troops to Darwin as part of the Pivot (Baron 2011). As a result of past US involvements in military conflicts abroad, there were also millions of new veterans starting lifetimes of expensive medical care and benefit payouts (2011).

Obama's vice president, Joe Biden, has reiterated that "we are, and we will remain, a resident Pacific power . . . our resident power status is the reason why this area of the world is able to grow and be stable" (Chan 2013). Yet the departure of Hillary Clinton as secretary of state and Kurt Campbell as assistant secretary for East Asian and Pacific affairs in early 2013 left big shoes to fill, a fact not helped by Obama's foreign policy concerns in his second presidential term being dominated by the Middle East—the rise of the militant "Islamic State," Iran's nuclear program, Syria's civil war, and continuing violence in Afghanistan as US troops began departing (Solana 2012). With John Kerry preoccupied with the intricacies of the Arab-Israeli peace process and the Syrian civil war, the time and effort that he could allocate to Asia was reduced, as was the substance of Washington's Asia policy. In hindsight, the Obama Administration's Pivot to Asia seems to be much ado about nothing, or to use a Chinese proverb, "loud as thunder with little rain." However, the US demonstrated its desire to contain China, not least in Chinese perceptions, to stir up trouble in China's own neighborhood, and payback was on the way. If offense is the better part of defense, then it is no coincidence that China's Belt-and-Road vision was enunciated by the Xi leadership at this juncture. Although the US had invited China, beginning in 2014, to participate in the Rimpac exercise, a large-scale naval drill that Washington conducts with its friends and allies, this invitation was discontinued under the Trump presidency.

Multilateral arrangements to tie America to Southeast Asia might have helped maintain US economic interest and security commitment in the region beyond the Obama presidency, but they might have also made the region an area of unbridled contest between Washington and Beijing. The embrace of the US Pivot initiative was what led Philippines president Benigno Aquino III to internationalize the South China Sea dispute by filing a case against China's sovereignty claims in the Permanent Court of Arbitration, the proceedings of which China refused to participate in or acknowledge. It seems unlikely that any Asian country, with the possible exception of Japan, would wish to be drawn into an anti-China coalition or be put in a position of "choosing" between Beijing and Washington, arguably their most important economic and security partners, respectively (Bush 2012).

China's Response to the Pivot

Power Transition and Direct Cause of the Belt-and-Road Initiative

It is widely acknowledged that differential economic growth rates and their concomitant effects on military budgets and technological innovations alter relative power capabilities between states, especially large ones, and one byproduct of this is the high potential for conflict when a major state that is dissatisfied with the status quo reaches relative or near equivalence with a dominant state in the international system. This dominant state currently holds preponderant power within a hierarchy of states with different capabilities and attempts to manage the global or regional system with a coalition of stable, satisfied supporters as friends or allies, who accept its rules that guarantee international security and trade. Students of international relations will recognize this argument as the power transition theory (Tammen, Kugler, and Lemke 2017). In the power transition literature, power as a collective measurement typically includes population, GDP, resources, and the government's material extractive capacity, particularly its ability to tax (Kugler and Tammen 2012). Certainly in terms of population China far exceeds the US, and may be closing in on its GDP, but with the other measures of power, even if one cares to include military budget, offensive weapons, or dual-use civilian-military technology, China is still very much behind the US. However, all indications are that China has been trying very hard to catch up in these aspects. One can read in the US Pivot to Asia an attempt to recover some ground in the face of China's rising relative power, which poses a challenge to US preeminence in Asia and the Pacific. Obama's initiative was a response to the rise of China, but this rise, demonstrably from about 2008 to 2013, was essentially a patchwork of economic or territorial moves and not yet a coherent strategy to expand China's influence beyond its own neighborhood. However, China's post-Pivot challenge to America, even if it is only a prospective or emerging one, would not be that easily parried, especially if China is perceived to be less than satisfied with the world order dominated by the US. This challenge would take the form of the BRI.

For power transition theorists, satisfaction is indicated by a favorable view of the existing international system or world order and its rules, including security alliances and economic regimes, and the dissatisfied state would reject working within the established order and desire to replace the old one with a new one deemed more favorable to its own interests, values, and image (Yilmaz and Wang 2019, 325), hopefully one that it would be in charge of or at least highly influential in. There is no debate anymore that China is a great or world power, but the jury is still out on whether it is a satisfied or dissatisfied great power. Even if we assume that it is dissatisfied, its economic development needs dictate that it still requires a stable and favorable international political and economic environment to operate in, or to fall back on, especially in times of domestic economic difficulties. Under the guidelines of the General Agreement on Tariffs and Trade and with membership in the WTO, China, as with other manufacturing-driven, export-oriented East Asian countries, has seen its foreign trade grow exponentially, resulting in positive balances of payments, while the US has over

Introducing China's Belt-and-Road Initiative | 39

time amassed the highest external debt in the world and huge and increasing trade deficits with China. While the US under the Trump presidency has withdrawn from the TPP and renegotiated the North American Free Trade Agreement, China has been participating in existing international regimes rather than attempting to overthrow them; it has not demanded radical restructuring of the international system or order; and it has not directly sought to confront the preeminent power.

As such, we can safely say that China is not yet *directly* challenging the US as the preeminent world power. However, this does not mean that Beijing has not been setting itself up for that challenge, particularly should America stumble badly again as in the GFC of 2008 and the resultant great recession. American primacy in world affairs is reflected in the institutions and multilateral rules that undergird the international society of states (Nye 2015). As a possible rising contender, China is not only well integrated into all existing international regimes in which it is always prepared to voice its demands and expectations. It is demonstrating its capacity to actively provide alternative ideas and mechanisms for global governance in its desire to be perceived as a major responsible power authoritative enough to direct world events, or serve as an effective check on US ambitions and actions. By introducing and promoting mega state-driven infrastructure projects in the BRI, together with the associated AIIB and Silk Road Fund for funding these projects, China is putting in place an alternative political-economic model that might be attractive to the developing world or less wealthy first-world countries. In the context of Chinese thinking, the overriding purpose of the BRI is for China to create *shi* (势), the strategic configuration of forces or propensity of perception that world political conditions and larger socioeconomic and technological trends are tilting its way. The hope and belief is that, given that *shi* is increasing on China's side, even if some US allies and friends verbally support America's position against China on Taiwan's autonomy, the South China Sea disputes, human rights in China, trade, and alleged theft of critical US technologies, they would be unwilling to endorse a policy of containment or encirclement against China that endangers China's and their own economic and security prospects.

Military strength aside, one of the key elements that allows the US as a dominant nation to affect international interactions is control over the US dollar as the global currency, rules for commercial and financial relations among the world's major industrial states, and international economic institutions that support these relations, such as the World Bank, International Monetary Fund (IMF), and WTO. China has not yet achieved power parity with the US, at least as of 2024. However, as China rises, both the dollar and euro areas are likely to shrink, and with the Chinese renminbi already the fourth most-used currency after the US dollar, Euro, and British pound, a challenge for monetary control of the international system is coming.

Economically, in response to the TPP, China has pushed for the realization of the Regional Comprehensive Economic Partnership (RCEP), which would cover the ASEAN countries, China, Japan, South Korea, Australia, New Zealand, and India, since the RCEP proposal was floated by ASEAN in February 2011. As a free trade proposal, the RCEP is narrower in scope than the TPP as it does not cover intellectual property rights, reform of state-owned enterprises, or regulatory standards, but it would allow members to drop trade policies that they disagree with and protect sensitive industries from competition (ChinaPower 2020). China hoped that such exclusionary provisions would make RCEP more attractive to fellow developing nations. After the US, under President Trump, withdrew from TPP negotiations in January 2017, China applied to join the reconstructed Comprehensive and Progressive Trans-Pacific Partnership (CPTPP) under Japanese leadership in September 2021 and managed to bring the RCEP free trade group that it has always championed to fruition in December 2020, albeit without the participation of India.

Militarily, Beijing saw in Obama's Pivot to Asia a naked attempt to contain China's rising power and influence in its own Asia-Pacific neighborhood, and a clear effort to exclude China from claiming a commanding stance in regional and world affairs. However, development of weapons technology such as the DF-21D anti-ship ballistic missile, aircraft carriers, and cyber warfare capabilities have given Beijing greater hardware to enforce its maritime territorial claims. At the 2014 Conference on Interaction and Confidence-Building Measures in Asia, Xi spoke of a new Asian security concept (Piekos and Economy 2015), which seems to imply a desire on the part of the Chinese leadership to see a heightened security and military role for China in the BRI, at least with its Asian members. Despite assurances by Xi to Obama at the Rose Garden of the White House in September 2015 that the islands created or expanded by China in the South China Sea would not be militarized, it was discovered that China went on to do just that (Mahbubani 2020, 79–80). According to professor Yan Xuetong, dean of the school of international relations at Qinghua University, "China could no longer be expected to insist on the principle of non-alignment and not have military alliances as the U.S. consolidates its relationships with its allies" (Chua 2011). "A strategy that was meant to check a rising China has sparked its combativeness and damaged its faith in cooperation," said political scientist Robert Ross of Boston College of the US Pivot (Anonymous 2013a, 85). Even so, from the relatively favorable receptions given by Southeast and Northeast Asian countries to the visits and pronouncements of President Obama and Secretary Clinton during the Pivot, China realized that if it was seen as a bully, other countries would join the US to confront it.

China would soon retaliate against what it considers to be US containment efforts, not in the form of enacting worldwide security alliances, as this may lead to a headlong clash with the US over conflicting interests, but by promoting a grand global geoeconomic-strategic scheme that would be called the Belt-and-Road Initiative, shortened to BRI. Particularly for other developing countries, but also for advanced countries as well, China would depict its own rise as a good thing, "as China will not behave like previous great powers that treated their colonies as unequals [*sic*] to be exploited . . . China's rise also benefits developed states, as China has emerged not only as a potential major source of much needed investment, but also, through its own domestic demand" (*People's Daily* 2010). As such, the BRI is about more than protecting China's friends and virtual allies, or entrapping them with bad debts for which concessions will have to be given to China. It is an imposing stratagem to tie the vital economic and other interests (including security) of Russia, the countries of Asia, Eurasia, South Pacific, Middle East, Africa, Europe, and perhaps Latin America to China so that it can ultimately replace America's influence in these parts of the world and compel the US to share power with it, or even yield leadership to it, in directing and guiding the international system.

As the BRI is President Xi's personal project, it has been dubbed by some analysts as "the number one project under heaven" (Cai 2016). Indeed, Xi's "China dream" is also portrayed as an "Asian dream," with the goal of returning China to "its natural, rightful and historical position as the greatest power in Asia" (Shull 2017). Central to such dreams is the ambitious BRI, which takes its cue from the ancient Silk Road trading routes and aims to connect different regions in China's near and distant neighborhood through a massive program of infrastructure building. Christopher Johnson, of the Center for Strategic and International Studies in Washington, DC, initially considered the BRI to be more a sweeping vision than an operational blueprint (Cai 2016). However, as China's global ambitions must start with adopting a position of regional preponderance, this visionary scheme has since witnessed China building "roads, railways and industrial corridors" across the adjacent Eurasian landmass, and also contains a complementary maritime component, which portends a robust Chinese presence in the neighboring South China Sea and Indian Ocean (Shull 2017). By furnishing the countries of the Silk Road Economic Belt (SREB) and Maritime Silk Road (MSR) with new investments and development opportunities, particularly through the two financial arms of the initiative fashioned by China in the form of the AIIB and the Silk Road Fund, China has sought to diversify its markets and sources of energy supply, but even more so to create a network of economic dependencies and strategic advantages that will consolidate its leadership and undercut America's alliance and partnership structure in Asia and further afield, if possible. *The China Dream*, a book first published in 2010 by Liu Mingfu, a PLA senior colonel, describes the relationship between the US and China in terms of a marathon, as a contest based on endurance. This was also the description in another book, *The Hundred-Year Marathon*, published in 2016 by Michael Pillsbury, a US military analyst. If the contest is indeed a marathon, then the BRI is a national endeavor by China to generate the wind behind its back, to enable it to catch up with the US in this long-distance race for primacy or at least equality. As the BRI is an international relations endeavor, the domestic politics of the countries involved will be dealt with in this study only to the extent that they are directly relevant to the initiative.

Map 1. Map of the Silk Road Economic Belt (SREB) and 21st century Maritime Silk Road (MSR). *Source:* Public domain.

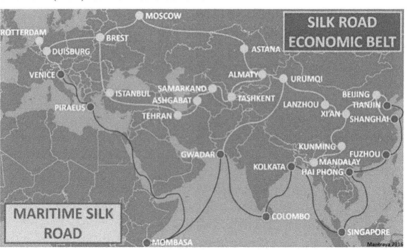

Chapter 2

The Silk Road Economic Belt

Bringing Together China's Eurasian Forums

After Xi Jinping assumed supreme power as the secretary general of the CCP in late 2012 and state chairman of the PRC in early 2013, he began to champion *fenfa youwei*, or "striving for achievement" in foreign affairs, thus signaling a more assertive foreign policy stance for China (Clover and Lin 2016). A key facet of this proactive turn in Chinese foreign policy involves manifesting a more ambitious international agenda, particularly in putting effort on an evolving "Eurasian engagement." This engagement focuses on the Shanghai Cooperation Organization (SCO) and the China-Central and Eastern European Countries (China-CEEC or "17 + 1") forum, which are multilateral arrangements of states initiated and led largely by China in Eurasia before the Xi Jinping era but became essential components of the Silk Road Economic Belt (SREB) of Xi's BRI. For those who doubt the strategic nature of the BRI, it should be recalled that the SCO was set up at China's behest to deal with terrorism-related security issues at its western borders with the former Central Asian Soviet republics, which are still major concerns for the organization despite its subsequent economic development focus.

The SREB was thus not put together from scratch but built on two existing multilateral frameworks that China was already involved with before the advent of the BRI, but now they are considered part of the initiative: (1) the SCO, which covers China, Russia, Central Asia, and later South Asia and (2) continuing westward, the China-Central and Eastern European Countries summit mechanism, which links China with initially 16 and later 17 countries in Central and Eastern Europe. As such, the SREB is not really a novel endeavor of inter-state connectedness but has rather developed out of linkages between China and the countries and mechanisms of the SCO and China-CEEC. Still, the maintenance of these two regional groupings is useful for demonstrating the cooperative nature of China's multilateral involvements in forums where China is very much the leader or agenda-setter. A major branch of the SREB, which extends from the city of Kashgar (Kashi) in China's northwestern Xinjiang (Uyghur) Autonomous Region to the port of Gwadar on Pakistan's Indian Ocean seaboard to meet the MSR, is the China–Pakistan Economic Corridor (CPEC). All three of these frameworks serve to reflect and promote Chinese foreign policy priorities for the broad Eurasian region, centering on regional stability and economic cooperation, but more so to create and cement a bloc of states friendly to and supportive of China's national interests and the exercise of its diplomatic influence. The form of the SREB may be multilateral, but within the setup its content is decidedly bilateral, usually involving just China and the specific country concerned.

China and the Shanghai Cooperation Organization

The bulk of China's SREB network runs through the countries of the SCO. The SCO is a regional Euro-Asian or Eurasian political, security, and economic grouping. It can be considered the most important security-oriented organization of states that the PRC has played an instrumental role in helping to create and develop. The cooperation of member states and development of the SCO is underpinned by the so-called Shanghai spirit, which is enshrined in the SCO charter, and features mutual trust, mutual benefit, equality, consultation, respect for diverse civilizations, and pursuit of common development (Yamei 2018). Notwithstanding such enlightening sentiments, the approach to regionalism cultivated by the Chinese political elite, particularly with regard to the SCO, is undergirded by a realist logic of calculating strategic and economic costs and benefits. China's vision of regionalism, guided by its own national interests, is in line with its vision of regional order to secure greater compliance for Chinese interests from other regional actors (Yeo 2019, 22), or at least greater cooperation.

Membership

The SCO originated on April 26, 1996, as the Shanghai-Five forum, in which China discussed its outstanding border issues with Russia, Kazakhstan,

The Silk Road Economic Belt | 45

Kirghizstan, and Tajikistan in Shanghai and tried to build security confidence with these four countries, chiefly through the reduction of troops on both sides of their border with China. Central Asia was given added emphasis in 2000 by exhortations from China's Jiang Zemin leadership to Chinese traders and investors to "zouchuqu" (go outwards) for the purpose of promoting Xinjiang's economy under the *Xibu Dakaifa* (Western Great Development) scheme. With the inclusion of Uzbekistan, the six countries created the SCO on June 15, 2001, and became its full members. The SCO's regular membership expanded to eight countries on June 9, 2017, when India and Pakistan joined the group at the SCO heads of states' summit in Kazakhstan's capital Astana, 12 years after they were given observer status in the organization. The SCO includes four observer states with no voting rights: Mongolia, Afghanistan, Belarus, and Iran. Iran was accepted in principle as the eighth full member of the organization during its annual summit in Tajikistan's capital, Dushanbe, in September 2021. All these countries can be considered to be involved in the SREB except India, which has remained non-committal to the BRI. China, together with Russia, are the largest and most powerful member states of the grouping.

STRUCTURE

The SCO consists, from the top down, of a council of heads of state, council of heads of government, council of foreign ministers, council of national co-coordinators, and secretariat. The council of heads of state is an annual summit of the presidents and chairmen of member states to decide the future directions and priorities of the group. The council of heads of government is an annual meeting of premiers or prime ministers of member states to discuss issues of multilateral cooperation, and most importantly to approve the budget of the SCO. The council of foreign ministers works on the external relations of the organization. The council of national co-coordinators, consisting of one representative from each SCO member state, orchestrates and coordinates cooperation among the countries.

Reflecting China's instrumental role and influence in the SCO, its permanent secretariat was erected in Beijing in 2003. The secretariat deals with the administrative work of the SCO. This includes drafting proposed documents, implementing and monitoring organizational decisions, functioning as a document depository, and promoting the group by providing information on its visions and activities (SCO). Parallel to the secretariat is an intelligence-gathering organ of the SCO, known as the Regional Anti-Terrorist Structure (RATS) and located in Tashkent, Uzbekistan, which aims

46 | China's Belt and Road Power Transition

to improve the organization's ability to respond to threats from terrorism, and lately, cyberattacks. The organization's structure, principles, goals, and prescribed activities are outlined in the SCO organizational charter. SCO's official languages are Russian and Chinese.

SCO Achievements

The major achievements of SCO are in the aspects of security, economics, cultural and educational exchanges, external cooperation, and membership expansion.

Security

SCO is first and foremost a regional security organization, more than a confidence and security building mechanism but less than a multilateral treaty alliance. It is not organized for the purpose of collective self-defense, but the original mandate of the SCO was for member states to assist one another to jointly cooperate in opposing what the organization has designated as the "three evils" of separatism, terrorism, and extremism. To this end, the SCO has been holding regular biannual joint anti-terrorism ("peace mission") operational planning and field exercises since 2003, involving military forces from most if not all SCO member states. Their governments have maintained databases and shared intelligence on suspected terrorists and terrorist groups through the RATS and also harmonized anti-terrorism legislations and practices. In 2017, at the time of its membership expansion, SCO reported that it had foiled 600 terror plots and extradited 500 terrorists through RATS (*Asia Times* 2018).

The SCO initially supported US military intervention in Afghanistan after the terrorist attacks of September 11, 2001, by allowing the US to lease air bases in Uzbekistan and Kirghizstan for bombing raids. However, after the riots in Andijan, eastern Uzbekistan, in May 2005, which led the leaderships of Uzbekistan and other SCO member states at that time to suspect Western involvement in the disturbances, the SCO took a decisively anti-American turn. At the organization's head of state meeting in Astana in July 2005, the SCO called for a timetable for the withdrawal of US-led forces in Afghanistan and for a deadline to terminate the use of military bases in SCO countries.

To monitor and interdict cross-border opium and terrorist trafficking from Afghanistan into SCO countries, an SCO-Afghanistan contact group was established in 2004. After the complete withdrawal of US military forces from that country, SCO member states, in particular China, helped stabilize Afghanistan by providing reconstruction assistance to its government. Afghanistan is a formal member of the BRI, and a senior-level delegation from Afghanistan attended China's Belt-and-Road forum in 2017. With the fall of the Ashraf Ghani government in Afghanistan backed by US military troops in August 2021, the PRC was quick to acknowledge the legitimacy of the return of the Taliban regime to protect its BRI metal mining investments in Afghanistan. However, the SCO had also refocused its attention on border security and domestic stability by announcing, at its September 2022 summit at Uzbekistan's Samarkand, that the organization had thwarted 40 terror attacks, more than 480 terrorism-related crimes, and 26 international terror group funding channels, with Xi, China's president, committing his country to training 2,000 law enforcement personnel for SCO member states (Kasonta 2022).

Economics

To Xi Jinping, "security is the cornerstone of development" (China Global Television Network 2018). To Xi's predecessor as state chairman and party secretary general, Hu Jintao, "without universal development and common prosperity, our world can hardly enjoy tranquility" (Hu 2005). Recognizing that poverty is a major source of instability in Central Asia and China's Xinjiang, the SCO has since 2003 been encouraging investment, trade, and infrastructure development among its member and observer states. As some SCO links start from Xinjiang, particularly Kashgar and Khorgas, Beijing hopes that economic development will bring social peace and stability to this occasionally restive Muslim Uygur-dominated region. Kashgar, China's westernmost city administration, almost 4,400 kilometers from the coast, was awarded the status of special economic zone in 2010 and since its inception has grown at a rate of 17 percent on average annually, while Khorgas, home of the China-Kazakhstan-Khorgas International Border Cooperation Centre, the Khorgas Free Trade Area (between both territories), and an export processing area, attracted nearly 2 million traders in 2014, the year of its creation (Ramon-Berjano 2018, 173, 183).

To finance investment projects in SCO member countries, the *Shanghai Cooperation Organization Interbank* Consortium was established by the council of heads of *SCO* member states in 2005. The consortium funds the construction of large infrastructure projects, particularly in energy (oil and gas pipelines), transportation (railways), and telecommunications, which are provided by government banks of member states, particularly those of China. The state-owned China Development Bank and Exim Bank are major financial backers of the consortium (Filippov 2018). Since the SCO heads of government meeting in 2017, China has committed the AIIB and the Silk Road Fund as well to provide financing to the consortium. In 2018, Xi announced that China would offer $4.7 billion, the equivalent of RMB 30 billion in loans under the consortium's aegis (Filippov 2018).

Within the SCO collective, Russia's Siberia, Central Asia, and Iran provide the energy resources, particularly oil and natural gas, and Mongolia and Afghanistan produce rare metals to fuel China's industrial economy. Strategically, the SCO creates alternative energy supply routes to the choke points of the straits of Hormuz and Malacca, through which most of China's maritime oil imports pass. India and Pakistan could constitute major markets for technological and household electronic products from China, although as a result of Sino-Indian border clashes in 2020, India has been systematically banning Chinese electronics and mobile apps. In return, China could provide them with a market for trade and a source of investment.

By 2017, when Xi first proposed the creation of an SCO free trade zone (Filippov 2018), trade between China and other SCO member states had totaled $217.6 billion, increasing on average around 20 percent per year (Xinhuanet 2018). In 2018, trade between Russia and China reached a high of more than $100 billion (Xinhua News Agency 2019b), and China became the largest trading partner of Uzbekistan, Turkmenistan, and Kyrgyzstan (Akita 2019).

By 2018, cumulative Chinese investment to SCO member states had exceeded $84 billion (Xinhuanet 2018b), a lot of which was channeled through China's state-owned Exim Bank, and between 2005 and 2020, Chinese companies invested nearly $50 billion in Kazakhstan, Kyrgyzstan, Tajikistan, and Uzbekistan, according to the China global investment tracker of the American Enterprise Institute, a Washington-based think tank (Zhang 2018). China has become the largest source of foreign direct investment in Kyrgyzstan and Tajikistan, principally for gold mining and hydroelectric power development, respectively, and overtaken Russia as an investor in Kazakhstan (Akita 2019). The Kazakhstan–China oil pipeline transports 12.3 million tons of oil and 44 billion cubic meters (bcm) of natural gas, while the Central Asia–China gas pipelines from Turkmenistan deliver more than 34 bcm of natural gas (Oseledko 2018). Between 2015 and 2019, exports from Uzbekistan to China have increased over 50 percent, while imports from China rose by 126 percent (China Briefing Team 2021).

However, the Chinese have encountered economic difficulties in Central Asia. Due to the lack of strong local content requirements, projects in Central Asia typically involve a high percentage of contractors, workers, and imported raw materials from China; Chinese officials have privately admitted that up to 30 percent of investments in the region are lost to corruption, with corruption scandals having dogged the Bishkek Power Plant and the Dushanbe-Chanak Highway; and Kyrgyzstan and Tajikistan have the highest debt default risk among BRI countries (Sim and Aminjonov 2020). In Kyrgyzstan's Naryn region, a deal with China to build a $275 million logistics center on 200 hectares of land leased for 49 years to a joint Kyrgyz-Chinese venture had to be canceled in February 2020 due to sustained local protests against the project (Putz 2020).

With Beijing stepping up its investments in Central Asia, there has been growing unease in the region over the expanding Chinese footprint. Polling from the Central Asia Barometer showed that while the governments in those countries welcomed closer ties with China, public opinion was mixed, with 30 percent in Kazakhstan and 35 percent in Kyrgyzstan viewing China unfavorably, compared to single-digit unfavorable ratings for Russia in those countries (Zheng 2021). Although Central Asian countries are concerned about domination of their economies by China, they must oftentimes consider much-needed Chinese investments.

External and Sino-Russian Cooperation

Following Xi's assumption of power, the SCO formalized nontraditional security ties with the Collective Security Treaty Organization and is pursuing greater economic ties with the Eurasian Economic Union, both created and dominated by Russia and consisting of Armenia, Belarus, Kazakhstan, and Kyrgyzstan. With Russia under US and EU sanctions, imposed following its annexation of Crimea in 2014, and China facing increasing scrutiny of its technological research and industry amid the US-China rivalry, the two countries designated 2020 as the "year of Russian-Chinese scientific, technical, and innovation cooperation." While Moscow has supplied Beijing with S-400 mobile, surface-to-air anti-aircraft missile systems, Beijing has identified communications technology, artificial intelligence, and facial recognition as fields for collaboration with Moscow, having Chinese telecommunications

50 | China's Belt and Road Power Transition

giants Huawei sign deals in May 2019 to build 5G (fifth-generation) networks with MTS, Russia's biggest mobile carrier, and Chinese companies Alibaba and Tencent working with Russian companies to develop e-commerce (Elmer 2019). In December 2019, Russia launched the $55 billion Power of Siberia natural gas pipeline to China, the first gas pipeline linking both countries (Simes and Simes 2021). In 2021, Sino-Russia trade reached $146.9 billion, an increase of almost 36 percent from 2020, and in February 2022, on the eve of Russia's attack on Ukraine, gas deals worth $117 billion were signed between China and Russia (Wion 2022). Should relations between Russia and the West worsen even further, then more natural gas could be expected to be piped to China from Siberia and elsewhere in Russia. One may go so far as to argue that the basis of Xi's SREB is his friendship with Vladimir Putin, with whom he made a point to meet in person at the SCO heads of state summit in Samarkand, Uzbekistan, in September 2022, after cloistering himself at home in China for more than two and a half years due to the COVID-19 virus.

If possible, SCO countries are keen to avoid the SWIFT international financial managing system backed and monitored by the US, which had been used to cut off countries that did not follow US trade and political policy, keeping them from making global banking transactions. Following Russia's annexation of Crimea in 2014, Moscow began developing its financial managing system SPFS amid Washington's threat to disconnect the country from SWIFT. SPFS was introduced to the banks in countries of the Russia-led free trade Eurasian Economic Union in October 2019 and will be linked to China's cross-border interbank payment system CIPS (Chaudhury 2022). While the US dollar is still the dominant currency in global transactions, the Chinese renminbi is second in international trade finance, and China has already engaged in bilateral use of local currencies with Russia, India, Iran, and Turkey for trading purposes (Devonshire-Ellis 2020). India and Russia have been trading through the rupee-ruble exchange mechanism since the Western sanctions on Russia in 2014, and Iran, which officially joined the Eurasian Economic Union in February 2022 (Chaudhury 2022), is working with Russia to link Russia's SPFS to Iran's homegrown financial messaging system SEPAM (Motamedi 2023).

Cultural-Educational Exchanges

To promote people-to-people exchanges, music fairs, concerts, art festivals, photography expositions, museum exhibitions, and youth camps are held among SCO artists in member states with increasing frequency. The University of Shanghai Cooperation Organization was established in 2008 as a network of universities from SCO member and observer states. It provides degree programs at the bachelor, master's, and doctoral levels; language courses; professional programs; and distance learning, focusing on information technology (IT), pedagogy, nanotechnologies, regional studies, economics, ecology, and energetics, all of which reflect China's development priorities first and foremost. Member states have made suggestions to promote public health, such as countering the spread of infectious diseases.

Membership Expansion

After the 2017 membership expansion, the SCO constitutes about 70 percent of the Eurasian area, almost half of the world population, and nearly 20 percent of the world GDP (Xinhuanet 2018a). The inclusion of India and Pakistan as regular members has the potential to increase the SCO's world influence. China and Russia gained an ally against trade protectionism when Indian prime minister Narendra Modi called for a "rules-based, anti-discriminatory and all-inclusive WTO-centered multilateral trading system" at the June 2019 SCO heads of states summit (Press Trust of India 2019). India also has experience combating groups that use violence to achieve political aims in Kashmir, which it disputes with Pakistan, and this experience may be useful for other SCO states involved in fighting or monitoring their own armed non-state actors. Pakistan may be more amenable to India's desire for the construction of a Turkmenistan-Afghanistan-Pakistan-India gas pipeline now that both countries are member states of the SCO.

India is extremely dependent on imported fuel and Pakistan faces energy shortages. India and Pakistan will constitute major markets for oil (from Kazakhstan and Russia), natural gas (from Kazakhstan and Turkmenistan), cotton (from Uzbekistan), uranium (from Kazakhstan), hydroelectricity (from Tajikistan), and technological and household electronic products (from China). However, membership expansion may pose the biggest challenge to the SCO.

SCO Challenges

The major challenges to SCO are in the areas of institutionalization and priorities, India's membership, the group's relations with Iran and Turkey, and potential China-Russia rivalry.

52 | China's Belt and Road Power Transition

INSTITUTIONALIZATION AND PRIORITIES

According to Article 22 of the SCO charter ("Settlement of Disputes") enacted in 2002, policies of the group are decided and implemented by consensus and differences settled through consultations and negotiations, which would only be harder to achieve with more members. Furthermore, there are existing issues of different taxation, labor visas, and internet regulation policies among the SCO members that have yet to be harmonized. The SCO might remain a principally regional security organization rather than one that prioritizes economic development or exchanges should its anti-terrorist function intensify, since both Pakistan and India have their own problems with armed separatist groups from Baluchistan and Kashmir, respectively. These difficulties undercut the cohesiveness, effectiveness, and evolution of the organization.

INDIA

The membership of India, which has always prized its democratic political tradition and nonaligned foreign policy orientation, may dilute the SCO's authoritarian political values, multipolar (anti-American) outlook, and internal cohesion. This is all the more so because India has been courted by Presidents Donald Trump and Joe Biden for America's Indo-Pacific Strategy, and India is a member of the Quad with the US, Japan, and Australia. Furthermore, India has serious territorial disputes with Pakistan over Kashmir. A suicide attack on an Indian paramilitary convoy in Indian-administered Kashmir in February 2019, which killed 40 Indian soldiers and was claimed by the Pakistan-based Jaish-e-Mohammed (JeM) group, led to Indian airstrikes on a JeM training camp in Pakistan, marking the first time since the 1971 Indo-Pakistan war that strikes were launched beyond the Line of Control, the de facto border between Indian- and Pakistani-controlled parts of disputed Kashmir (Seiwert 2019). India also has disputes with China over their common border. Doklam, where India's protectorate of Bhutan adjoins China's Tibet Autonomous Region, witnessed a tense standoff between Indian and Chinese soldiers in the summer of 2017. With the fatal Chinese attacks on Indian soldiers along another stretch of the disputed China-India border in 2020, China and India went into a deep chill. New Delhi has, as of yet, refused to support Beijing's BRI. India has objected to the CPEC, where energy, road, rail, and communications conduits would be built between Pakistan's port of Gwadar and China's Kashgar in the Xinjiang Uyghur

Autonomous Region, because it traverses Pakistan-held Kashmiri territory claimed by New Delhi. India's opposition to the BRI would make it more difficult for China to use the SCO as a platform to promote the initiative. Furthermore, as India is fast catching up with China in its oil and gas demands, it may become a keen competitor of China for influence and hydrocarbons in Central Asia.

TROUBLESOME PARTNERS: IRAN AND TURKEY

Iran remains an observer member of the SCO, although it has applied for regular membership since 2008. Accepting Iran as a regular member seems like a natural progression for SCO membership expansion, as Iran is in the neighborhood of Central Asia and friendly to both China and Russia. However, doing so would antagonize the US, given Iran's anti-US foreign policy stance and on-and-off sanctions against it by Western countries over the issue of its nuclear development. Still, membership is a move that might be contemplated should US relations with China and Russia markedly worsen. Since 2019, China and Russia have conducted biannual naval exercises with Iran in the Gulf of Oman. As a sure sign of worsening relationships for China and Russia with the West, Iran was accepted in principle as the eighth full member of the organization during its annual summit in Tajikistan's capital, Dushanbe, in September 2021, joining the SCO in July 2023.

Turkey has been an SCO dialogue partner since 2012. In 2017, Turkey ordered batteries of the advanced S-400 ballistic missile air defense system from Russia, despite opposition from the US, receiving the first installment in July 2019 (Marcus 2019). As such, given the state of Ankara's uneasy relationship with Washington, there is an opportunity for Russia and China to expand their influence over Turkey by upgrading it to an SCO observer. However, Turkey is a member of the North Atlantic Treaty Organization (NATO), and encouraging Turkey's further involvement with the SCO may increase America's suspicion of the territorial ambitions of the organization.

POTENTIAL CHINA-RUSSIA RIVALRY

With regard to the SCO, Russia prefers a focus on security, given its military bases in Central Asia and arms sales to India, while China prefers a focus on economics, as it has extensive and increasing trade, investment, and energy ties with Central Asian states and Pakistan. However, wary of China's growing economic influence in Central Asia compared to Russia's,

Moscow has so far not agreed to the establishment of an SCO development bank (Gabuev 2017) or an SCO free trade area. Despite persistent attempts by Russia to keep Central Asia within Moscow's defense perimeters, Beijing may pursue security ties unilaterally with Central Asian states to safeguard its vital energy investments in these countries, and the presence of a small Chinese military base in southeastern Tajikistan, bordering Afghanistan and China in the Pamir Mountains, was confirmed in February 2019 (Shih 2019). As such, although this can be considered the best of times for the relationship between China and Russia, standing together against US trade tariffs targeting China and Western sanctions on Russia, there is still potential for Sino-Russian rivalry over Central Asia and the future development of the SCO.

When President Xi met his Russian counterpart Vladimir Putin at the opening of the Beijing Winter Olympics in February 2022, they issued a joint statement describing bilateral relations as "superior to political and military alliances of the Cold War era" and cooperation as having "no limits" (Eurasianet 2022). And although China did not refer to the advance of Russia's army into Ukraine as an invasion, it also did not provide material support for Russia's action. Russia would have noticed this studied, self-serving neutrality on the part of China. Furthermore, with disruption in the supply of oil from Kazakhstan and natural gas from Uzbekistan to the West through Russia due to the Russo-Ukraine War, these Central Asian countries are looking to reorientate their sale of fuels eastward toward China. China's imprint on Central Asian and interregional politics and its ambition to make a distinctive Chinese contribution to its brand of globalization may yet come into conflict with Russia's vision of a "greater Eurasia" in which Moscow stakes out a place for itself as an indispensable power.

To What Extent Does China Still Need the SCO?

Certainly, as the world enters the third decade of the 21st century, the other SCO member and observer states are still respectful or at least circumspect toward China's vital economic interests and security role in the organization. However, it seems that already by the mid-2010s, after the BRI/SREB was operationalized and given the challenges faced by the SCO, China no longer felt the need to pursue its objectives in Central Asia with SCO member states solely through the organization. China's oil pipeline from Kazakhstan, four gas pipelines from Turkmenistan across Central Asia, and the CPEC were negotiated individually with the countries concerned. China's "strategic partnership" with Russia can and does operate independently from the SCO. In the 12 years from 2007 to 2019, China and Russia conducted five bilateral military exercises on the land and sea of either or both countries. In October 2016, China held its first-ever joint bilateral counterterrorism exercise with Tajikistan, independent of the SCO (Indeo 2019).

China's relations with Central Asia and West Asia have also undergone significant changes. On July 16, 2020, China held its first meeting with the foreign ministers of all five Central Asian countries in the "5 + 1" format. The online meeting was initiated by Beijing and focused on joint cooperation to fight the pandemic and restore the economies in the region. The second China + Central Asia (C + C5) forum, held on May 21, 2021, in Xi'an, Xi's home province of Shaanxi, had the same priorities as the first meeting but also celebrated 30 years of diplomatic ties between China and the post-Soviet Central Asian republics. On the whole, Central Asian governments still discuss the possibilities of the BRI with China for much-needed trade, investment, and employment. However, there has been a discernible undercurrent of anti-Chinese sentiment among the population, sometimes championed by opposition or nationalist political forces, which could disrupt China's relations with Central Asian countries and its BRI plans in the region if not properly handled.

Kazakhstan is a major part of the Iron Silk Road, with the Alashankou-Dostyk border being the busiest point on the Silk Road. Until October 2020, freight traffic was operating smoothly with an estimate of 18 trains passing per day, but China's border closure due to the COVID-19 pandemic caused a severe backlog that has negatively impacted Kazakh exports to Beijing (RailFreight.com 2021). A massive wind farm in the south of Kazakhstan, completed in June 2021 as a BRI project partly built by China Power International Holding, has a 100-megawatt capacity and can power a million homes with clean electricity when all 40 wind turbines become fully operational (Darabshaw 2021). However, responding to public fear of land being sold to foreigners, now mainly from China, in May 2021 the Kazakh government placed a ban on leasing and selling agricultural lands to foreign investors. However, judging by the 2021 protests organized by Kazakhstan's political opposition over Chinese BRI investments, it appears that distrust is yet to be quelled (Bartlett 2021).

Kyrgyzstan's government vows that China's upgrades to the Bishkek power plant will solve the power shortages in the country's energy sector. However, the Kyrgyz government is also accused of ignoring allegations of health damage and environmental degradation in Bishkek by the BRI project of a major Chinese oil refinery for the sake of promoting local employment (Aizat 2021a). Since the presidential election in November 2020, anti-Chinese and anti-BRI sentiments have been growing. The Kyrgyz ambassador in Beijing was even summoned by Chinese Foreign Ministry officials to express their displeasure over the attacks on Chinese citizens working in Kyrgyzstan (Standish 2021b). In 2021, a notable ultranationalist group called the Kyrgyz-Chorolor (Forty Knights) began raiding clubs and establishments frequented by Chinese visitors, allegedly with the support of the Interior Ministry of Kyrgyzstan (Aizat 2021b). Kyrgyzstan owes 40 percent of its foreign debt (US $1.8 of $5 billion) directly to China's Exim Bank. With the economy shrinking 8.6 percent in 2020 and repayments for debt due soon, Bishkek asked China for concessions. Beijing has allowed deferred payment of $35 million by two years at 2 percent interest but added provisions that would prevent Kyrgyzstan from bringing debt disputes to international courts, regarding which only the use of Chinese arbitration courts are allowed (Standish 2021b).

Uzbekistan, similar to Kazakhstan, relies heavily on China for renewable energy, especially solar energy, as China is the largest global provider of solar panels, but Chinese businesses have complained to their own government that arbitrary regulation enacted by the Uzbek authorities have led to unfair negotiations and heavy delays in BRI investment progression (Hashimova 2021). Still the Uzbek government signed an agreement with Huawei after the second Belt-and-Road forum in April 2019 to start the construction of a "safe city" project, whereby a converged digital technology communications center will be established to streamline surveillance security protection and urban management (Sukhankin 2021).

Although China voted for five United Nations Security Council resolutions to impose sanctions on Iran for its nuclear program before 2012, under the leadership of Xi Jinping China has opposed US efforts to tighten those sanctions (Anonymous 2013b, 105). During a two-day visit to Iran's capital, Tehran, by Chinese foreign minister Wang Yi on March 24, 2021, Wang and his Iranian counterpart Javad Zarif signed a bilateral 25-year "comprehensive strategic partnership" cooperation agreement between China and Iran worth $400 billion under the Belt-and-Road framework, committing the Chinese government to invest in and purchase oil from the Islamic Republic (Shahla 2021). Although this deal was raised in August 2020, Beijing was reluctant to sign on for fear of angering the US, as the latter had imposed sanctions on Iran due to the impasse in their nuclear negotiations. However, with the US presidential election results out and US-China tensions increasing after failed trade talks in Alaska, Beijing reached out to Iran to deepen bilateral economic and strategic cooperation (Mehdi 2021). By mid-2021, Chinese oil refineries were the largest importers of crude oil from Iran. In March 2023, Saudi Arabia and Iran agreed to reestablish diplomatic relations in a deal mediated by China. The agreement signaled a sharp increase in China's influence in the Gulf region, where the US has long been the dominant power broker. Iran became a full member state of the SCO on July 4, 2023.

On November 6, 2019, as a milestone of connectivity between China, Central Asia, West Asia, and Europe, the first Chinese freight train passed uninterrupted from China's Xi'an via Kazakhstan, the Caspian Sea, Azerbaijan, Georgia, and Asiatic Turkey before entering European Turkey through the China-built Marmaray tunnel below the Bosporus Strait to Istanbul. In 2020, a Chinese consortium consisting of the Chinese highway company Anhui Expressway, China Merchants Expressway Network and Technology, CMU, Zhejiang Expressway, Jiangsu Expressway, and Sichuan Expressway bought a 51 percent stake in Turkey's Yavuz Sultan Selim Bridge connecting Europe and Asia via the Bosporus Strait. In March 2021, China's Export and Credit Insurance Corp. signed off $5 billion to Turkey's Wealth Fund specifically for BRI projects, and Turkey's Hunutlu Thermal Power Plant, worth $1.7 billion, is primarily financed by Shanghai Electric Power Company (Alemdaroglu and Tepe 2020). Erdogan, Turkey's president, is hoping to attract Chinese investment under the BRI framework to fund his $15 billion pet project, the Canal Istanbul, which would connect the Black Sea to the Sea of Marmara to reduce congested traffic in the Bosporus Strait (Writer 2021).

Amid the US-China "trade rivalry" or "tariff war," which started in 2018, the SCO can and does function in a limited way for China as a fallback economic sphere, as an important alternative source of raw material, export market, investment destination, and anti-protectionist platform. Soon after Russia sent troops into Ukraine in February 2022, Apple, Samsung, and other foreign electronics companies stopped selling smartphones in Russia, creating a vacuum for such devices in the Russian market that was quickly filled by Chinese smartphone brands such as Xiaomi, Huawei, Oppo, and Vivo. To ensure China's own vital food security, because of the trade war with the US and worsening ties between China and Western countries, Beijing has been trying to diversify the country's wheat import sources from Russia and Central Asian BRI countries such as Kazakhstan (Donnellon-May and Zhang 2022). Beijing's push to secure more wheat supplies during the Russia-Ukraine war, in spite of the economic sanctions that many countries

58 | China's Belt and Road Power Transition

have placed on Russia, would bring more uncertainty to the global wheat market. The SCO could also be an arrangement for China and Russia to maintain a lock on the geopolitics of the Asiatic landmass should their relations with the West collapse. BRI member Belarus joined the SCO in July 2023. However, although the SCO remains a useful platform for the advancement of the SREB, which as a broader initiative also encompasses the China-CEEC group, the SREB operates independently for China.

China-Central and Eastern European Countries

China was able to construct and deepen its relationships with countries in Central and Eastern Europe (CEE) in the years following 2011 because while the CEE economies were hitherto able to rely on the support of the relatively more developed and wealthier EU countries like France and Germany, EU countries could no longer provide assistance due to the European financial crisis. The China-CEEC arrangement would not only serve as a bridge or transportation corridor for China between the SCO and Western Europe, or an employment destination for Chinese engineers and technicians, but it could also function as a venue to garner support for China's foreign policy positions from more than half the countries of Europe, and may well provide Chinese companies with a beachhead to penetrate the markets of Europe and Britain in the future.

Membership

The China-CEEC is an intergovernmental platform initiated by the Chinese government in 2012 to expand cooperation between Beijing and a group of 11 EU member states (Bulgaria, Croatia, the Czech Republic, Estonia, Hungary, Latvia, Lithuania, Poland, Romania, Serbia, Slovakia, and Slovenia), with Greece joining in 2019, plus five non-EU Balkan countries (Albania, Bosnia and Herzegovina, North Macedonia, Montenegro, and Serbia). The 16 + 1, and later 17 + 1, cooperation mechanism took root as the China-CEEC Economic and Trade Forum in Budapest, Hungary, in 2011, as a precursor to the first China-CEEC leaders' summit in Warsaw, Poland, in 2012, which marked the founding of the mechanism. Both these forums and summits have since become annual events involving the prime or foreign ministers of China and the European member states.

Structure

The China-CEEC secretariat is located in Beijing, with one "national coordinator" from each of the CEEC countries. The investment component is the China-CEEC Investment Cooperation Fund, which was announced in 2012, established in 2013 with a commitment of $435 million, supported by the Export-Import Bank of China and Hungarian Export-Import Bank, and headed by a Chinese national (China-CEE Fund 2022). At the sixth meeting of the heads of China-CEEC governments in Budapest, Hungary, in November 2017, PRC prime minister Li Keqiang announced the establishment of the China-CEEC Interbank Association and a second expanded phase of the fund (Xinhua News Agency 2017c). Subsequent to the meeting, the fund was accordingly raised to $800 million (China-CEE Fund 2018). It was also decided at the meeting to create a new Sino-CEE Fund by the Industrial and Commercial Bank of China as a holding company, headed by a former chairman of the bank (Xinhua News Agency 2016a). The Sino-CEE Fund focuses on financing joint projects that purchase equipment and products made in China (Hu 2016).

China-CEEC Achievements

Infrastructure Building

The heads of China-CEEC governments meeting in Budapest in November 2017 was a high point in the economic, particularly financial and investment, cooperation between China and the CEE countries, but Chinese assistance was already in place well before the summit. Identifying infrastructure, advanced technologies, and green energy as the priority areas for increasing cooperation, China has contributed more than $15.4 billion toward infrastructure and other investment in the CEE countries from 2012 to 2019 in areas such as energy, transport, information and communication technology (ICT), manufacturing, real estate, and mergers and acquisitions (Hillman and McCalpin 2019). The energy and transportation sectors accounted for 64 percent of Chinese-involved activities and 79 percent of Chinese investments in the six non-EU countries plus Croatia, and Serbia received the highest level of Chinese funding and investment, totaling over $9.5 billion, with an increasing focus on digital infrastructure and ICT (Conley et al. 2020, 6). Serbia, Poland, and Hungary are the three CEE countries with comprehensive strategic partnerships with China, with Hungary attracting about one-third of the Chinese investments in CEE nations and becoming China's largest source of imports in 2016 among CEE states (Hu 2017). The Czech Republic, Poland, and Romania are also major recipients of Chinese foreign direct investment, although Prague also touted the possible cybersecurity risks of using Huawei's 5G system. In Greece, the state-owned China Ocean Shipping Company Limited has a controlling 51 percent share of the port of Piraeus (Kavalski 2019), which has been leased to China until 2052. The attraction of Chinese infrastructure investment is such that Greece vetoed an EU condemnation of China's human rights record at the United Nations in 2017 (Smith 2017). Addressing the China-CEEC Summit, held online on February 9, 2021, with CEE heads of state, government, and ministries, Xi stated that China had plans to import over $170 billion in goods from CEE countries over the next five years. He also said that by the end of 2020, Chinese trade with CEECs had exceeded $100 billion for the first time, with an average growth rate since 2012 approaching 8 percent annually (Xu and Cao 2021).

Health Assistance

To position China as a global health leader and responsible state actor in dealing with the worldwide spread of the COVID-19 pandemic since 2020, which to the best of existing knowledge originated from the Chinese city of Wuhan, Chinese leaders have raised the notion of building a Health Silk Road internationally by providing medical supplies, test kits, protective medical suits, healthcare experts, and later China-made COVID-19 vaccines to afflicted countries. In Europe, the medical support was delivered to CEE states through railways such as the Europe–China Railway Express, the so-called Iron Silk Road, of which many lines were built across Eurasia for freight with heavy subsidies by China, as well as through ports and logistic hubs (Shepard 2020a). The number of freight train journeys rose from 17 in 2011 to 12,406 in 2020, accumulating more than 45,000 freight trains along 73 routes between more than 50 Chinese cities, in addition to 175 cities in 23 European and Asian countries by October 2021 (Wang, Yang, and Peng 2021). Poland is a major rail node on the Europe–China Railway Express and also hosts Huawei's regional headquarters (Sweeney 2022).

China's provision of vaccines to European countries such as Serbia and Hungary offered fertile ground for China to strengthen bilateral ties with those country's populist leaders, who are often critical of the EU. When the first medical supplies and health experts from China arrived in Serbia in March 2020, Serbia's president, Aleksandar Vucic, who had earlier complained of European tardiness in providing his country with medical aid to fight COVID-19, was on hand at Belgrade's airport to receive them and kiss the Chinese flag (Standish 2021a). At the China-CEEC online forum in February 2021, Xi said that Chinese companies had already supplied 1 million doses of COVID-19 vaccines to Serbia (Ng and Lo 2021), about two-thirds of the amount ordered, making Serbia the first country in Europe to start inoculating its population with China's vaccines, which constituted the majority of the country's supply (Wu and Gelineau 2021). In Hungary, the first 550,000 doses of the Sinopharm vaccine arrived from China in February 2021, with another 1 million doses expected by April, followed by another 3.5 million in May (Euronews and AFP 2021). However, it should be noted that the state of China's relations with a CEE country is dependent on the person in charge, such as Serbia's president Aleksandar Vucic and Hungary's prime minister Viktor Orban, and may not survive their tenure in office unless it expands to a broader and more popular national base.

China-CEEC Challenges

Project Controversies

Chinese projects in the CEE countries have not been without controversy. Attempts to circumvent EU rules requiring open tenders for infrastructure construction of the China-CEEC's flagship Budapest–Belgrade railway project triggered investigations by the EU, entailing delays and cost overruns (European Parliament 2018). After a change of government in North Macedonia, it was discovered that the Chinese company Sinohydro had been selected without open and competitive bidding as the main contractor for the Kicevo–Ohrid and the Skopje–Štip motorways, and the contracted Chinese loans were directly allocated to local subcontractors linked to the ruling elite (European Parliament 2018), resulting in a large national debt to China. Also new coal-fired plants financed and built by Chinese companies in Serbia and Bosnia and Herzegovina have increased these countries' carbon emissions beyond EU allowable standards (European Parliament 2018). In April 2021, Montenegro's government asked the EU to help it pay off an almost $1 billion loan owed to China's Exim Bank for the construction of one section of the Bar–Boljare Highway, connecting its Adriatic Sea coast to Serbia (Bermingham 2021b). The request was initially rebuffed, and

62 | China's Belt and Road Power Transition

a deal was struck only with the involvement of US banks later. Even in Serbia, in April 2021, many Serbians protested the damage and pollution caused by Chinese-run Zijin copper mine in the southern town of Bor, which led the government to shut down the project (Standish, Cvetkovic, and Zivanovic 2021). Both the European Commission and European Parliament have voiced concerns that by exploiting existing weak governance, rule-of-law, and environmental frameworks in some CEE countries, the China-CEEC mechanism could undermine EU unity on policies toward China. A cold-eyed observer may remark that, if anything, undercutting European accord or unity in dealing with China is Beijing's chief purpose in this China-CEEC arrangement.

Political Problems

There are rife suspicions in the Baltic states of Estonia, Latvia, and Lithuania, which were once annexed by the Soviet Union and see the US as their guarantor of independence, that in the face growing confrontation with the US and the West, China's goals are to create a division between the US and Europe through the "17 + 1" initiative (Bermingham 2021a). In 2021, when entrepreneur Peter Vesterbacka, developer of the video game Angry Birds, proposed building an underwater rail tunnel from Finland to Estonia with $17 billion in Chinese government financing, his idea was met with widespread political opposition in Estonia, and Lithuania blocked a state-owned Chinese company, Nutech, from supplying equipment for three of its airports over national security concerns (Bermingham 2021a). In May 2021, Lithuania withdrew from China-CEEC altogether, turning it back to "16 + 1." After canceling a project with China to build two new nuclear reactors in May 2020, Romania banned Huawei, and in June 2021, a demonstration of 10,000 people took place in Budapest to protest the building of a Chinese Fudan University campus in Hungary (Brînză 2021). After Belarus's controversial presidential election in August 2020 ended in the reelection of Alexander Lukashenko, whose power is maintained by the Kremlin, China's land links with CEEC countries are very much in the hands of Russia. Furthermore, Putin's war on Ukraine has made it harder for private companies to transact between the West and Russia, and the flow of goods along the Iron Silk Road, the Eurasian rail system across which $75 billion worth of Chinese products traveled to Europe in 2021, is likely to slow (Sweeney 2022). However, China remains the biggest customer for Ukraine's corn export in the first half of 2023, although 60,000 tons of agricultural products destined for China were destroyed by Russian attacks on a port terminal, according to Ukrainian president Volodymyr Zelensky. There has also been no indication that such concerns have made the major European economies of Italy, Germany, and Britain any less interested in trade with and investment from China than their CEEC counterparts, particularly by making use of the Europe–China Railway Express network. China, particularly its Da Jiang Innovation company, remains a major supplier of drones to Germany and several other European companies, despite their fears of espionage.

To What Extent Is China-CEEC Still Useful to China?

If the salient purpose of the SCO for China is to stabilize and consolidate relations with post-Soviet Russia and the countries of Central Asia first as a Sino-Russian condominium and later on a bilateral basis, the China-CEEC forum of more recent vintage demonstrates Beijing's primary interest to develop and enhance "China plus" forums that are multilateral in form but essentially bilateral, with the agenda set by China. Prominent examples include the China + ASEAN forum, Forum on China-Africa Cooperation, China-Arab States Cooperation Forum, and Regional Comprehensive Economic Partnership. Perhaps the Chinese leadership feels that pursuing this model of relations with smaller, weaker, or poorer states would best parlay China's burgeoning economic size, hard-power strength, and authoritarian efficiency in development and governance as a political paradigm and channel attention into means of influencing, if not directing, the affairs of other countries and the world. The China-CEEC relationship is certainly a reflection of such an ambition, as it is indeed the entire BRI, and China-CEEC could conceivably expand in the future to security cooperation.

It is not surprising that China may prefer not to deal with an enlarged "EU + China" or "27 + 1," because unlike Central and Eastern Europe, Western Europe contains several economies, such as Germany, France, Italy, Spain, and Britain, that are of some size, technological sophistication, and financial wealth and therefore difficult if not impossible for China to dominate economically, especially if they were to stand together and act in unison. Still, there are loopholes to exploit should Western Europe again lapse into economic troubles. Italy was the first EU member state to officially join the BRI, and in the aftermath of its financial crisis, the People's Bank of China purchased shares worth more than $5 billion in the Italian stock market, acquiring holdings in important companies such as Unicredit, Eni,

Enel, and Telecom Italia. To protect the country's strategic economic assets, the Italian government issued "golden power" measures in April 2020 to safeguard national assets, special powers through which the government can oppose or require adherence to specific conditions for the purchase of shares of Italian firms by external buyers (Tagliapietra 2020). Germany enhanced its FDI screening process (although it did allow a Chinese company to purchase a minority stake in the port of Hamburg in 2022), France lowered its threshold for notification of FDI from 25 percent to 10 percent, and Spain introduced new restrictions on FDI (ICLG.com 2020).

In May 2021, the European Parliament voted overwhelmingly to put on hold indefinitely the legislative process for ratifying the EU's investment pact with China, negotiated over the previous seven years, unless Beijing lifts sanctions against EU lawmakers that were imposed after the 27 EU countries slapped Xinjiang officials with sanctions over mass internment of the region's Uyghur minorities (Lau 2021). In response, the Chinese foreign minister soon afterward invited his counterparts from Poland, Hungary, Serbia, and Ireland to China for meetings on furthering cooperation. CEEC countries have trade deficits with China, which they are eager to narrow or eliminate by attracting more Chinese purchases of their products, and in the world of realpolitik, EU laws or the laws of individual countries could be changed to permit or even encourage Chinese buyouts should the economic situation demand. China would then be in a position to challenge the US for world dominance, with or without the BRI or SREB.

China–Pakistan Economic Corridor

Perhaps nothing demonstrates the geostrategic nature of the BRI more vividly than the CPEC. The CPEC, which connects China and Pakistan, is considered by China as a flagship project of the BRI, for which Beijing has committed some $62 billion (SCMP 2020). Pakistan's attraction and commitment to the CPEC is the consequence of its lack of infrastructure connectivity, electricity, industrial development, skills training, and investment funds. The CPEC is also a means for Pakistan to join with China to counter India, with which both countries have territorial disputes. For China, the CPEC would shorten oil and gas routes from the Middle East by transporting hydrocarbon over land into western China instead of thousands of kilometers of water around South Asia and Southeast Asia by ship. Oil from the Persian Gulf could reach China via Gwadar in just

10 days instead of 45 days without the use of this route (Hussain, Yuan, and Ali 2016). For Pakistan, under the CPEC, several coal-fired and wind energy generation projects, a number of highways, an optical fiber cable, and the mass transit light-rail system in Lahore are already completed and operational, but proposed hydropower stations, mass transit systems in other major cities, the Pak-China Friendship Hospital in Gwadar and expansion of its deep-sea port, and nine special economic zones or industrial zones were still under review or construction as of 2022 (CPEC 2020; CPEC-Gwadar 2022). For China, promotion of the CPEC is pivotal to the development of Xinjiang (Uygur) Autonomous Region and the western provinces of China, which have benefited less from the economic boom of the previous two decades than the eastern seaboard. The CPEC aims to give China's vast landlocked western region access to overseas markets by connecting Kashgar in Xinjiang with the port of Gwadar in Pakistan's Baluchistan province, by means of a planned 3,200-kilometer trade route across Pakistan that would include roads (some of which have already been completed), rail links, and oil and gas pipelines, reducing the overland distance by about 50 percent from Xinjiang to the Arabian Sea (Chand 2014).

Pakistan and China have been described as having shared "a great history of brotherly and time-tested relations" (Arifeen 2016). If so, it is no wonder that Pakistan has been the most consistently enthusiastic supporter of China's BRI and is for China the most important economic and strategic partner in the region of South Asia. China is Pakistan's largest trading partner, and Pakistan is China's second-largest trading partner in South Asia. Trade volume between the two countries grew from $5.7 billion to $100.11 billion during a 15-year period from 2000 to 2015, while the total value of contracts signed in this period went from $1.8 billion to $150.8 billion (Arifeen 2016). However, according to the American Enterprise Institute, a quarter of investments or projects undertaken by the Chinese from 2005 to 2014, worth $246 billion, have stalled due to various reasons (Viswanath 2016).

CPEC Achievements

The CPEC was proposed during Premier Li Keqiang's visit to Pakistan in May 2013, which was also the year that Nawaz Sharif became prime minister of Pakistan. In connection with CPEC, Chinese companies were expected to invest at least $45.6 billion in Pakistan—$33.8 billion in electricity and $11.8 billion in transport infrastructure (UNCTAD 2015). Of the 53 agreements and memorandums of understanding signed by Li and Nawaz, a total of 31 were accords in the private energy sector, which would allow Pakistani energy companies engaged in power generation projects to access debt financing from Chinese commercial banks (Arifeen 2016). Expected Chinese investments on CPEC are equivalent to the value of all FDI inflows into Pakistan from 1970 to 2012 (Javaid 2016, 257).

Pakistan's peak power demand is 18,000 megawatts, but since the country's present power generation capacity is just 12,000 megawatts, the power shortfall creates opportunities for China to cooperate with Pakistan in this field. As part of its commitment to the corridor, the Chinese government is reported to have agreed to build 18 new power plants, half of which will be coal-powered. One of the first projects in Pakistan to benefit from the Silk Road Fund is the 720-megawatt, $1.4 billion Karot Hydropower Project on the Jhelum River in the northeast of Pakistan, which has been jointly developed by China Three Gorges South Asia Investment and Pakistan's Private Power and Infrastructure Committee, with the co-investors being the People's Bank of China and the World Bank's International Finance Corporation and loans provided by China Exim Bank and China Development Bank (*Global Capital* 2015). The plant, scheduled to be built by 2020 and transferred to the government after 30 years of operation, was expected to create about 3,500 local jobs and generate enough power to provide electricity for 7 million homes (*Global Capital* 2015). China's plans include adding 10,400 megawatts of electricity to the supply capacity at a cost of $15.5 billion by 2018, since this would be the time when President Sharif was expected to seek reelection and the project would fulfill one of his major election pledges (Chowdhury 2015, 2). China would also establish 10 projects of 6,600 megawatts in the Thar Desert, costing another $18.6 billion and doubling Pakistan's current production level of power (2). Chinese companies would disburse $35 to $37 billion in FDI for power production based on solar, wind, coal and hydropower generation of 16,400 megawatts and for the construction of a transmission system (Javaid 2016, 262).

The southern terminus of CPEC, Pakistan's Gwadar, is regarded by China as a strategic link to the Middle East, Africa, and Europe, since the deep-water port positioned close to the Strait of Hormuz would give China easy access to key shipping routes in and out of the Persian Gulf (*Global Capital* 2015). As early as 2006, at Pakistan's request, China had provided $198 million for the first phase of the port, which was completed that year (Ali 2013). As a signal commitment to the CPEC, Pakistan signed an agreement with the state-owned China Overseas Port Holding Company in

The Silk Road Economic Belt | 67

2015 to pass over control of Gwadar port's operation, which was previously under the Port of Singapore Authority, and allow it to manage the port until 2059 (Bokhari, Kazmin, and Kynge 2017). Gwadar was expected to be upgraded to a special economic zone spread over 152 hectares and expanded to allow for docking of heavy ships with deadweight capacity equivalent to 70,000 tons (Javaid 2016, 263). Oil is expected to be imported from the Middle East, refined and stored in refineries at Gwadar, and sent to China via roads, pipelines, or railway. Since security patrols in the Strait of Malacca are carried out by the US Navy, China's existing dependence on deliveries of oil through that strait was a major reason behind Beijing's attempts to diversify the routes of oil transportation (Belokrenitsky 2007). China has helped to build some roads in Pakistan, but thousands of kilometers of gas and oil pipelines and railway tracks still have to be laid to make Gwadar and the CPEC economically useful to China. Pakistan's first highway project under the CPEC financed by the China-backed AIIB is a 64-kilometer stretch of the M4 highway connecting Shorkot to Khanewal in Pakistan's Punjab province that broke ground in August 2016 (*Financial Post* 2016) and will eventually be linked all the way to Gwadar.

Gwadar's development holds additional advantages for both Pakistan and China. Pakistan lacks ports for shipping and maritime security; in successive conflicts, the navy of its neighboring rival India quickly blockaded Karachi, severely limiting the Pakistani navy's maneuverability (Ali 2013). As such, Gwadar, with its deep harbor 470 kilometers away from Karachi, seemed an ideal place for a new outlet to the Indian Ocean, and not just for Pakistan. Gwadar could lend itself to being a Chinese naval listening post, allowing Beijing to monitor Sea Lines of Communications, keep an eye on US maritime movements in the Persian Gulf, and oversee India's naval bases of Mumbai and Gujarat from a strategic location close to the Strait of Hormuz. China's interest in having a military presence astride the strait arises from the fact that this narrow 3.2-kilometer-wide maritime corridor is the route for the transportation of 17 million barrels of oil per day and through which about 60 percent of China's oil supplies pass from the Gulf to the Arabian Sea and Indian Ocean. In 2001, Pakistan's former president Pervez Musharraf told an audience in his country's capital, Islamabad, just after the visit of then Chinese prime minister Zhu Rongji, that in the event of a conflict with Pakistan, India would find the Chinese navy positioned in Gwadar (Parthasarathy 2016). Apart from Gwadar, China's engagement in proximate ports such as Chittagong in Bangladesh, Hambantota in Sri Lanka, and Sittwe in Myanmar has been viewed by some Indian political

68 | China's Belt and Road Power Transition

analysts as reflective of a wider encirclement policy against India (Javaid 2016, 262). This is a perception that is not in Pakistan's interest to discourage.

CPEC Challenges

By 2017, China's realized investments in Pakistan have exceeded $25 billion, and four industrial parks under the CPEC are planned for operation (Phoenix Television 2017). By 2020, 11 projects were said to have been completed, 11 more were underway, and the CPEC already provides one-third of Pakistan's electricity supply (Ng 2020). However, there were indications that although Pakistan was deriving great benefits from the CPEC, it is not entirely satisfied. In 2017, Pakistan removed China from the construction of the $14 billion Diamer-Basha Dam astride the Indus River after the Chinese demanded that ownership of the dam be transferred to China after completion. Notwithstanding, a contract for the construction of the Mohmand Dam located on the Swat River in Khyber-Pakhtunkhwa (KPK, the former Northwest Frontier Agency) was awarded to a joint venture between China Gezhouba and Descon, a company founded by one of the advisers of Imran Khan (*Nikkei Asian Review* 2019), who succeeded Nawaz Sharaf as prime minister of Pakistan. With the completion of many CPEC projects delayed, deep and rising indebtedness to China, and a soaring current account deficit, Pakistan had to borrow $6 billion from the IMF in May 2019, agreeing in return to cut fuel subsidies, increase interest rates, raise taxes, and further devalue the Pakistani rupee (Masood 2019). Due to the adverse economic impact caused by COVID-19, Pakistan slashed its annual budget for the CPEC from $241 million in 2019 to $159 million in 2020 (Leng 2020). As of mid-2020, completed CPEC projects amounted to less than one-third of those announced, valued at about $19 billion, with no signs of factories operating at Gwadar's free trade zone, which was established in 2015 and operated by the state-owned China Overseas Ports Holding Company, and the planned airport and oil refinery in Gwadar, as well as railway and oil pipeline from the city to China, have all yet to materialize (SCMP 2020). Scheduled completion of the Karot hydropower plant was pushed back from 2020 to mid-2022 (CPEC 2022).

Furthermore, both Pakistan and CPEC are expected to face security challenges, especially in the regions of KPK and Baluchistan, where militants in armed uprisings target power pylons and gas pipelines. Four rebel groups operating under the umbrella of the Baloch Raaji Aajoi Sangar are violently opposed to Chinese activities in Baluchistan, where Gwadar is located (Hussain

2021). Given such security concerns and opposition to Chinese workers and engineers in Pakistan, several of whom have been harmed or killed throughout the years, the Pakistani government has formed a 12,000-strong security force to stand guard over Chinese workers (Viswanath 2016). Even so, armed separatists from Baluchistan have attacked government and Chinese personnel and attempted an assault on the Chinese consulate in Karachi. Despite these setbacks, Khan's appointment of Asim Saleem Bajwa, retired army general, as the first chairman of the CPEC Authority in November 2019 demonstrates the strategic significance of the ostensibly economic CPEC initiative to Pakistan. For security purposes, Gwadar port will be equipped with an air defense unit, a military garrison, and an airport (Chand 2014). However, in Pakistan, concerns remain about the country's ability to service the interest and principal on the Chinese loans and the actual number of jobs created for Pakistani workers, technicians, and engineers by the CPEC projects (Ranade 2017) relative to those brought in by China. The political parties of KPK and Baluchistan have complaints about the allocation of funds and designated routes, which they claim have favored Punjab (Ahmed 2019), Imran Khan's home province. Apparently, much remains to be done by both Pakistan and China to ensure the economic success of the CPEC, but since the scheme is in the strategic and military interests of both the leaderships of Pakistan and China, in simultaneously strengthening Pakistan against India and China against its world power rivals, they will in all likelihood do everything in their power to see that it will not fail.

Chapter 3

Reimagining the 21st Century
Maritime Silk Road

The BRI's 21st century Maritime Silk Road (MSR) is basically China's initiative to invest in, collaborate with, and lift up the economic welfare of countries in Southeast Asia, South Asia, East Africa, and continental Europe along ancient sea trading routes from eastern China through the East China Sea, South China Sea, Indian Ocean, Red Sea, and Mediterranean Sea. Harking back to the golden age of maritime trade and travel by Chinese mariners during the Tang, Song, Yuan (Mongol), and early Ming dynasties from the 7th till the mid-15th century, the PRC is propagating the MSR to project itself as a true maritime power. However, such an attempt, although understandable from the standpoint of its economic and military strength, will inevitably attract anxiety and attention from the US, the world's largest sea power, and its allies such as Japan and Australia. The MSR starts from China's engagement with Southeast Asia, traverses South Asia, encompasses the countries of East Africa, and passes through the Red Sea and out to the Mediterranean Sea. Compared to the SREB, the truly novel MSR has attracted many more policy discussions and material resources from China in its realization.

From China's perspective, securing energy supply from the Persian Gulf region via the Arabian Sea, Indian Ocean, Malacca Strait, and South China Sea is the way to guarantee the country's energy and economic security, and therefore sustain the economic growth that underpins its domestic political stability. Given the strategic importance of maritime linkages to China, it is not surprising that an official white paper on military strategy published in 2015 avers that "the traditional mentality that land outweighs sea must be

71

abandoned, and great importance has to be attached to managing the seas and oceans and protecting maritime rights and interests" (Bokhari, Kazmin, and Kynge 2017, 11). Certainly, China's priority is to develop and expand maritime infrastructure along its major trading routes. At the time of the MSR's launch, China was already the world's largest exporter and second-largest importer, controlling 20 percent of the world's container fleet, and its shipping companies carry more cargo than those of any other nation, with 5 of the top 10 container ports in the world in mainland China plus another in Hong Kong (Chand 2014). China possesses a 300-ship navy and a 200-ship maritime law enforcement fleet, more than Japan, Indonesia, Vietnam, Malaysia, and the Philippines combined (Oxford Analytica 2016a). China has asserted that its network of ports from Port Sudan to Mainland China is only to guard its commercial and energy interests, but this statement has been questioned, as the network also includes the building of naval facilities abroad. Indeed, China's National Defense Transportation Law stipulates that overseas infrastructure projects of the country's state-owned enterprises must be designed to meet military standards (Sharma 2021a). This, if anything, is proof that just like the ports constructed by China, the MSR and BRI itself has more than just an economic purpose.

Southeast Asia

The region of Southeast Asia, located south and southeast of China, can be considered the geographical starting point of the MSR. In this section, the political and economic benefits and cost ramifications of the MSR are examined from the vantage point of both China and the countries of the Association of Southeast Asian Nations (ASEAN), which is a regional organization of states in Southeast Asia that includes Indonesia, Malaysia, the Philippines, Thailand, Singapore, Brunei, Laos, Myanmar, Vietnam, and Cambodia. For the MSR to be successful, China's leadership role is important but active participation from ASEAN countries is needed. An ASEAN country is unlikely to react favorably to China's MSR initiative if it expects little accruable political and economic benefits. This section thus examines the incentives or disincentives, for ASEAN countries, of the MSR's development. Since political and economic factors are closely intertwined, the political benefits and costs are weighed against the economic benefits and costs to more objectively evaluate the effects of the MSR's implementation on ASEAN countries.

Southeast Asian countries that signed on to the MSR are first and foremost interested in receiving infrastructural investments and FDI inflows from China. They also hope to use the initiative to create more opportunities for exporting goods and services to China, considering that until the early years of the MSR Southeast Asian countries generally experienced trade deficits with China due to their declining net exports (value of exports minus imports) and unfavorable trade terms vis-à-vis China, as they generally export cheaper primary commodities and import dearer manufactures and capital products from China (Chung and Voon 2017, 437–44).

It is imperative to understand the geopolitical calculations of the parties involved in the MSR, namely, (1) the major political considerations of China's MSR initiative with regard to Southeast Asian states, (2) why there are differences in the reactions of these governments to the initiative, and (3) what actions the Chinese government is taking to address these reactions. Economic cost-benefit calculations aside, it is hypothesized that the political receptivity of Southeast Asian countries to MSR initiatives are functions of (1) existing territorial disputes with China over islands in the South China Sea, (2) fear of Chinese expansionism or assertion of hegemony, or, conversely, (3) attempts to use a rising China as a counterweight against neighboring countries.

China's Geopolitical Calculations

It should be recalled that China's MSR initiative was first proposed by Xi Jinping during a speech to the Indonesian Parliament in October 2013 during his official visits to Malaysia and Indonesia. In Jakarta, Chairman Xi called for the creation of a "China-ASEAN community of common destiny." The choice of venue for the address was not incidental; Indonesia is the largest country in Southeast Asia, and its decision to join the initiative would largely determine its success or failure. Since the outbreak of the global financial crisis in 2008, it has been widely perceived that the center of world economic and political power has shifted remarkably from the West to the Asia-Pacific. Shortly after the China-ASEAN Free Trade Area was inaugurated and China surpassed Japan to become the world's second-largest economy in 2010, Washington announced its Pivot to Asia security strategy and Trans-Pacific Partnership for free trade. With a more assertive China, words and actions from its leadership could also be more easily interpreted as threats, and along with deepening contact between China and its neighbors, conflicts of interest between them have also been on the rise. Strategically, therefore, the MSR initiative could cushion China within its defined "good neighborliness" policy and overcome any effects of the US' "rebalancing" and expanded security cooperation with Japan, the

Philippines, Australia, and India. As the US sees China as a competitor, and some Southeast Asian states have territorial disputes with China, China is seeking a proactive stance in global governance, and the MSR places Southeast Asia within the context of shaping a modern, global strategic layout for Beijing. Beijing is not yet ready for military confrontation with the US, but it is seeking a long-term transformation in the character of contemporary international relations, from an international system dominated by America to a more genuinely multipolar international order in which China would have greater influence. If the MSR project in Southeast Asia proves to be a catalyst that accelerates the relative decline of US world hegemony, it would also position China as a true maritime power.

Xi has spoken of the "Chinese dream" of boosting China's living standards and restoring it's past greatness, in a way playing up nationalistic sentiments to buttress the Party's legitimacy. In scale, ethos, and routing, the MSR initiative can be seen as a systemic approach to revitalize China's historical legacy of external engagement that has existed for centuries, and consequently heighten its standing in the world. With Fujian province's Quanzhou city as the designated starting point, the MSR project harkens back at least to the Ming dynasty (1368–1644) when the diplomat and navigator Zheng He (1371–1433) was commissioned by his emperor to lead seven expeditions to Southeast and South Asia, the Middle East, and East Africa, pioneering for China regional diplomacy, trade, and perhaps most important for the Chinese leadership today, influence among the countries that he visited. To expand cooperation, China has made efforts with Southeast Asian countries to upgrade CAFTA; speed up construction of interconnectivity infrastructure; enhance regional cooperation on finance and risk prevention; stimulate exchanges and cooperation on security issues, people-to-people contact, science, and technology; and promote environmental protection (Chen 2015). More than half of global piracy incidents occurred in Southeast Asia in 2014, so navigational safety, joint law enforcement patrols, and search-and-rescue could be either challenges to the smooth implementation of the MSR or areas of Sino-ASEAN cooperation (*Beijing Review* 2015).

THE GEOPOLITICAL CALCULUS OF SOUTHEAST ASIAN RECEPTIVITY TO THE MSR

To attract countries to China's MSR, the peoples and governments of the targeted states have to approve of a Chinese presence, and to a certain extent,

China's involvement in their countries' affairs. At the Conference on Interaction and Confidence Building in Asia (CICA) security meeting hosted by China in May 2014, Xi pointedly stated that it was for the people of Asia to run the affairs of Asia. The problem for Beijing is that this sentiment is not reciprocated everywhere in the region since it could be read as a desire to remove the US as an external balancer to China for regional states. China's rise has led countries such as Japan, the Philippines, and Vietnam, with which Beijing has taken a hard line on maritime territorial sovereignty disputes, to conduct more frequent and larger-scale military exercises with the US (Krishnan 2015). Political mistrust toward Beijing and its unwillingness to compromise on territorial disputes remain the biggest challenges. China's neighbors welcomed closer economic ties with it, but doubts about Beijing's intentions, and whether unfavorable conditions may be attached to an MSR project, appear to be making some countries reluctant to embrace a vision of comprehensive political and security cooperation with China. To make the MSR diplomatically and economically attractive to Southeast Asian states, China has specifically earmarked RMB 3 billion to set up a China-ASEAN Maritime Cooperation Fund, ostensibly for the purposes of promoting maritime security and environmental protection (Liu 2014). However, many ASEAN countries have been reluctant to draw on the fund as they fear there would be political strings attached (Kwok 2013).

Southeast Asians recognize that there is a real risk that Beijing's MSR efforts, well intentioned or not, will heighten geopolitical tensions in their region. This is because there are direct security implications of the project, since deepening ports under the MSR initiative will likely expand China's capacity to project its growing naval power abroad, while increased Chinese involvement in building ICT infrastructure in Southeast Asia could create new channels for Beijing to exert its influence in the region (Kennedy and Parker 2015). While Southeast Asian states do not want to be seen as taking part in any effort to contain China, thus compromising their burgeoning economic relations with Beijing, they also do not want to be perceived as facilitating China's efforts to check an opponent. Unless China is able to convince would-be participating countries that the MSR would not be used as a geopolitical ploy to outmaneuver a rival power, these countries will hesitate to get involved to any extent.

Suspicions of China's intentions in Southeast Asia are rife and cannot be simply brushed off with blandishment of trade and investment carrots. Its assertive behavior in the South China Sea, where it is engaged in reclaiming and construction sprees to turn disputed rocks into fortified military bases, has given the impression that it will simply do what it wants regardless of the preferences of its smaller neighbors. There is uneasiness that China may also use MSR plans to provoke division among its neighbors, luring some countries into immediate economic interests to support China's MSR and thus undermining the interests of others. Unsurprisingly then, the initial reactions in Southeast Asia to the MSR were skeptical, particularly in the countries where the initiative was first publicly floated.

Malaysia's defense minister Hishamuddin Hussein said that the MSR has "raised questions" and must come across as a joint (i.e., regional) initiative rather than as a solely Chinese one, but even so, Malaysia's prime minister Najib Razak welcomed the initiative as conducive to the country's development (SCMP 2015). Despite overlapping claims in the South China Sea dispute, Malaysia's relations with China have been better than cordial, with both countries' navies holding their first ever bilateral drills on search-and-rescue in the Strait of Malacca from September 11 to 18, 2015. Indonesia's president Joko Widodo, who had said he wanted to turn his country into a "global maritime fulcrum," was doubtful at first but later appeared inclined to the view that he could attract massive investment in ports and other infrastructure from China with the MSR, although he made clear that Indonesia does not accept China's territorial claims in Southeast Asian waters (Kapoor and Sieg 2015). Like China, Indonesia has always considered itself a large maritime nation. The significance of Jakarta's support for the MSR cannot be overemphasized, particularly in the beginning as a "strategic distraction" to the US "rebalance." In February 2014, a Chinese People's Liberation Army Navy (PLAN) task force crossed the Indonesian straits of Sunda and Lombok to conduct unprecedented and unannounced exercises off Australia (Khurana 2015). For all Indonesia's interest in investments from China, it's involvement in the MSR has been and will be limited by nationalist and Islamist sentiments, which could be mobilized by hard-liners in the government and opposing sociopolitical groups (Kuik 2021, 265).

Cambodia, a major recipient of Chinese aid for its railway infrastructure and agriculture development, has officially and unsurprisingly expressed its support for the MSR proposal. Phnom Penh particularly desires a Chinese presence in Southeast Asia to ward off military pressures from both Vietnam and Thailand, with which it has border disputes. Furthermore, multisectoral cooperation with China provides the capital and technology required to industrialize and stimulate growth in Cambodia, while enabling the ruling Cambodian People's Party to mobilize patronage resources to sustain its power (Kuik 2021, 266). Laos is a fellow socialist one-party state of China on which it is heavily dependent for trade and investment, particularly in road, rail, and hydroelectric dam constructions.

Thailand supports and actively participates in the MSR, chiefly to strengthen infrastructure cooperation with China (Huang and Zhong 2015). The Chinese government sees Thailand's current military-backed government as providing fast-track trade and investment opportunities to circumvent democratic political processes in Thailand and further map out the blueprint of an emerging Sino-Thai quasi-alliance. As energy security is a major strategic purpose behind MSR initiatives for China, Myanmar's oil and natural gas transportation corridor, 2,400-kilometers long through its Kyaukphyu Port via railway and pipeline to China's Yunnan province, completed in 2013 by the China National Petroleum Corp., will enable China to reduce its dependency on the Strait of Malacca, patrolled by the US Navy (McCoy 2015), through which 80 percent of China's energy supplies now pass (Rolland 2015). For its part, the Brunei government wants to diversify its overwhelming dependence on the oil and gas sector and so welcomes rice, agriculture, and fishery cooperation with China under the MSR plan (Song 2015).

As for Singapore, it cannot expect much benefit from participating in the MSR. Since the Sri Lankan government announced that it intended to develop itself into a maritime hub, in contest with Singapore and Dubai, China's investments in Colombo's port facilities as part of the MSR would be aiding a competitor of Singapore's (Johnson 2015). Also, if China were to maximize its use of the oil and gas pipeline and railway through Myanmar, Chinese ships and oil tankers would reduce their use of the Malacca Strait, and the commercial importance of Singapore to China would also be correspondingly diminished. Inhabiting the smallest country in Southeast Asia in terms of land area, Singaporeans are also worried about possible domination of their region and state by any one single power to the exclusion of others. Nonetheless, Singapore remains China's top Southeast Asian investor, and Singapore's prime minister Lee Hsien Loong has indicated that the MSR could act as a catalyst for development of the region (Fu 2015).

Vietnam and the Philippines have signed on to the MSR but have been carefully balancing nationalistic feelings over their territorial sovereignty disputes with China in the South China Sea against the financial incentives offered by China. Vietnam experienced anti-China riots in mid-2014 after a Chinese oil rig was discovered parked in waters claimed by Vietnam. The Philippines infuriated Beijing by unilaterally asking a United Nations arbitration panel in The Hague to rule on the legality of China's "nine-dash line," which it did rule against, that encloses China's claim to almost the entire South China Sea, part of which is contested by Manila. Maps denoting the "Maritime Silk Road" released by the Chinese media have shown the route running through the disputed areas, which could not have won adherence to the initiative in Vietnam and the Philippines (Dasgupta 2015). Still, both the governments of Vietnam and the Philippines appear interested in expanding trade with and infrastructure investment from China.

Despite Vietnam's quarrels with China over the South China Sea, the general secretary of the Communist Party of Vietnam, Nguyen Phu Trong, said that his country was "studying the 21st Century MSR" (Anh and Zhang 2015). Beijing and Hanoi subsequently agreed to upgrade the container port facilities of Haiphong, in northern Vietnam, to service cargo bound for inland areas of China (Phuong 2016). When the president of the Philippines, Rodrigo Duterte, paid a state visit to China in October 2016, shortly after his election, not only did he not mention the South China Sea ruling, but he announced his country's foreign policy realignment from Washington to Beijing, for which Duterte returned with business deals worth $17 billion (Huang 2016). Although China's maritime assertiveness remained, Duterte prioritized the attractiveness of development benefits from China's BRI. The recalibrations were motivated by Duterte's domestic political agenda: closer relations with China provided not only much-needed developmental capital to pursue his "build, build, build" infrastructure program but also political support to fend off the Western countries' criticism of how he allegedly condoned arbitrary police action in the conduct of his "war on drugs" (Kuik 2021, 260).

The BRI's buzzword *large infrastructure construction projects* was quickly put into operation. For the Southeast Asian region-wide portion of the MSR, the pièce de résistance is the Pan-Asian railway network proposed by Chinese prime minister Li Keqiang in 2013. This railway, when completed, would connect China to a market of 260 million consumers in Myanmar, Thailand, Laos, Cambodia, and Vietnam (Mok 2015). China has its own national standards for high-speed rails, which means that it will provide the specifications for connecting railways in the Pan-Asian railway network and integrating them into the Chinese rail system (Chan 2015). Separate high-speed railways would start from Kunming, capital of China's Yunnan province, with three routes passing through Vietnam, Cambodia, Laos, and Myanmar, respectively, to merge at Thailand's capital, Bangkok, before traveling down to Malaysia's capital, Kuala Lumpur, and reaching its final destination of Singapore. The rail line extending into Laos from

China actually began construction in 2011, at an estimated cost of $6.2 billion (McCoy 2015). However, when the Laos section of the railway from the Yunnan border to the Laotian capital of Vientiane was completed in December 2021, borrowed money within Laos accounted for 60 percent of the railway's investment (AP 2021), and Laos's debt to China was standing at 45 percent of its GDP (Strangio 2020). When the Thai section of the railway, which began construction in 2015 but has been delayed by haggling over cost sharing between Thailand and China, eventually opens to traffic, Bangkok will be the Southeast Asian rail hub of the 21st century. This is a major reason for Thailand's support of the MSR. After years of negotiations and delays, contracts were finally signed on March 29, 2021, for the Bangkok–Nong Khai high-speed railway, with costs estimated at $5.75 billion and completion expected by 2027 (Xinhua News Agency 2021). Thailand stands to benefit as the line will increase connectivity from Bangkok to the remote northeast, driving economic growth in towns along the route (Hart 2021). The Cambodian government asked its Chinese counterpart in 2015 to provide funds under the MSR to finance the missing railway links from both Oudong district in Kampong Speu province and Snuol district in Kratie province to Loc Ninh in Vietnam (Leng 2020). Besides, there is also the 150-kilometer, $5.1 billion Jakarta–Bandung high-speed railway in Indonesia being built by a joint venture formed by China Railway International, a subsidiary of China Railway, and Indonesian firms for which Xi has pledged to enhance local procurement, a move expected to create 40,000 jobs for Indonesians each year from its inception (Zhou 2016).

Railway construction aside, in 2020 the Cambodian government requested MSR funding for laying the Phnom Penh–Sihanoukville Expressway and gave the Chinese-owned company Angkor International Airport Investment exclusive rights to construct and manage the new Siem Reap international airport concession for 55 years under a build-operate-transfer scheme (Johnson 2021). The construction of Laos's $6 billion Vientiane–Boten Expressway, which stretches from Vientiane to the town of Boten at the Chinese border, began in 2018. The expressway, 60 percent of its construction funded by loans from the Exim Bank of China, is 95 percent owned by China's Yunnan Construction Engineering Group and only 5 percent by the Laotian government, with Chinese investors operating the expressway under a 50-year concession agreement (*The Star* 2021). A state-run Chinese company, the Guangxi Beibu Gulf International Port Group, had as early as 2013 drawn up plans to double the capacity of the deep-water container port at Kuantan on the east coast of West Malaysia with $2 billion MSR funding earmarked (Kwok 2013). In 2014, the company also began jointly developing, with Malaysian authorities, an industrial park in Kuantan, and in 2015 agreed through its subsidiary to invest $1 billion in a steel plant there (Page 2014). Considering that Kuantan lies far away from consumer markets and mineral deposits, what makes sense about this project is its strategic significance, given that it borders the South China Sea. In 2016, China's Guangdong province announced that it would invest $10 billion in a deep-sea port in Malacca (Yong 2016). It is possible that, once constructed, both ports of Kuantan and Malacca would have dual civilian and military uses for the Chinese navy. In the Philippines, the Exim Bank of China extended $62.09 million for the Chico River Irrigation Pump project, $211.21 million for the Kaliwa Dam, $219.78 million for a project management consultancy on the National Railways South Long-Haul project in Mindanao, and $337 million for the Safe Philippines Project to install high-definition, closed-circuit television cameras on public roads, with $750 million from the AIIB in June 2020 for combating the coronavirus (Robles 2021). However, by the end of 2021, most of these promised funds had yet to be dispensed. In Indonesia, where China is the largest country of export and import, as of 2021 Weda Bay Industrial Park's projects include a plant to produce nickel sulfate and a $2.8 million copper smelter, involving partnerships between multinational firms and the Zhejiang-based Tsingshan Holding Group. At Morowali Industrial Park, a collaboration between Tsingshan and Indonesia's Bintang Delapan Group, plans are underway to build a $350 million lithium chemical plant (Yuen 2021).

SOUTHEAST ASIAN REACTIONS AND CHINA'S RESPONSE

Although attractive, the investment schemes attendant to the MSR have caused concerns among some Southeast Asian governments that China's Silk Road program will enmesh their roads, railways, and ports, financed and constructed by Chinese companies, into China's economic, political, and strategic space. Many Southeast Asian states have deeper concerns that Beijing may leverage economic ties to coerce non-economic decisions in China's favor. Witness China's unofficial halting of rare earth exports to Japan in 2010 at the height of Sino-Japanese tensions in the East China Sea, and its delayed inspection and quarantine of fruits from the Philippines by Chinese customs officials in the aftermath of a bilateral flare-up in April 2012 over the contested Scarborough Shoal in the South China Sea (Miller 2015). Southeast Asian countries also may feel that closer integration between China and Southeast Asia, as envisaged by the MSR, will threaten or undercut the consolidation of ASEAN as a regional community of states. Whether as a work in progress or a master plan, China's grand connectivity MSR project has as many as 12 central government agencies involved in its drafting, funding, implementation, and reporting, ranging from the ministries of foreign affairs, commerce, transport, and agriculture to the National Development and Reform Commission (Chan 2015). Perhaps unsurprisingly then, Indonesia's officialdom sees the MSR as a contest for influence in Southeast Asia between mainland China and the US (Zhou 2015). Given the chain of events between China and the US since 2008, which in many ways affected Southeast Asia, this is a none too insightful but comprehensible perception.

Many Southeast Asians are concerned that by building multilevel intergovernmental macro-policy mechanisms to coordinate economic development strategies and policies for regional cooperation, China's MSR initiative will tie the national planning of Southeast Asian states to Chinese priorities. As such, sovereignty concerns, public opinion, and regime or leadership transformations will ultimately be the principal factors affecting the degree of success in the MSR's implementation in Southeast Asia.

Regarding Sovereignty Concerns

Sovereignty is a paramount and sensitive issue for Southeast Asian states, as they are all postcolonial entities except for Thailand and can still be considered developing countries.

China has tried to interest neighboring Vietnam in building two cross-border railroads into China and refurbishing its ports as part of the MSR, and China is financing the construction of a metro line in its capital, but Vietnam is worried that closer cooperation may entail Beijing demanding concessions from Hanoi on its South China Sea territorial claims. Vietnam claims not only all the Spratly Islands but also the Paracel group, which China's navy seized from South Vietnam in January 1974. Vietnam has been courting American companies, rather than Chinese, for the development of liquefied natural gas projects for its electricity needs (Hiep 2021). In February 2020, Duterte, president of the Philippines, decided to end the Visiting Forces Agreement, which allows US military aircrafts and vessels free entry into the Philippines, but he rescinded that decision four months later in response to China adding to the number of maritime militia vessels amassing around Thitu, the largest Philippines-occupied Island in the Spratlys

(Lendon 2020). As the smallest country in Southeast Asia in terms of land area, with the region's highest ratio of foreign trade to GDP, Singapore is persistently worried about possible domination by any one powerful state and thus allows the US Navy to use its port to balance any possible assertion of hegemony from China. However, sovereignty concerns over the MSR are felt not just by countries that have reason to be suspect of China's intentions.

Malaysia under Prime Minister Razak made a determined effort to align itself with China's MSR by allowing Chinese construction companies to take charge of the building of the $20 billion East Coast Rail Link joining Kota Bahru to Port Klang across Peninsula Malaysia, the Malacca Gateway and Kuantan port-industrial park complexes, and the Forest City project, a $100 billion mixed housing and commercial development built by the Chinese real estate company Country Garden and a local partner on four reclaimed islands in the Malaysian state of Johor across from Singapore. The buyers of Forest City were principally Chinese citizens given the right to reside in Malaysia. After the political opposition won the general election of May 2018, new Malaysian prime minister Mahathir Mohammed (temporarily) halted all MSR projects, hinting at a new version of colonialism (McGregor 2021).

In aiming to become the "battery of Southeast Asia" and escape poverty by exporting electricity to its neighbors, Laos has welcomed China as a major player in its ambitious hydropower plans to construct dams on the Mekong River and its tributaries, with Chinese companies involved in the construction of half of these facilities by providing around $11 billion in development financing, and for which Laos owes about half of its external debts to China (RFA 2019). In March 2021, the Chinese state-owned enterprise China Southern Power Grid, which became the majority shareholder of the Laotian state-owned enterprise Electricite du Laos, in September 2020 signed a concession agreement with the Laotian company that would position it to "serve as the country's national power grid operator to invest in, construct and operate 230kV-and-above power grids in Laos and implement grid interconnection projects between Laos and its neighboring countries" (Guerreiro 2021). Environmentalists are concerned that the dams will affect downstream fishers and farmers by disrupting fish migration patterns and blocking sediment flows needed to refresh farmland in the Mekong rice-growing regions of Laos, Thailand, Cambodia, and Vietnam, thus threatening the economic and food security of these countries. Paradoxically, it was sovereignty concern that led Cambodia, already a longtime recipient of Chinese aid for its railway infrastructure and agriculture development, to

Reimagining the 21st Century Maritime Silk Road | 83

express unwavering support for the MSR, as Phnom Penh desires a strong Chinese presence in Southeast Asia to ward off military pressures from both Vietnam and Thailand, with which it has border disputes.

Still, it appears that neither Laos nor Cambodia is putting all its eggs in China's basket. On September 26, 2021, leaders of the ruling parties of Vietnam, Cambodia, and Laos held a rare conclave in Hanoi, which included Nguyen Phu Trong, the general secretary of the Vietnamese Communist Party; Hun Sen, president of the Cambodian People's Party; and Thongloun Sisoulith, the chief of the Lao People's Revolutionary Party. Vietnam maintains close historical, political, and ideological ties to the ruling parties of its two "fraternal" western neighbors, which it helped attain power in the 1970s, and the unusual meeting of party heads speaks to the rising concern in Hanoi that its two erstwhile clients are being drawn slowly into China's widening orbit at a time of ascendant Chinese power (Strangio 2021). In January 2020, Jakarta sent warships and fighter jets to waters off Indonesia's Natuna Islands, located in the southern reaches of the South China Sea, after Chinese fishing vessels escorted by China's coast guard entered Indonesia's exclusive economic zone (RFA 2021b). Out of sovereignty concerns, Southeast Asian countries have also been diversifying when it comes to the purchasing of arms. Between 2000 and 2019, in addition to spending $2.6 billion on weapons from China and $8.2 billion from the US, Southeast Asian states imported $10.7 billion worth of arms, including submarines and fighter jets, from Russia, of which China's friend Myanmar is a major customer (Heydarian 2021).

Concerning Public Opinion

In Cambodia, the rapid inflow of Chinese citizens to the port city of Sihanoukville, where China was given control of a special economic zone for 99 years to run factories and casinos, is generating loud complaints from local communities for bidding up the rental and property prices (Leng 2019, 250–51) and allowing transnational gangs to set up shop. As noted, Vietnam experienced brief but serious anti-China riots in mid-2014 after a Chinese oil rig was reported to be parked in South China Sea waters claimed by Vietnam. Concerns are voiced in Laos over displacements of villagers and lack of compensation from the government for construction of the China–Lao railway line (RFA 2021a). In Thailand, work on a $15 billion high-speed railway joint venture with China was suspended in 2016 following local complaints that too little business had gone to Thai companies (Mcdonald, Ahmed, and Domasa 2018, 6). Indonesia's estimated $6 billion 150-kilometer Jakarta–Bandung high-speed rail project, to be built by China Railway and four Indonesian state enterprises, was scheduled to be completed within three years of 2015, but it has been delayed because the Indonesian government has yet to secure all the land needed for its construction because of compensation negotiations with the landowners (Hutton 2018, 8). In April 2022, to prevent the depletion of state coffers, the Indonesian government asked the China Development Bank to finance 75 percent of the nearly US $2 billion cost overrun for the construction of the rail line, which was then projected to be completed in 2023, to which the bank was unresponsive (Koswaraputra 2022). Since 2015, Myanmar has been cooperating with China's state-owned CITIC group to develop a port at Myanmar's Kyaukpyu to connect with southwestern China via the railway-cum-pipeline China–Myanmar Economic Corridor. However, due to public and official complains in Myanmar regarding the high cost of borrowing from China, both countries reduced the scale from $7.2 billion to $1.3 billion (Mobley 2019, 62) and renegotiated China's initial 85 percent stake in the project to about 70 percent, with 30 percent accruing to Myanmar (Wheeler 2018). Sightings of Chinese warships and fishing boats near the Philippines have typically been met with howls of protests by Filipino fisherpersons who believe that their rights would be affected by China's presence in the South China Sea. Flows of capital are increasing organized crime in BRI countries Cambodia, Thailand, and Myanmar, where gangs involved in internet gambling have engaged in human trafficking, mainly from other Asian countries, to lure and confine unwilling workers to the country to conduct international online fraud. This causes bad press internationally for the three countries involved.

Considering Regime or Leadership Changes

A different national leader or government would be expected to have different policy priorities for the country. In Myanmar, the Myitsone Dam, constructed by the Chinese state-owned China Power Investment, became a focus of local protests because nearly 12,000 people needed to be relocated from the site (Miller 2017, 199–200). After taking over power from the pro-China military junta in the parliamentary elections of 2011, the civilian administration relaxed its grip on media censorship. As a result, protests against the Myitsone Dam led to such nationwide popular resentment that Myanmar's president Thein Sein had to issue an order to suspend work on the project indefinitely, leading to an immediate fall in Chinese FDI into Myanmar. As Myanmar's population is 88 percent Buddhist, in order to assuage the Myanmarese public, China sent a Buddha's tooth relic for a 48-day tour in 2011 to build relations between Lingguang Temple in China, where the relic is lodged, and Shwedagon Pagoda in Yangon, Myanmar's most revered Buddhist shrine (Xinhua News Agency 2011). The tooth was conveyed through the capital city of Naypyitaw with a palanquin and a rare white elephant before departing for Yangon, Myanmar's largest and main commercial city, drawing large crowds wherever it went (*Wall Street Journal* 2011). During unrests in Yangon in March 2021, some Chinese-financed businesses were torched, as China was viewed as being supportive of the military coup that overthrew the elected government of Aung San Suu Kyi on February 1, 2021 (SCMP 2021). However, Myanmar is expected to grow closer to China, as Western countries have opposed its return to military rule.

After Mahathir Mohammed's political coalition came to power in the 2018 elections, he announced a halt to China's BRI projects in Malaysia and then vowed to renegotiate the deals during his visit to China in August 2018. After discussions, the port-industrial park projects were reinstated, and the East Coast Rail Link was revived in April 2019, with Malaysia's construction cost reduced by one-third, from approximately $16 billion (MYR 65.5 billion) to $10.68 billion (MYR 44 billion) (Gong 2020, 84), and the right to contribute up to 70 percent of raw materials and labor for its construction (Rocknifard 2019). Although Mohammed's successors as prime minister, first Muhyiddin Yassin and then Ismail Sabri Yaakob, both hailed from Najib's political party, they maintained Mohammed's stance toward the MSR, as did Ismail's successor Anwar Ibrahim. These changes of direction with the national leadership changes in Myanmar and Malaysia demonstrate the pitfalls for China in putting all its BRI eggs in one political or personal basket.

Even the changes in foreign policy toward China that are based on a country's current government may not be permanent. Upon election as president of the Philippines in 2016, Duterte altered his predecessor's confrontational policy toward China by choosing China for his first state visit, but even so, the Philippines under Duterte has not rescinded its claims to the South China Sea. Given that anti-China sentiment remains a live, nationalist issue for Filipinos, doing so would be tantamount to committing political suicide. Duterte's successor, Ferdinand Marcos Jr., has been decidedly less reticent in conducting military exercises with the US to assert his country's South China Sea claims vis-à-vis China. However, as China's influence in

Southeast Asia gets more established, it is also conceivable that domestic political forces in Southeast Asian countries may vie for Beijing's support and largess, leading to internal division and disunity.

There is an important non-state nexus to China's calculations for Southeast Asia that is often overlooked in discussions on the MSR. Except for Singapore, of which 75 percent of the population is ethnic Chinese, the Chinese constitute the biggest ethnic or cultural minority in all other countries of Southeast Asia. Chinese people in Southeast Asia have continued to exhibit an enduring cultural connection to China despite assimilating and naturalizing to the countries in the region. The royal family of Thailand has Chinese blood and several of its prime ministers were ethnic Chinese. The Malaysian government minister most enthusiastic and supportive of the MSR initiative was Liow Tiong Lai, transportation minister in the Najib cabinet, who was also then president of the biggest Chinese political party in Malaysia, the Malaysian Chinese Association.[1] Although not integral parts of the BRI, Confucius Institutes and the Chinese mass media serve as useful soft-power tools to advance China's image among citizens of the countries where it invests. In addition to the English China Global Television Network, China's mass media have a significant impact on the Chinese diaspora, with popular programs such as Chinese New Year celebrations. Confucius Institutes, which promote the study of the Chinese language and Chinese civilization overseas, are attached to universities in foreign countries where there are also Confucius Classrooms established in local schools. In ASEAN, as of 2021, there were 33 Confucius Institutes and 35 Confucius Classrooms (Tan 2022).

Altogether, approximately 32 million of the 50 million ethnic Chinese who live outside the PRC and Taiwan reside in Southeast Asia, where they account for a considerable share of the wealth, play key roles in the production and trading networks (Huang 2014), and are politically active or maintain good relations with local government leaders. Many recent immigrants from China are also operating businesses in Southeast Asian countries. This diaspora could facilitate Chinese investment and diplomacy in regional states or could rekindle doubts regarding loyalty, whether diaspora members would be loyal to China or to the Southeast Asian country of which they are citizens. It bears recalling a Chinese ambassador to Malaysia making known that although China's official foreign policy stance is non-interference, if China's economic interests were threatened, it would pursue means to protect them (*Straits Times* 2016). This statement could not have been well received by non-Chinese Southeast Asians. Management of the

Confucius Institutes under the Chinese Ministry of Education also adds to the suspicion that China has ulterior motives (Tan 2022).

Questions for Resolution over the MSR in Southeast Asia

China's Belt-and-Road Initiative, particularly in the form of the MSR, is potentially one of the most significant developments in relations between China and Southeast Asian states in this century. However, for the initiative to find eventual acceptance in Southeast Asia, two key political questions often raised by critics of China's MSR must be answered: What are China's deeper motivations behind the enterprise? And what roles will the Chinese navy and maritime law enforcement agencies eventually play in the MSR? Claimant states to the Spratly and Paracel Islands are concerned that China may highlight past maritime trade linkages as ways to reinstate its historical presence in the region, legitimize its increased military presence, and fortify its claims in the South China Sea. For the MSR to bear fruit, China will have to lay to rest Southeast Asia's doubts about its geostrategic intentions and reduce the perception of Chinese dominance in the region. This means that Beijing may have to negotiate away some territorial claims and come up with a binding South China Sea code of conduct that all claimants to unresolved titles can accept and abide by. However, given the strength of nationalism in China today, this will be no easy task for Xi's leadership, assuming that it has any inclination for it.

Will MSR membership by countries along the proposed routes permit the regular deployment of China's navy or coast guard vessels in maritime Southeast Asia? China may request some preferential access to Southeast Asian ports, rightfully, in light of its MSR investments in constructing warehouses, adding piers, streamlining customs, and dredging harbors. However, if China's regional rivals such as India or Japan see the MSR as a strategy that would eventually lead to basing rights or easy access for China's PLAN, they may discourage countries from participating in the initiative, if not deploy their own navies or coast guards in Southeast Asian waters. Japan in particular relies heavily on the sea lanes of the South China Sea for its exports and imports and has already made efforts to prevent China from controlling the sea by providing patrol boats and related weaponries to the Philippines and Vietnam (Guo 2014). For South China Sea littoral states, Chinese naval and coast guard assets patrolling vital shipping sea lanes and waters adjacent to MSR ports in Southeast Asia may be seen in the region as jeopardizing their own territorial and maritime claims in the disputed sea.

88 | China's Belt and Road Power Transition

To address this, China may need to increase maritime security cooperation with Southeast Asian states. This may include funding to support exercises and operations on search-and-rescue, combating maritime piracy and terrorism, responding to maritime pollution and marine environment degradation, or even initiating joint management of shared fisheries resources and joint development of offshore oil, gas, and other seabed minerals.

ASEAN countries are likely to benefit from more trade with China and more investment from China. ASEAN jumped ahead to be the number one trading bloc with China in 2020, with the trade volume hitting $731.9 billion (*Global Times* 2021), twice that of US-ASEAN trade at $362.2 billion (USTR 2021). Furthermore, in 2021 Xi pledged that China would provide $1.5 billion in development assistance for ASEAN countries in the following three years (Hoang 2023). However, these huge economic benefits projected from implementing the MSR are expected to be constrained by several costs. It is important to address the operational risks, trade distortion and trade diversion polemic, and other political-economic constraints in order to preserve ASEAN's economic interests and enhance the success rate of the MSR. For example, government-level cooperation and policy measures may be instituted to alleviate the operational risks inherent in poorer ASEAN countries. To alleviate ASEAN's deteriorating trade imbalances with China, the goal of the MSR should not be to facilitate China's export push into ASEAN markets or to compel more trade with China via strings and conditions attached to the AIIB funds. Such action, should it be undertaken by China, will reduce ASEAN's benefits from trade and investment with the rest of the world and may diminish its support for the MSR.

Chung and Voon (2017) found that GDP growth for a Southeast Asian country participating in the MSR in its first four years correlates positively to higher levels of investments in machinery, infrastructure, and transportation equipment, elevated by increasing trade flows between China and ASEAN economies. However, the anticipated investment benefits may be overestimated if the operational and political-economic risks reduce the success rates of the large-scale infrastructure projects. The expected benefits from trade expansion may be reduced by the reluctance of ASEAN countries to participate in the MSR due to their unfavorable trade balances with China, which aggravate the debt burdens of the relatively impoverished developing countries in Southeast Asia. It is also possible that China intends to push its manufacturing exports and excess raw materials, impose strings or conditions in the disbursements of MSR funds, or divert ASEAN's trade away from other countries. If the above concerns could be mitigated, then huge economic benefits can be generated even beyond ASEAN countries and China.

Even though the political or South China Sea disputes have yet to be resolved, and the pace of Chinese construction projects in Southeast Asia has slowed due to the COVID-19 pandemic, the promised economic benefits from the MSR seem to be attainable for Southeast Asian states, and the management of costs that restrict its development potential appears to be tractable. The economic benefits from the MSR may outweigh or mitigate the political costs, which is good geostrategic news for China, but trust will have to be developed and effort made from both China and ASEAN for the MSR to be mutually beneficial in the long run.

SOUTH ASIA

Given the saliency of the MSR enterprise to the Chinese government, how this ambitious scheme would impact China's relations with South Asian states along the MSR's route (i.e., India, Pakistan, Sri Lanka, Bangladesh, and the Maldives) merits investigation. The extent of the MSR's success will be determined by China's relations with the maritime states of South Asia, since South Asia is in the middle of the sea lanes of communications and commerce between East/Southeast Asia and Middle East/Europe.

This section first introduces the objectives and projects of China's MSR in South Asia, particularly with regard to Sri Lanka, Bangladesh, Maldives, and India (China's involvement with Pakistan in the CPEC has been analyzed in chapter 2). It then evaluates the political-economic costs and benefits of participation in the MSR for the region's states. The political calculations and reactions of South Asian states to the MSR initiative are explained by the extent to which Pakistan, Sri Lanka, Bangladesh, and the Maldives attempt to use a rising China as a counterweight to possible domination by neighboring India and India's uneasiness, even nervousness, about the expansion of influence or assertion of preeminence by China in the Indian Ocean rim. In economic terms, this section analyzes two dominating pathways through which benefits from the MSR could be realized for South Asian states: increases in Chinese state-backed infrastructure investments and expansion in bilateral trade with China. The attractiveness of the former may be reduced by China's insistence on dual military-civilian use of communications facilities, and the latter, by loans owed to China or conditions attached to commercial agreements. Lastly, this section identifies

90 | China's Belt and Road Power Transition

actions taken by South Asian states that may potentially enhance or diminish the MSR's success for China.

CHINA'S MARITIME SILK ROAD OBJECTIVES AND ACTIVITIES IN SOUTH ASIA

Many of the key recipients of China's government-backed lending in connection with the MSR are on important Asian sea routes, reinforcing Beijing's maritime ambitions. Indonesia, Pakistan, India, Sri Lanka, Vietnam, and Cambodia all are among the top 20 beneficiaries, with the South Asian states of Pakistan, India, Sri Lanka, and Bangladesh being the leading recipients (Kynge 2016). The CPEC, which China is investing in to link directly to the Arabian Sea, is where the SREB "belt" meets the MSR "road," particularly at Gwadar in the southwestern coast of Pakistan where China is building and expanding a deep-sea port. It has constructed a similar sea port in southern Sri Lanka, where it is now implementing several other major infrastructure projects. Chinese companies are also engaged in large-scale development projects in the Maldives, including the construction of a resort and expansion of the airport to handle the growing volume of tourists, where before the COVID-19 pandemic Chinese tourists constituted about 30 percent of the country's tourist arrivals (PTI 2018). During President Xi's visit to New Delhi, India, in September 2014, he offered a $20 billion investment for the Indian economy, particularly in infrastructure (Oxford Analytica 2015). An annual China-South Asia exposition to promote bilateral trade has been held in Kunming, China's Yunnan province, since 2013.

In response to Chinese investment along the Indian Ocean littoral, the phrase "string of pearls" has been used to describe China's development of sea ports in Bangladesh, Burma, Sri Lanka, and Pakistan as a strategic move to surround and constrain India (Marantidou 2014). This purported string of pearls strategy has led China to develop and expand port facilities in Pakistan's Gwadar, Sri Lanka's Hambantota, Bangladesh's Chittagong, and Myanmar's Kyaukpyu, raising concerns among many, particularly in New Delhi. As reported and termed by the US Department of Defense, the string of pearls strategy represents a long-term geostrategic approach for China to expand its naval influence over crucial sea lines of communication and choke points in the South China Sea and the Indian Ocean region, for which China has constructed, or planned to construct, military bases, ports, and other facilities (Athwal 2008, 44). The ports developed and managed by China in Pakistan, Sri Lanka, Bangladesh, and the Maldives, as well as

Djibouti, were viewed as military stepping stones to consolidate friendships and counter India's dominance in the Indian Ocean region (Lu 2016, 42). China has vehemently denied the existence of such a strategy. According to an article in China's *Global Times*, "Western scholars forged and hyped China's 'string of pearls strategy' in the Indian Ocean, and some Indians believe that MSR is just an alternative wording that sounds more pleasant and is used to replace the string of pearls strategy. . . . The so-called string of pearls strategy is a military and geo-strategic design, but Chinese leaders define the 'Belt and Road' initiative as the top-level design of China's opening-up and economic diplomacy in the new era" (*Financial Express* 2016d).

Analytically speaking, the MSR in South Asia suffers from divergent Chinese and Indian perspectives. China talks up the "complex interdependence" virtues of the initiative for connectivity, a globalized liberal trading order, and inter-civilizational exchanges, but uncertain of India's receptivity to the enterprise, Beijing has mostly targeted surrounding countries, particularly Pakistan and Sri Lanka but also Bangladesh and the Maldives. However, doing so only caused a concerned India to see a more "realist" approach to the design, regarding it as a disguised attempt to expand Chinese influence in the Indian Ocean and undercut New Delhi's sway over its neighbors by actively involving them in the project. These contrasting perceptions could well lead to a full-blown contest for influence between China and India over South Asia, which may allow the region's smaller countries to benefit in the near term, but would ultimately increase regional tension and mistrust. For the success of China's grand connectivity project, by whatever name it is referred to, the importance of Beijing's relations with all countries in South Asia cannot be gainsaid, and it would have to reconcile conflicting perceptions and allay suspicions of its intention in forming and executing the MSR.

MSR and Sri Lanka

Sri Lanka hosts two key projects along the MSR that are financed and constructed by Chinese interests—the Port City project in the country's capital, Colombo, and the port of Hambantota project. They were first approved by Mahinda Rajapaksa when he was president of Sri Lanka between 2005 and 2015. Isolated from the West over allegations of human rights abuses during the country's civil war, which he ended with much bloodshed in 2009, Rajapaksa was one of the first leaders in South Asia to publicly support China's MSR. Indeed, one major reason for Rajapaksa's failure to get reelected was public opposition to his perceived excessively close ties with China and alleged corruption involving Chinese firms, although Sri Lanka had received $1 billion dollars a year since 2009 in military credits from Beijing without any conditionalities (Oxford Analytica 2015). Both port initiatives then for a time fell victim to domestic Sri Lankan politics when the incoming president, Maithripala Sirisena, challenged the fairness of Chinese investments and ordered reviews of various China-aided projects, but relations between the two countries recovered enough for the development to proceed according to plan.

China's largest MSR investment plan in Sri Lanka, estimated at $15 billion and scheduled for completion in 2040, is the Colombo International Financial City, a metropolis in the capital city with residential, business, and recreation facilities (Fernando 2020), close to which an international container terminal or port city is also being constructed. A rather noncontroversial project, Colombo Port City was the product of a joint venture between two local companies and China Merchants Holdings (International) Company, which together invested $500 million in the Colombo International Container Terminals, making it the largest actualized foreign investment project in Sri Lanka when the port began operation in August 2014, after two years of construction (UNCTAD 2015). The port city was blessed by Chinese president Xi Jinping during his visit to Sri Lanka in September 2014 and expected to include housing, a marina, and a Formula One racetrack (Shrivastava 2016). By then, China had become the largest source of FDI to the country, and negotiations on a China-Sri Lanka free trade agreement had begun. The Port of Colombo has a current capacity of over 4.5 million TEUs (twenty-foot equivalent units), which will increase by another 7.2 million TEUs in three separate phases, making it one of the world's 20 largest container ports (Chand 2014). This $1.4 billion plan for Chinese companies to build on land that they reclaimed next to Colombo's main harbor was suspended by President Sirisena shortly after he took power in January 2015, but it has been subsequently given the green light (Shrivastava 2016). Colombo Port City is being developed by China Harbor Engineering Company, a subsidiary of state-owned China Communications Construction Company, which was blacklisted by the US Trump administration for helping China build militarily strategic islands in the South China Sea, an action the US considers to be in contravention of international law.

There is, however, a more controversial project. In the early stages of the MSR, China partnered with Mahinda Rajapaksa to build infrastructure megaprojects such as a new deep-sea port, an airport, a stadium, a giant conference center, and roads and railways in Hambantota, on the island nation's southern coast, with loans from China. China may have plans to use the port as a refueling and docking station for its navy. Other controversies associated with the MSR in Sri Lanka include air pollution from power stations, trade deficit with China from increasing Chinese imports related to infrastructure building, and state-owned enterprises recruiting workers from China at the expense of local labor (Wignaraja et al. 2020). However, Hambantota remains particularly noteworthy as an indicator of China's geostrategic interest in Sri Lanka and the South Asia/Indian Ocean region.

The port of Hambantota, which on completion should make it one of the largest ports in South Asia, was actually started before the MSR in January 2008 by the Chinese state-owned enterprises China Harbor Engineering Company and Sinohydro Corp. (Chand 2014). Hambantota was selected as it has a natural harbor and is located on the southern tip of Sri Lanka, close to international shipping routes traversing the Indian Ocean. Furthermore, Rajapaksa is a native of Hambantota. Under the original deal negotiated by Rajapaksa during his presidential tenure, the container terminal at Hambantota was to be operated by a joint venture between China Harbor Engineering and state-run China Merchants Port Holdings for 40 years, and the port authority of Sri Lanka would retain control of all other terminals in the harbor as well as a jointly developed 6,000-acre industrial zone (Reuters 2017). Funds for the Hambantota project were made available at near commercial terms by China's Exim Bank, which extended credit of over $1.2 billion for construction of the port and $1.35 billion for an adjacent power plant (Parthasarathy 2017).[2]

Sirisena, after much ado about canceling the contracts with China following his election, reached an agreement with Beijing in late 2016 to further develop the strategic port of Hambantota and build a huge industrial zone nearby. When Sri Lanka later struggled to pay back its debts to China, the Sri Lankan government negotiated and approved a deal to lease 80 percent of the port, later reduced to 70 percent, to China Merchants Port Holdings for $1.12 billion for 99 years (Shepard 2020a), and announced a bigger lease of 15,000 acres around the port to the same Chinese company to build an industrial park, which evoked protests from locals (*BBC Monitoring* 2017). Despite his reluctance, Sirisena's hand was forced by the country's high debt burden—by the end of 2016, Sri Lanka's national debt stood at around $64 billion, or 76 percent of its GDP, one of the highest among emerging economies, and it already owed China over $8 billion (Reuters 2017).

94 | China's Belt and Road Power Transition

At the start of 2017, China had already spent $1.7 billion building Hambantota port and the adjacent Mattala Rajapaksa airport, named after the former president, and according to China's ambassador to Sri Lanka, Yi Xianliang, Beijing would invest $5 billion more in the next three to five years and create 100,000 jobs in the country (*Sunday Times* 2017). Notwithstanding China's past spending and promises of more spending in the future, opposition to Chinese investments in Sri Lanka turned violent when hundreds of Sri Lankans clashed with police at the opening of the Hambantota industrial zone in January 2017. The clashes, in which demonstrators threw stones and police responded with tear gas and water cannons, underlined the depth of resentment felt by local people who feared they would be forced from their homes (*Daily News* 2017). Leading the campaign against the deal was Sri Lanka's former president Mahinda Rajapaksa, who said that the deal was too generous to China. According to Rajapaksa, the 99-year lease on Hambantota impinges on Sri Lanka's sovereign rights because a foreign company would enjoy the rights of the landlord over the free port and the main harbor, and he also questioned the 15,000-acre lease, which he said was more than three times the area of all other economic zones in the country combined (Reuters 2017). Adding to the troubles bedeviling the Hambantota project, according to the Sri Lankan finance ministry, were losses at the port, which added up to around $230 million in the five years from 2012 to the end of 2016 (Reuters 2017). Against annual interest repayment liabilities of around $65 million, revenues from trade shipments amounted to only about $1.3 million (Parthasarathy 2017). Apart from a few vehicles that India, Japan, and South Korea export to Sri Lanka, Hambantota receives virtually nothing else from international trade, and despite offering free landing facilities to foreign airlines, very few flights have made use of Hambantota airport (Parthasarathy 2017).

Although the Chinese authorities say that Hambantota's development is a purely commercial, albeit long-term, venture, its strategic location makes it a valuable alternative asset for future use. China may have plans to use the port as a refueling and docking station for its navy as it patrols the Indian Ocean to protect supplies of oil from the Middle East (Shrivastava 2016). Having ready access to ports in Sri Lanka would also allow Chinese warships to break their voyages on their way to or from Pakistan or anti-piracy operations in the Gulf of Aden. In 2014, Colombo hosted the visit of some Chinese submarines. Colombo is a "trans-shipment" hub for India's container traffic, as larger ships unload containers at Colombo and feeder boats trans-ship them to India's smaller and often aging ports.

When the new terminal operates at full capacity, Colombo's trans-shipment share of India's container traffic may grow from the present 13 percent to 28 percent, which would raise security issues for India as China runs this port and can hinder smooth movement of essential goods to and from India during a crisis (Chand 2014).

Because news that the Sri Lankan government leased Hambantota port to China for 99 years in lieu of debt payment had aroused much grumbling and disaffection on the island state, China sought to reaffirm its historical ties and Buddhist "people-to-people" bonds with Sri Lanka, whose population is more than 70 percent Buddhist. It was propitious for China that the Lotus Tower was in the thick of construction at that time, allowing China to send out a message of peace and Buddhist affinity to Sri Lanka. The Lotus Tower is a 350-meter-high communication tower shaped like the lotus flower that China started building in Colombo in 2012, with the Exim of China providing $100 million for its construction by two Chinese companies (APBU 2012). The lotus is a symbol of purity and detachment in Buddhist iconography. Upon completion of the tower in September 2019, it was reputed to be the tallest freestanding tower in South Asia.

In presenting a softer and more personal side of the BRI, China hoped to recall its initial engagement with Sri Lanka, by the famous Chinese Buddhist scholar-monk Faxian (377–422), who arrived on the island when it was the epicenter of Buddhist learning and teaching. This engagement continued with the illustrious Admiral Zheng He of the Ming dynasty, who visited the island during his seven voyages (1405–1435). In May 2017, a large Chinese delegation consisting of the head of the Buddhist Association of Guangzhou, abbot of Guangzhou's Dafosi (Great Buddha Temple), abbot of Shantou's Jueyuansi, members of the Guangdong People's Political Consultative Committee, chairman of a Buddhist foundation, and chairman of a Guangzhou Buddhist broadcasting company visited the Sri Maha Bodhi Temple in Anuradhapura. As much as the visit was to admire the sacred Bodhi tree, grown from a sapling brought over from the spot in India where the Buddha had achieved enlightenment, it was also to impress upon the Sri Lankan audience the connection between Buddhism and the traditional Silk Road, which passed by Ceylon or ancient Sri Lanka, particularly since President Sirisena was less than enthusiastic at that time about the benefits that the BRI could bring to his country. This qualm about the initiative would not be shared by Sirisena's successor, Gotabaya Rajapaksa, who was elected president in 2019 and who promptly appointed his brother, the former president Mahinda Rajapaksa, as his prime minister. However, by

April 2022, facing serious economic troubles from the COVID-19 pandemic, which had destroyed Sri Lanka's tourism revenues and increased costs of food and consumer goods imports due to the Russo-Ukrainian War, the Rajapaksa brothers had to borrow $1 billion from India, the World Bank, the IMF, and China to pay down existing Chinese loans due in July 2022, out of about $3.5 billion owed to China for infrastructure construction, in addition to raising another $1.2 billion of principal and interest payments for dollar-denominated bonds and loans by the end of 2022 (SCMP 2022a).

MSR and Maldives's Reactions

When Xi became the first Chinese head of state to visit the Maldives in 2014, he took the opportunity to encourage then Maldivian president Abdulla Yameen to get his government involved in the MSR. With Chinese loans and assistance, Beijing announced the construction of a $210 million Friendship Bridge that would connect the capital to the western corner of the island of Hulhule, where the international airport is located. In 2018, the four-lane China–Maldives Friendship Bridge spanning 2 kilometers across the Indian Ocean connecting Male with the airport was opened, and property prices in Hulhule soared. China later agreed to expand the airport by building a new runway, as well as construct a port in the atoll of Laamu (Dorsey 2017). According to Yameen's office, the country reached nine agreements with China during Xi's visit, including the above-mentioned projects (Visham 2014).

Beijing was engaged for its $800 million construction and expansion work on the Ibrahim Nasir International Airport when the Maldives government changed in November 2013 and a privatization award to an Indian company was canceled (Oxford Analytica 2016). For this project, the Exim Bank of China in December 2016 granted an initial loan of $373 million to the Maldives (Shaahunaaz 2016). However, sovereign guarantees on loans from Chinese companies amounted to more than $1.5 billion, about 30 percent of the GDP of the Maldives, such that the government of new president Ibrahim Mohamed Solih has accused officials in the Yameen administration of pocketing some of the loans and vowed to lower interest rates and extend repayment schedules in negotiations with China (Mundy and Hille 2019). To combat China's massive influence in Maldives, India launched the Greater Male Connectivity Project with Solih worth $400 million, consisting of a number of bridges and causeways, spanning 6.7

kilometers, to connect Male to Villingili, Thilafushi, and Gulhifahu islands (*The Hindu* 2020).

Still, helping to expand the airport was not only good diplomacy for China; it was also necessary to accommodate the rising number of tourists from China. The Maldives, a nation of 1,192 tiny coral islands scattered some 850 kilometers across the equator, received over a million tourists in 2013 and more than 30 percent of them were Chinese. Tourism accounts for more than a quarter of the $2.3 billion economy, and Chinese tourists have become the largest single group of holidaymakers to visit the Maldives (Shaahunaaz 2016). However, there were reports that some Maldivians had been recruited to fight for the Islamic State in Iraq and Syria (Visham 2014). If true, rising Islamist radicalism could be a source of concern for Chinese tourists and a potential threat to the Maldives tourism industry, a very important sector of its economy, which took a hit during the most serious COVID-19 years of 2020 and 2021.

MSR and Bangladesh's Reactions

A proposal to create an economic corridor connecting China, India, Bangladesh, and Myanmar, first coined as the Kunming initiative in 1999, faced years of apathy, but once translated into the Bangladesh-China-India-Myanmar (BCIM) initiative, it garnered much policy traction through official recognition from all the four governments involved. This economic corridor, which transverses through northeast India, Bangladesh, Myanmar, and southwest China, links some of the least economically developed parts of the world together, but the BCIM subregion possesses a potential market size of 2.8 billion people (Hussain 2015), at the heart of which lies Bangladesh.

The development of a more modern and efficient 2,800-kilometer transportation infrastructure connecting the BCIM countries could be expected to increase regional trade, if and when China delivers on its plan to construct a high-speed rail link between Kunming, in China's Yunnan province, and Kolkata, in India's West Bengal state. The proposed railway, reportedly a candidate for funding from the AIIB and the Silk Road Fund (*Global Capital* 2015), would start from Kolkata; cross Benapole, Dhaka, and Sylhet in Bangladesh; reenter Silchar and then Imphal in India; hit the Tamu–Kalewa friendship road in Myanmar; and proceed onward to Kunming (Viswanath 2016). There were also reports that the rail line may pass through the port of Chittagong (*Global Capital* 2015), in Bangladesh's southeastern Cox's Bazar District. Additionally, a Kolkata to Kunming

(K2K) Highway plan was unveiled at the tenth BCIM forum meeting in Kolkata in 2012, though not much detail has yet been officially released about it. China and Bangladesh have also been negotiating a highway project to connect Chittagong and Kunming through Myanmar (*Financial Express* 2016c), which, if realized, would give Bangladesh an entry into the Mekong subregion, which includes not only southwestern China but also the mainland Southeast Asian countries of Myanmar, Thailand, Lao, Cambodia, and Vietnam, and enable Bangladesh to accelerate trade with these places. It would also allow Bangladesh to raise revenues by collecting toll charges or transit fees on vehicles using the highway. China has also expressed interest in Chittagong's port, which India also covets, to protect China's sea lanes of communication, particularly guaranteeing its flow of oil from the Middle East (Shrivastava 2016). With the Chittagong–Kunming highway and proposed development by Dhaka of a deep-sea port linking the Sonadia-Matabari islands to Chittagong, Bangladesh would be a significant part of the MSR (Ahamed 2016).

On bilateral relations, trade between Bangladesh and China has grown rapidly, making China Bangladesh's largest trading partner, with two-way trade accounting for about $12 billion in 2014, Chinese investment in Bangladesh exceeding $200 million, and imports from China growing at about 20 percent and export growth to China averaging 40 percent between 2011 and 2016 (*Financial Express* 2016a). Furthermore, Dhaka has granted China exploration rights for developing Bangladesh's natural gas fields at Barakpuria (Shrivastava, 2016). President Xi Jinping, during his state visit to Dhaka on October 14 to 15, 2016, presented a gift in the form of a cornucopia of investment proposals amounting to $24.5 billion (*Financial Express* 2016b), a hefty sum for a poor country like Bangladesh. In the course of this visit, 27 were deals signed, comprising 15 agreements and memorandums of understanding (MOUs), and 12 loan documents. Among these was a cooperation agreement on increasing investment and production capacity building, under which 28 development projects were to receive $21.5 billion in concessionary Chinese co-funding (Chowdhury 2016, 4). A number of MOUs came under the purview of the MSR initiative, and the agreements span a large range of economic activities, such as maritime cooperation, a joint feasibility study on a free trade area, new ICT framework, counterterrorism collaboration, information sharing, tackling climate change, rail links and communications, and power and energy development.

The economic agreements between China and Bangladesh could in part help Bangladesh narrow its manufacturing "catch up" gap by attracting low-end, labor-intensive industries that are being hollowed out from the east coast of China. However, much of the loans and assistance from China are debt-based. The debt-to-GDP ratio was 13.6 percent and the proportion of export earnings needed to service foreign loans was 5.1 percent in fiscal year 2014–15 (ERD), not by any means unmanageable. However, borrowing can be alluring, and once the trend is set in motion, it may spiral out of control. If all the Chinese proposals materialize, the ratios above will more than double in a few years. In an editorial, the Chinese state-run *Global Times* stated that Xi's visit to Dhaka was "seen by *some* as being designed to 'snatch the South Asian country from the embrace of New Delhi,'" going on to say, "it would not necessarily be a bad thing if an increasingly close relationship between China and Bangladesh puts pressure on New Delhi to rethink its strategy in the region and encourages it to put more effort into improving relationship with China" (Chowdhury 2016, 3). If this editorial was reflective of the thinking of China's leadership, then the danger remains of Bangladesh being used as a pawn in China's struggle for economic and strategic influence over India in South Asia.

It is perhaps to forestall Sino-Indian rivalry over Bangladesh that Dhaka accepted a Japanese bid to lead construction on a port at Matarbari, starting in early 2016, while a similar Chinese bid to construct a container port on Sonadia Island was put on hold (Oxford Analytica 2016a), although it is still in the offing. It is also possible that Bangladesh encourages a strong Japanese economic presence to diversify investment risks. At around $100 million, Japanese FDI in Bangladesh kept rising, comprising 5 percent of FDI in Bangladesh in 2016, significantly outweighing China's (1 percent) (Oxford Analytica 2016a). Bangladesh's investment hedging strategy seems to have put off China to some extent. After Bangladesh asked for a reduction in the costs of the Joydebpur–Jamalpur double rail and the Akhaura–Sylhet dual-gauge rail by more than half a billion dollars, China withdrew funding from these two BRI projects altogether.

Nepal's Reaction

Nepal is not exactly on the SREB or MSR, but as it is located between the two routes, it is a major target of Chinese influence dissemination in South Asia. With the abolition of the Nepali monarchy on May 28, 2008, the succeeding republican government formed by Maoist rebels starting drawing closer to socialist China in terms of foreign relations. After Nepal signed on to the BRI in 2017, China has been exploiting common cultural-religious ties by developing Lumbini, birthplace of Gautama Buddha and the only significant Buddhist site not situated in India. Nepal welcomed the BRI and was offered $3 billion for the Lumbini tourism development project, to build a new airport, hotels, convention centers, temples, and a Buddhist university (Bhaumik 2013). Facilitating an increase in the number of Chinese tourists to Nepal would provide Beijing with more economic and political leverage over Nepal. The $76 million Gautam Buddha International Airport, 19 kilometers from Lumbini, was inaugurated in May 2022 (*Hindustani Times* 2022). The funds to transform the small town into "the premier place of pilgrimage for Buddhists from around the world" comes from the Asia Pacific Exchange and Cooperation Foundation, whose executive vice president, Xiao Wunan, is a member of the CCP and holds a position at the PRC's National Development and Reform Commission (Dorjee 2018). There is already a Chinese Temple in Lumbini, which is sponsored by China and headed by a Chinese monk (Chen 2015). In 2013, the ostensibly nongovernmental Buddhist Association of China announced plans to take over coordination of the Lumbini project (Devaranade 2017). This announcement might well be related to China's proposal to link Lumbini by road and rail to Tibet. As Lumbini is very close to Nepal's border with India, although road and rail tunneling and bridging is extremely challenging with Nepal's mountainous terrain, some Indians are concerned that China's construction projects would have security implications for India. In the wake of Nepal's ratification of the Millennium Challenge Corp., a $500 million US grant for building electricity transmission lines and improving roads (India Briefing 2022), Beijing has been trying to restart the road and rail projects, its hydroelectric plans, and a China-Nepal industrial park joint venture, which have been stalled by COVID-19. However, the Nepalese government prefers grants and soft loans from China to commercial loans, it wants the interest rate and repayment time to be in line with that of multilateral funding agencies like the World Bank and Asian Development Bank, and it believes the BRI projects should be open for competitive bidding (Brunnersum 2022).

India Holding Out

The attitudes of Pakistan, Maldives, Sri Lanka, and Bangladesh to China's economic and possible military presence in these countries may be labeled, respectively, as passionately enthusiastic, very enthusiastic, welcoming for want of an alternative, and cautiously welcoming, for reasons described. For them, economic and security advantages accruing from the MSR largely go together, and drawbacks are (as yet) absent or obscure. As for India, the biggest and most powerful state in South Asia, its receptivity to the BRI was cool from the beginning. India knows that infrastructure investment arising from the initiative can help the country boost its economic growth. On the other hand, India thinks that the scheme will allow China to increase its influence in the India Ocean region to India's detriment because China can provide financial support to attract other South Asian countries, which India cannot match, for which these countries would support China rather than India (China-US Focus 2015). The historical baggage of the 1962 border war and unresolved border with China still looms large in India's nationalist imagination, and New Delhi has been concerned that Beijing is establishing a "string of pearls" to contain India's influence in the Indian Ocean, particularly with Beijing's friendship with Islamabad, as Indian political leaders see the subcontinent at a minimum to be "their" area and seek to exclude other powers (Li 2013, 15–21). Thus, China's MSR projects, although slowed down since early 2020 due to the COVID-19 pandemic, risk making India feel encircled when it perceives its neighbors are tilting toward China.

China's relations with the South Asian states, particularly that of the largest one, India, are crucial in determining the success of the MSR, as the sea lanes of communications and commerce between East/Southeast Asia and Middle East/Europe must pass the waters of South Asia. India's disinclination to join the MSR therefore creates the biggest obstacle to South Asia's regional integration with the initiative.

Security Relationship between China and India

Indian foreign policy analysts have been divided as to whether Xi Jinping's signature initiative of the BRI represents a strategic threat or economic opportunity to their country. Srikanth Kondapalli, a researcher at the Center for East Asian Studies of India's Jawaharlal Nehru University, opined that China only pretends to cooperate with Pakistan, Bangladesh, Nepal, Myanmar, and Sri Lanka in order to contain India through the BRI (*Lianhe Zaobao* 2016). He also believes that One Belt, One Road is aimed at establishing "a new (world) order," and with India-US ties warming up, New Delhi should not be seen signing up for a project that is perceived as anti-US (Roche 2017a). India's then foreign secretary Subrahmanyam Jaishankar clearly saw China's construction efforts in the region as instruments of Beijing's intention to build influence in India's neighborhood and natural sphere of influence, and

102 | China's Belt and Road Power Transition

at Singapore's International Institute for Strategic Studies Fullerton Lecture in 2016 he said that the "'One Belt, One Road' initiative was China's own unilateral effort and that India would not commit to buy-in without significant consultation" (Cai 2016).

India has not signed on to Beijing's MSR principally because, as it officially stated, "no country can accept a project that ignores its core concerns on sovereignty and territorial integrity," that project being the CPEC, which traverses Pakistan-held Kashmir, known in the official Indian discourse as Pakistan-occupied Kashmir or PoK, that is claimed by India (Ayres 2017). India and Pakistan have had a territorial dispute over the region of Kashmir for several decades, so if India accepts CPEC, it would imply that it accepts Kashmir as part of Pakistan, which it does not. India's prime minister Narendra Modi has declared that "the entire Kashmir belongs to India" (Jamil 2016). Furthermore, Pakistan's port of Gwadar is located by the Arabian Sea close to India's sea lanes, which links India to the Persian Gulf/Strait of Hormuz, where it gets over 70 percent of its oil supplies (Parthasarathy 2016). Some Indians perceived that China's development of Gwadar for dual civilian-military use could, in the event of military hostilities with India, allow China to interrupt India's oil shipments. India's suspicion about China's motives was aggravated when Chinese submarines visited Colombo in 2014. At India's 2016 Independence Day speech, Prime Minister Modi condemned human rights violations in Baluchistan (Chandran 2016), where Gwadar is located. Although invited to the BRI summit in Beijing in 2017, India sent no official to the event (Kasturi 2017), nor did it send any to the subsequent BRI summits in 2019 and 2021.

India has long been holding joint naval exercises with Sri Lanka, and Maldives' coast guard joined this set of exercises in 2012. In 2013 former Indian prime minister Manmohan Singh announced that India should be seen as a "net security provider to the region," and unsurprisingly, initial focus was on the nearby Indian Ocean islands of Sri Lanka and Maldives. In March 2015, sensing an opportunity to influence the new government of Sri Lanka, given its suspicions of China's MSR, as well as to forestall possible Chinese inroads into Mauritius and Seychelles, Modi paid state visits to these three countries in hopes of securing for India a dominant position in the Indian Ocean through bolstering military and security cooperation with these island nations (*Financial Express* 2016d). Shiv Shankar Menon, India's national security advisor, then announced on March 7, 2015, that Seychelles and Mauritius had joined India's naval arrangement with Sri Lanka and Maldives in a new Indian Ocean security grouping that some have called the IO-5 (Rafique 2015, 4 to share information and develop capabilities to counter maritime terrorism, piracy, and illegal fishing (Chand 2014). However, as of yet, the IO-5 is no match for China's "string of pearls" or MSR in terms of scale of vision and financial investment.

To throw China off guard, India has enforced its military and strategic coordination with the US, Japan, and Southeast Asian countries, which have island disputes with China in the South China Sea. India's navy began making port visits to Southeast Asia around the time when the BRI was announced. In June 2016, Modi visited the US and stated that India hoped to have a closer relationship with Washington on Asian affairs (*Liberty Times* 2016). India, the US, and Japan also conducted military exercises in waters near Okinawa, which raised speculations that China was the exercises' target. In November 2016, India confirmed its intention to buy around $1.6 billion worth of US-2 amphibious search-and-rescue aircrafts at a possible discount from Japan to send a message to China that Japan and India were enhancing their military and political cooperation (*Japan Times* 2016).

After the withdrawal of Western sanctions on Iran in January 2016, Modi offered to help build Iran's southern port of Chabahar with funds from India's Export-Import Bank. The port is located on the strategic Gulf of Oman, not far from Pakistan's Chinese-built Gwadar port. According to then Indian minister for shipping, highway, and road transport, Nitin Gadkari, Indian investment in the Iranian port could amount to $100 million (6.5 billion Indian rupees) (*Financial Express* 2016c). Expansion of Chabahar is expected to take a long time, but if India gets to make use of the port, it might, if strategically necessary, be better able to monitor shipping and naval activities around neighboring Gwadar by Pakistan and China.

Economic Relationship between China and India

The BRI could potentially create many opportunities for China and India to strengthen their economic cooperation. China's capacity for manufacturing and infrastructure and India's capacity for providing services and IT could complement each other (Bajpai, Huang, and Mahbubani, 2016, 102). In 2014, Modi paid a state visit to China, where the Chinese leadership promised to increase its investment value in India. In 2015, China boosted its investments in India to $1.2 billion, an increase of seven times compared with its investments in 2011 (*21st Century Economic Times* 2015). In 2016, China set up an industry area in Haryana State, mainly concentrating on locomotive manufacturing, and bid for two high-speed railway projects in

India, from New Delhi to Mumbai and New Delhi to Chennai, of 1,200 and 2,200 kilometers in length, respectively (*Sina* 2015). The construction of India's first bullet train between Mumbai and Ahmedabad was ultimately awarded to Japan. Besides, China also began to develop two industrial areas in Maharashtra and Gujarat, which mainly focus on car manufacturing and power generation, with investments of $5 billion and $1 billion, respectively (*China Times* 2014).

With IT cooperation, major Chinese telecommunications firms like Huawei, LeEco, and Xiaomi have set up research and development centers in Bangalore to take advantage of the Indian IT talent pool. China also invited India to set up an IT industry area in Guizhou province to help India's IT industry enter the Chinese market (Channel News Asia 2015). Renewable energy is another area for China and India to cooperate. At the Fourth China-India Strategic and Economic Dialogue, held in October 2016, both countries agreed to enhance their cooperation in developing wind and solar energy and work on solar cell/module manufacturing in India (*The Hindu* 2016).

However, since 2001, India has been suffering a deficit with China-India bilateral trade. The trade deficit has grown 36 times from $1 billion in 2001–02 to $36.2 billion in 2013–14 (Bajpai, Huang, and Mahbubani, 2016, 57). Even as China increases its investments in India, India's trade deficit with China has been rising. From 2015 to 2016, while the value of exports from India to China was $9 billion, the value of exports from China to India was $61.7 billion (Suneja 2016). In order to reduce India's trade deficit and protect its local industries, Indian politicians conducted heated discussions on whether to eliminate existing import tariff concessions on some manufactures from China. Yet those were the good old days of "Chindia" relations.

Following a bloody border clash between Chinese and Indian troops in June 2020, Indian officials and trade groups called for boycotts of China-made goods and Chinese apps, such as Tik Tok on Indian cellphones, and made plans to raise tariffs on some 300 products from China (Lee 2020). Although bilateral trade was worth $88 billion and Chinese companies' total investment in India exceeded $26 billion, India's trade deficit with China stood at about $47 billion and India's smartphone market is dominated by Chinese companies such as Xiaomi and Vivo (Lee 2020). Given the bad state of relations between China and India, in August 2021 Chinese carmaker Great Wall Motor decided rescind its decision to make a $1 billion investment in India to make cars, batteries, and parts and instead relocated up to $300 million of the proposed sum to purchase a Daimler plant in Brazil (Macrae 2021). With China standing firm on territorial sovereignty over its border claims with India, India's participation in the MSR is practically a dead issue. Unsurprisingly, the hitherto much-touted BCIM proposal to connect Kolkata in India's West Bengal state to Kunming in China's Yunnan province via Bangladesh and Myanmar by road and rail, to be constructed and funded by China, is on indefinite hold.

IMPLICATIONS FOR CHINA'S MSR IN SOUTH ASIA

In 2016, facing a severe economic slowdown at home, China's trade surplus fell for the first time in five years, slipping 14 percent to $510 billion; imports also slipped 5.5 percent even after depreciation of the Yuan; and FDI grew only at 4.1 percent to reach $118 billion, far lower than the 6.4 percent growth rate seen in 2015 (*Asia News Monitor* 2017). Still, China's government and state-owned enterprises investing overseas have deep pockets and a desire to offload excess production. Countries participating in the MSR would have uninterrupted access to the Chinese market, comprising one-fifth of the human population, and the initiative is lucrative for all governments involved, particularly those from developing countries because of China's longstanding aid and grant policy of not having "good governance" strings attached, such as anti-corruption measures, development goals, human rights protection, or political accountability.

China's building of ports and other infrastructure facilities in Pakistan, Sri Lanka, Maldives, and Bangladesh that may have dual civilian-military use, as has been pointed out by regional and extra-regional rivals of China, could be a design to gain strategic footholds in the region (Baqai 2015, 5). If so, the general receptivity of these states to the MSR also demonstrates a desire to use China to undercut India's sway over them, or bargain with New Delhi for more benefits. On a visit to India in April 2017, Bangladesh's prime minister obtained from her host $9 billion worth of business agreements, which went a long way toward correcting a massive trade deficit with India, and a $5 billion line of credit, of which $500 million was for the purchase of Indian military hardware (Roche 2017b). India funded and launched a $70 million satellite in May 2017 to provide telecommunications, weather forecasting, and early warnings of floods and cyclones to itself and Bangladesh, Nepal, Sri Lanka, Bhutan, and the Maldives (Pasricha 2017).

India is keeping a wary eye on the MSR and the CPEC because both schemes allow China to eclipse India's influence in the Indian Ocean region.

China can provide financial support to smaller countries in that region, like Sri Lanka or Bangladesh, as incentives for them to support China, while India has much less wherewithal to do so. "Dominance in the Indian Ocean translates in a way to dominance in Asia, because of the primary maritime trade routes and energy trade," said Caron Natasha Tauro, South Asia analyst for IHS Jane's. "This boosted competition between India, which sees the sea as its backyard, and China, which has potential to enlarge its influence with the One Belt, One Road project and the Maritime Silk Road initiative" (*Business Wire* 2016). The result it seems has been not only burgeoning Sino-Indian rivalry but also a potential arms race in the Indian Ocean rim, as total spending on warships by India, China, Pakistan, and Bangladesh has shown a strong upward trend since 2009 (*Business Wire* 2016). From an economic perspective, even if China were to invest billions of US dollars in India and help develop its infrastructure and manufacturing industry, India is worried that the resulting debt and increasing trade deficit may harm its local economy. Besides, under the MSR and CPEC, the tight relationship between Pakistan and China could drive India closer to the US and Japan. If so, this would not be a welcome development for China's involvements in the Indian Ocean region.

Although it is expected that the South Asian phase of the MSR will proceed with or without India's participation, for the initiative's smooth operation and Beijing's reputation, it would be in China's interest to allay India's suspicions regarding its motives and actions. As an essay in China's *Global Times* exhorted,

> China should step up efforts to improve maritime, economic, civil, disaster relief and legal cooperation, maritime interconnection, and other maritime security activities, provide more international public goods collectively with other countries, and ensure the security of sea lanes and freedom of navigation in the Indian Ocean . . . China should make clear its purposes in the Indian Ocean, especially the security of sea lanes of energy and trade, the security of overseas investment and the security of overseas Chinese, in order to build strategic trust with Indian Ocean countries, especially India . . . and improve connections and cooperation with the Indian Ocean Rim Association and other regional cooperation organizations in the Indian Ocean. (*Financial Express* 2016d)

The Indian and Chinese armies have conducted joint counterterrorism land exercises in southwestern China, although on a much smaller scale than India's military exercise with the US and Japan (Oxford Analytica 2016). Islamist terrorism, whether it emanates domestically or from Pakistan or the Maldives, constitutes a threat to both China and India and is an area where both countries can further their cooperation. China should stop blocking India's membership in the Nuclear Suppliers Group, the multistate group that regulates global trade in nuclear weapons and materials, even though India has not signed the Nuclear Non-Proliferation Treaty. China also needs to import more commodities from India to narrow the trade deficit. Since China and India are the biggest rising powers in the international system, disputed borders notwithstanding, the MSR offers an opportunity for both to become close working partners. The chances of the initiative's success will be greatly enhanced if it is pursued with the interests of all countries along its route, taking into account relevant authorities at all levels and affected local communities.

East Africa and the Red Sea

Africa is rich in mineral resources, but because of governance and development issues, the per capita income of Africans as a whole was only 60 percent of the world population average in 2016 (Varathan 2018). As good infrastructure is needed to attract FDI, Africa requires help in this aspect from the outside world. For years before the announcement of the BRI, Chinese state-owned petroleum companies had been conducting exploration and exploitation of oil and other hydrocarbon resources in oil-rich countries such as Sudan, Angola, Nigeria, Congo, and Angola, which is currently the largest recipient of Chinese loans. Since 2000, Chinese leaders have been hosting a triannual Forum on China-Africa Cooperation, typically attended by nearly all of Africa's heads of state, except Swaziland, which recognizes Taiwan as the Republic of China. In the following two decades, China's economic cooperation with Africa has been intensifying. In 2009, China-Africa trade volume at $1.3 billion exceeded that of trade between the US and Africa, rising to $170 billion in 2017 (Chen 2018). In 2017, Chinese investments in African countries amounted to $3 billion, focusing on infrastructure building, manufacturing, finance, tourism, and aviation industries (Chen 2018). By 2019, Chinese companies had invested at least

108 | China's Belt and Road Power Transition

twice the amount of money in African countries as American companies (Zhou 2019), and close to half of all types of aid dispensed by China had gone to Africa.

Nowhere are China's relations with Africa more important than in the countries of East Africa: Djibouti, South Sudan, Ethiopia, Kenya, and Tanzania, which are part of the MSR. As with China's MSR relations with its South Asian partners, East Africa, on the western shores of the Indian Ocean and the Red Sea, has both strategic and economic imperatives for China. Since the average wages of workers in these countries are lower than wages in China, Chinese firms are setting up factories there to produce labor-intensive consumer products and extract mineral resources, which accounts for China's interest in spending on infrastructure in the region. Kenya, Ethiopia, and Tanzania are also the three biggest African aid recipients from China (Morlin-Yron 2016). As such, China's relations with East Africa should be examined country by country to gauge the usefulness of China's projects and understand local reactions.

China's MSR Projects in East Africa

Djibouti

Although the MSR is mostly about economics, it also has a security aspect, which relates to the country of Djibouti, located strategically on the Gulf of Aden, a maritime choke point between the Red Sea and Europe to the west and the Indian Ocean and the rest of Asia to the east. Djibouti, if anything, is a demonstration of China's strategic intentions with its BRI. It was here that China's first foreign naval base was launched in July 2017, to complement the PLAN's ongoing efforts, since 2012, to conduct anti-piracy operations off the coast of adjacent warlord-ridden Somalia (Panda 2017), together with warships from other countries. China is mindful that its cargo ships to and from Europe have to pass through the Gulf of Aden, which could be subjected to attacks by pirates, or for that matter, warships from an unfriendly nation (Chan 2017). China's is the fourth military base in Djibouti after the US, France, and Japan. However, even though China has proclaimed that its naval base in Djibouti was established to fulfill its international obligation, Western observers have suspected that it is part of China's intention to project its military power far from its shores (Pautasso 2018), and the base could be expanded to accommodate China's aircraft carriers or other large warships (Hutton 2020). In any case, having a naval base in Djibouti will greatly increase China's strategic involvement and military influence in the Horn of Africa.

In addition to the base in Djibouti, a port and free trade zone was established, financed, and operated by Chinese enterprises, including China Merchants Holdings and Dalian Port Corp., together with the Djibouti government; another port was constructed by the China State Construction Engineering Corp. at Doraleh, the principal port just west of the capital city; and an electric railway from Doraleh to Addis Ababa, the capital of Ethiopia, was built between 2016 and January 2018 by two Chinese state-owned enterprises, creating "tens of thousands" of jobs for Djiboutians (Xinhua News Agency 2020) and reducing travel time between the two cities from a week to 10 hours (Xinhua News Agency 2018). China, through China Merchants Inc. in Hong Kong, has since 2012 controlled 23.5 percent of the port and free trade zone of Djibouti (Nyakazeya 2018). In January 2017, the Silk Road International Bank, a joint merchant banking venture between the government of Djibouti and Chinese interests, was opened for business in Doraleh (Xinhua News Agency 2017).

Ethiopia

As Ethiopia is a landlocked country, the 756-kilometer Addis Ababa–Djibouti railway—the first standard gauge electrified railway built with Chinese standards and technology in Africa—is crucial for providing economic access to the Aden Gulf and the Red Sea, as the railway terminus of Doraleh has terminals for handling oil, bulk cargo, and containers. The railway was built by two Chinese state-owned companies and funded by China's state Exim Bank to the sum of $2.9 billion, or about 70 percent of its cost, with the rest coming from commercial loans made by other Chinese banks (Zhou 2019). Still, due to debt pressure from the plan, on his visit to Beijing in September 2018, Ethiopia's prime minister Abiy Ahmed renegotiated some of his country's loan agreements with China and had the repayment period extended by 20 years (Zhou 2019). Aside from rail link, another major infrastructure undertaken by China in Ethiopia was the Addis Ababa city light-rail transit system, the first of its kind in sub-Saharan Africa. It was started in December 2011 with funding from China's Import-Export Bank and went into operation in 2015 (Tarrosy and Vörös 2018). Chinese funds were also instrumental in the construction of Addis Ababa's first six-lane highway for $800 million, a national sports stadium, and a general hospital, although these and other projects have resulted in Ethiopia owing almost half its external debt to Beijing (Marks 2020). The Chinese government funded Ethiopia's first ever remote satellite, the ERSST-1 (Ethiopian Remote Sensing Satellite-1), which was officially handed to Ethiopia by China in December 2020 (Abera 2020). China's infrastructure investment in Ethiopia is more than a case of "infrastructure for diplomatic support," as often alleged. Under the MSR, Ethiopia benefited from China's zero-tariff policy on agricultural imports, witnessing a dramatic growth in its sesame exports to China, and China became a major source of manufactured goods and machinery for Ethiopia (Chakrabarty 2016). Ethiopia, with 100 million people, and the rest of East Africa are becoming large and important markets for Chinese products. Aside from the Addis Ababa–Djibouti railway, another of Africa's MSR flagship projects is the railway built by Chinese companies in neighboring Kenya.

Kenya

On Moody's investors service's credit rating list, Kenya scored a B1 from 2012 to 2017, meaning that its credit worthiness was on watch and might possibly be downgraded anytime in the future, with investors advised to consider it a high speculative and credit risk for investment (Moody's 2017). Yet this did not dissuade China from completing a railway in Kenya in 2017, the Mombasa–Nairobi Standard Gauge Railway, linking the capital city of Nairobi to the county's major port of Mombasa. This was the most extensive railway project for Kenya since its independence from Britain in December 1963, and China built it to help Kenyans replace the old railway laid by the British and improve Kenya's economic development. Constructed with a loan of $3.2 billion from China to the Kenyan government, principally underwritten by the China's Exim Bank, the railway reduced transportation costs from $0.20 to $0.08 per ton per kilometer and significantly shortened travel time between Nairobi and Mombasa from 15 hours to 4 hours (Kacungira 2017). Construction of this railway created some 46,000 jobs for locals, and China coached about 45,000 people in railway operation, management skills, and technological application, many of whom spent time training in China (Mwakio 2017). The railway zone would make locating factories or settlements easier for the Chinese should they wish to invest even more in Kenya. And even though the railway had yet to turn a profit, it was later extended from Nairobi westward to the Rift Valley at a cost of $1.5 billion. However, it became the subject of a lawsuit when in June 2020 a Kenyan appellate court declared the rail contract between

Kenya and builder China Road and Bridge Corp. illegal on grounds that it was not put up for tender (Nyabiage 2020). To head off the controversy, the government-owned Kenya Railways Corp. announced in March 2021 that it would assume operation of the railway in May 2022 at the end of the five-year contract with the Chinese contractor Afristar, owned by China Road and Bridge, to which Kenya Railways owed $340 million in operation and maintenance fees (Oirere 2021). In response to a petition from two activists to reveal the contents of the contract, particularly its cost and to whom the debts are owed, the attorney general of Kenya refused to make the contract public on grounds of national security (Metropol TV Kenya 2022).

One of the major but unstated reasons for MSR's interest in Kenya is crude oil, not from Kenya itself but from adjacent South Sudan. South Sudan is a key exporter of crude oil to China. However, South Sudan has no direct access to the sea, and due to border conflicts between South Sudan and Sudan, from which it became independent in 2011, it has not been able to export its oil via Sudan's Red Sea port, although Sudan has been a friendly country to China. As such, China has proposed building a transport corridor with a railway, highway, and oil pipeline from South Sudan's capital, Juba, through southern Ethiopia and northern Kenya to a new port to be developed at Lamu on Kenya's coast, with its first berth scheduled for completion in June 2019 (Ziromwatela and Zhao 2016; Kazungu 2018). The infrastructure development would be funded through an export of crude oil from the South Sudan government to the Exim Bank of China, which increased from 10,000 barrels per day before February 2019 to 30,000 afterward (*Bloomberg* 2019). For fear of popular backlash against indebtedness to China or influence from it, neither the Kenya Ports Authority nor its government has been advertising Chinese involvement in the project. As of 2022, a new $353 million Kipevu Oil Terminal is being constructed in the port city of Mombasa, financed by Kenya Ports Authority and constructed by the China Communication Construction Company (Nyabiage 2021a).

Tanzania

Due south of Kenya is Tanzania, where the showcase MSR project is the 680-meter seven-lane Nyerere Bridge in its largest city, Dar es Salaam. The Nyerere Bridge is the largest cable-stayed bridge in East Africa. It was built by two Chinese companies, the China Railway Jiangchang Engineering and China Major Bridge Engineering Company, starting in 2014 and officially readied for operation in 2016. The Chinese claimed that the Nyerere Bridge effectively solved the severe problem of overcrowding on poorly maintained ferries, which, before the construction of the bridge, commuters and cars would have to take to cross the Kurasini Creek from the city's business district to the Kigamboni suburbs, and such ferries were often delayed due to breakdowns (BBC 2016). The president of Tanzania, John Magufuli, even said that the bridge "liberates" the residents, in the city of more than 4 million (BBC 2016), by providing a quicker and safer alternative to cross the creek.

Also in Dar es Salaam, an Internet Data Centre was built by the China International Telecommunication Construction Corp. This was part of Tanzania's national fiber-optic broadband cable network, with a total length of about 7,500 kilometers and built with a $250 million loan from China (Boyle 2012). The Centre would provide high-speed broadband connectivity even in the most remote villages, and Faustin Kamuzora, Tanzania's permanent secretary in the Ministry of Works, Transport and Communication, claimed that it would provide specialized ICT services that could attract stakeholders in the ICT sector to store information and data, effectively making Tanzania the center of ICT for countries in East Africa (Xinhua 2016).

Following Xi's first trip to Tanzania as president in 2013, China's largest public-port operator, China Merchants Holdings, set about to develop Bagamoyo, a small fishing port about 45 miles north of Dar es Salaam, into East Africa's biggest container port, with piers and docks extending along 10 miles of coastline and the capacity to handle 20 million containers a year, after securing funding of $10 billion from the Sultanate of Oman's sovereign wealth fund and China's Exim Bank (Servant 2019). The area south of Bagamoyo, seen by China as a new Shenzhen-type special economic zone, is projected to have factories in a fenced-off industrial area, apartment blocks to accommodate the estimated population of 75,000, and possibly an international airport (Mead 2018). If completed, Bagamoyo would be the largest and most significant Chinese project in Tanzania.

Notwithstanding the fact that the Bagamoyo port project was approved by Xi himself, it was suspended in June 2019 by the Tanzanian government because the financing terms presented by China were "exploitative and awkward," according to John Magufuli, Tanzania's president. In the terms, agreed to by his predecessor, China would lease the port for 99 years and Tanzania would not have a say in who can invest in the port once it is operational (Yan 2019). After protracted negotiations, on June 27, 2021, Magufuli's successor Samia Suluhu Hassan announced that Tanzania and China would work together to revive the Bagamoyo project (Su 2021). Still, two Chinese companies, China Civil Engineering Construction and

China Railway Construction Company, had earlier won a tender of $1.3 billion to construct phase 5 of the Tanzanian Standard Gauge Railway linking Tanzania to Rwanda and Uganda in January 2021 (Ayemba 2021b). If China's state-backed railway companies are able to link the railways of Djibouti, Ethiopia, Kenya, South Sudan, Uganda, Tanzania, and Rwanda into one rail system, China would be guaranteed quick and steady access to the natural resources of East Africa.

Egypt

Although the BRI is mainly focused on East Africa, China has integrated Egypt into the initiative where the Red Sea sails through the Suez Canal to Europe. Egypt received $4.95 billion in loans from China between 2015 and 2019, after the MSR when into operation, compared to around $332 million between 2002 and 2014 (Nyabiage 2022a). One of the biggest BRI projects in Egypt is the construction of the central business district in Egypt's new administrative capital by the Chinese State Construction and Engineering Company. The $3 billion project, which includes 20 skyscrapers, began in 2018 with 85 percent of the financing handled by Chinese banks (Ayemba 2021a). China's industrial developer Tianjin Economic-Technological Development Area is developing an industrial estate with a minimum area of 7.23 square kilometers in Egypt's Suez Canal economic zone, principally to receive investments from Chinese companies to produce outputs; China's AVIC International and China Railway Group Limited are building a light-rail transit to connect Egypt's new administrative capital with east Cairo; Chinese State Construction is constructing what will be the tallest building in Africa in Egypt's new capital; Chinese firms are building a coal-fired power plant and three solar power stations; and in 2018, Chinese banks have provided Telecom Egypt $200 million in financing, with the understanding that Huawei would develop a 4G network for Egypt (Telecom Egypt 2018). There are more than 1,600 China-funded enterprises operating in Egypt, with a total investment of about $7 billion by Chinese financial institutions, to create about 30,000 jobs for Egyptians, according to China's ambassador to Egypt Liao Liqiang in 2019 (*Belt and Road News* 2019). However, even though the first phase of the Suez venture, completed in 2014 with an area of 1.83 square kilometers, has attracted 85 enterprises with a cumulative investment of $1 billion, its second phase has until the end of 2021 attracted only eight enterprises with $200 million worth of investments (Nyabiage 2022a).[3]

114 | China's Belt and Road Power Transition

Reactions to China's MSR Projects in East Africa

Despite the stated benefits of the MSR in East Africa, China's growing activities and influence in Africa was criticized by former US secretary of state Rex Tillerson in 2018 for "predatory loan practices" (Chen 2014), by trapping African countries into incurring unserviceable debts with Chinese infrastructure investment loans. US concerns about its influence in Africa being challenged and eroded by China are fully understandable. However, from 2000 to 2016, China's loans to Africa accounted for only 1.8 percent of the continent's total debt. These loans were usually offered with relatively low interest rates and long repayment periods, and no African country has claimed to have been lured into a "debt trap" with China (Chen 2014). Furthermore, about 40 percent of the loans were used for power generation and transmission, and 30 percent for upgrading outdated transport infrastructure (Chen 2014), for which there were no political strings or conditions attached, as China adheres to a foreign policy of nonintervention in the internal affairs of other countries. As to China's purchases of Africa's hydrocarbon, metal, and other resources, it could only be a boon to the exporters of these resources to have another customer, particularly one that is large, deep-pocketed, and eager.

In addition to its significant investments and aid, China operates more than 40 Confucius Institutes in Africa with teachers posted from the country to instruct locals in Chinese language and culture (Heever 2017). In 2017, the country received 95,000 exchange students from Africa on scholarships, compared to 40,000 in both the US and the UK (Xinhuanet 2017). Since 2012, *China Daily*, China's leading English-language state newspaper, has been printing an Africa edition, published in Nairobi, Kenya, for free distribution (York 2013). In February 2022, the Mwalimu Julius Nyerere Leadership School, funded, built, and staffed by the CCP to train political leaders and enhance governing capacity in Mozambique, Zimbabwe, South Africa, Namibia, and Angola, was opened in Tanzania, where officials could learn from China's experience on law enforcement, digital surveillance, and its model of combining political authoritarianism with state-led capitalism (Nyabiage 2022b). Yet even if Confucius Institutes, Chinese scholarships, and newspapers with Chinese viewpoints are preparing the next generation of African business and political leaders to be fluent in Mandarin Chinese and friendly to China, it will take time for them to influence local economies and polities, as English and French are, for historical reasons, still the main languages of communication in Africa, particularly English in East Africa.

This is not to say that the MSR in East Africa does not have its problems. Data released by the Kenyan Ministry of Communications recorded a loss of $100 million for the Chinese-funded Mombasa–Nairobi Standard Gauge Railway for its first year of operation in 2018 (BBC 2018). The explanation for such loss, given by the Kenyan authority, was the compensation of affected communities. However, there were already two legal charges against officials for committing fraud relating to the railway. In August 2018, two senior government officials of Kenya, Muhammad Swazuri, chairman of the National Land Commission, and Atanas Kariuki Maina, chief executive officer of Kenya Railways, were arrested and accused of deliberate falsification when they paid more than $2 million as compensation to private companies that falsely claimed their properties were confiscated to make way for the construction of the railroad (BBC 2018). In November 2018, two Chinese and five Kenyan employees of China Road and Bridge Corp., which operates the railway, were accused of fraud by Kenya's Ethics and Anti-Corruption Commission for stealing money from train ticket purchases worth about $10,000 per day, or 15 percent of the railway's daily revenue (Salem 2018). The obvious lesson here is the need for tighter supervision over the construction and operation of MSR projects by both the Chinese and host governments in Kenya, East Africa, and elsewhere where corruption is endemic. Moreover, as the railway cuts through the middle of Nairobi National Park, environmentalists and scientists have complained that the construction noise and dust adversely affected the wildlife and vegetation of the park, which, with its stock of cheetah, zebra, lion, and leopard populations, is Nairobi's main tourist attraction (Ambani 2017). However, the disruption to animals should be greatly reduced with the completion of the track. Furthermore, al-Shabab, a jihadist fundamentalist group based in neighboring Somalia, has threatened the security of infrastructure facilities in Kenya, where previous terrorist attacks have forced the nation to send troops into Somalia (Nyabiage 2021a).

William Ruto, who became Kenya's president in September 2022, was highly critical of China's BRI during the presidential election campaign, promising to make opaque government contracts with Beijing public and threatening to deport all Chinese people from his country, whom he had accused of taking jobs that should be reserved for Kenyans (Bartlett 2022). However, once elected, perhaps mindful of China's importance to Kenya's development and trade, and the 400 Chinese companies operating in the country employing tens of thousands of Kenyans, Ruto said he had no plans to scale down China's investments in Kenya (Bartlett 2022).

In Tanzania, the construction of both the Nyerere Bridge and the Internet Data Centre by China has led to a surge of Chinese firms in the local consumer goods market that are competitive in terms of price, quality, and speed of delivery. This may be beneficial to the consumers but has invited complaints from local sellers. As such, Chinese traders in Tanzania and elsewhere in Africa should be aware of the impacts of their activities on their own communities and also watch out for their own safety. The flip-flop over Bagamoyo port also demonstrates the confusion that leadership changes may have on a BRI project that perhaps China is more eager to promote than the host country.

In Egypt, while the first phase of the Suez Canal economic zone, completed in 2014 with an area of 1.83 square kilometers, has attracted 85 enterprises with a cumulative investment of $1 billion, its second phase has until the end of 2021 enticed only eight enterprises with $200 million worth of investments (Nyabiage 2022a). This could be due to the COVID-19 pandemic but perhaps also the industrial zone expanding too fast.

Chinese security businesses are being hired to protect BRI infrastructure. DeWe Security Service, a privately owned Chinese security protection firm, has entered into a contractual agreement with the government of Kenya to provide training services for local security personnel tasked with safeguarding the Standard Gauge Railway infrastructure from terrorist threats (Zheng and Xia 2021). In 2016, DeWe reportedly enlisted and armed Sudanese individuals to safely evacuate several hundred Chinese oil workers in South Sudan during conflict between opposing groups. The presence of Chinese security firms at BRI projects only serves to highlight the security dimensions of the initiative.

It seems that overall, the drawbacks of the MSR in East African countries are only temporary, but the benefits of the initiative for both African and Chinese people will be long-lasting and profound. What is important is how the peoples and governments of Africa perceive China and the Chinese people. According to a recent Afrobarometer survey, almost two-thirds (63 percent) of Africans say China's influence in their continent is somewhat positive or very positive, while only one out of seven (15 percent) see it as somewhat or very negative (Morlin-Yron 2016). It seems then that China's investment and influence in East Africa, and the rest of Africa, will only increase.

Chapter 4

China's "Health Silk Road" Diplomacy

The visible donation and sale of masks and vaccines by the PRC authorities to foreign governments since the advent of the COVID-19 pandemic in early 2020 is not a new form of Chinese diplomacy, as is often supposed. Rather, this is a major aspect of the "Health Silk Road" (HSR), which was first announced in an international forum at the inaugural BRI summit in 2017 but has, since the spread of the virus, been the most conspicuous feature of the BRI. The HSR may be considered as a co-opting and attractive "soft power" counterpart to the exercise of China's influence through hard infrastructure and finances (Nye 2004). With the start of COVID-19 in early 2020 and the resultant economic difficulties, China has faced considerable pressure to restructure or forgive outstanding loans to BRI partners, which means that major new BRI infrastructure projects are unlikely to move ahead at the scale and pace of the previous five years. As such, the Chinese state has adapted the BRI by changing its focus, giving prominence to newer areas of engagement, such as the hitherto low-profile HSR. To promote the internationalization of health cooperation, Beijing has been organizing forums on health for foreign officials, providing direct and prompt medical assistance to those affected by the coronavirus in more than 100 countries and through the United Nations, and engaging in joint vaccine development and testing with foreign governments and laboratories. China has used the pandemic as an opportunity to increase its global influence, particularly in Europe, Southeast Asia, and the developing world. While China's HSR actions have won praise from most BRI countries, many Western states are concerned about medical overdependence on China, at least in the first two years when the virus went global.

The Origin of China's Health Silk Road Diplomacy

Contrary to popular perception, China's HSR diplomacy was not initiated after the onset of COVID-19[1] but actually predated it by years, although the pandemic certainly focused world attention and redirected the energies of Chinese authorities on this mode of diplomacy. As early as the 1960s, the PRC has dispatched medical teams to countries in Africa and the developing world with which it has diplomatic ties, as part of South-South cooperation, with a focus on treating maternal and child health problems. As an example, China began receiving donated corneas for transplant from Sri Lanka in 1967 and has in recent years built hospitals and given about $20 million annually to the healthcare sector in Sri Lanka (Ranaraja and Majueran 2020). Pakistan is another country in South Asia that joined the HSR before the outbreak of COVID-19, with plans to conduct eye health screening through smart medical methods and establish electronic eye health files for students under the Liaoning Health Silk Road Action Adolescents Eye Health Comprehensive Project, which is expected to benefit about 2 million adolescents and children (*The News International* 2020). For this project, Pakistan is the country paired with Liaoning province under China's system of "province for a country," which is responsible for providing medical material and healthcare talents for Pakistan. Pakistan has of course been very supportive of and involved in the BRI.

In 2015, to enhance international health cooperation under the "people-to-people exchanges" aspect of the BRI, which also includes policy coordination, facility connectivity, unimpeded trade, and financial integration, the PRC National Health and Family Planning Commission proposed policies titled a "Three-Year Implementation Plan for Advancing Belt-and-Road Initiative Health Cooperation (2015–2017)." According to the document, "Strengthening health cooperation between China and the BRI countries, and jointly working to counter public health crises, will help protect the health security and social stability of China and BRI countries, and thus the construction of the BRI" (Ngeow 2020).

Building upon this document, the concept of an HSR was first introduced to the world by Xi in an address to Uzbekistan's Supreme Assembly in Tashkent in June 2016, where he called for increased cooperation in infectious disease prevention and information sharing, medical assistance, and traditional medicine development as ways of building an HSR (Xinhua News Agency 2016a). The HSR was expected to cover a wide scope of activities, including offering the experiences and advice of China's medical teams on treating diseases, strengthening mechanisms of control to prevent cross-border infectious diseases, instituting bilateral and multilateral health policy meetings and networks, and building the healthcare industry and infrastructure together with other BRI countries.

The HSR has a domestic counterpart, the Health China 2030 program launched in October 2016, which is a comprehensive and ambitious nation-wide healthcare initiative to improve China's overall public health standards and environmental cleanliness through emphasizing the importance of both prevention and cure for sicknesses and diseases, focusing on prevention and control, Chinese and Western medicine, and changes in the service mode to reduce rural-urban gaps in the provision of basic health services (Tan, Liu, and Shao 2017). Although this plan is different from the external-oriented HSR, the synergy between the two came to the forefront when COVID-19 hit, as the production of face masks, protective suits, goggles, ventilators, infrared thermometers, test kits, pharmaceutical products, and medical equipment had already started under the domestic health plan.

Although the 2015 policy proposal never led to a fixed or detailed blueprint, it laid out a three-stage strategy to promote the BRI from the health angle (Ngeow 2020). The first stage would in the short term (2015–2017) consolidate existing health cooperation projects, initiate some new ones, and build consensus among the BRI countries on health cooperation. In response to the threat posed by infectious diseases such as the Ebola hemorrhagic fever, Middle East respiratory syndrome, and the Zika virus, ministers and senior officials from the health sector in China and other participating countries, as well as representatives from the World Health Organization (WHO), Joint United Nations Program on HIV/AIDS, Organization for Economic Cooperation and Development, Global Alliance for Vaccines and Immunization, and Global Fund, attended an inaugural "Belt and Road High Level Meeting on Health Cooperation towards Health Silk Road" in Beijing on August 18, 2017 (*China Daily* 2017). The second stage would have three-to-five-year goals (from 2017) of constructing a preliminary network of health cooperation among the BRI countries, ensuring adequate domestic policy support for such endeavors, launching several key health cooperation projects, and raising China's voice and influence in regional and global health governance mechanisms. International cooperation in the fight against COVID-19 and the development of a counteracting vaccine would later on fall into this stage. The third stage, which would span 5 to 10 years from the completion of the second stage, would reap the benefits from the earlier projects and demonstrate to the world the advantages of

120 | China's Belt and Road Power Transition

health cooperation with China. China by then should also have increased both its capacity and status in regional and global health governance matters.

The establishment of the HSR under the BRI was recognized by the WHO in January 2017 and praised by its director, Adhanom Ghebreyesus Tedros, as "visionary" and "accelerating the realization of universal health coverage" (Tedros 2017), with China dispatching medical teams, providing medical supplies, and deploying medical technologies to the international community. To promote the internationalization of health cooperation in accordance with the HSR framework, Beijing organized and sponsored various international health forums and invited health officials from different countries to attend. Forums such as the Silk Road Health Forum, China-ASEAN Health Cooperation Forum, China-Central and Eastern European Countries Health Ministers Forum, and China-Arab Health Cooperation Forum aim to provide a platform for China and participating countries to propose and review concrete plans for cooperation on health matters.

The China-Arab Health Cooperation Forum, for example, was initiated on September 11, 2015, in the Chinese city of Yinchuan, Ningxia (Hui) Autonomous Region. It was organized by China's National Health and Family Planning Commission, the Ningxia government, and the secretariat of the League of Arab States, with the participation of 400 members from 16 Arab countries and China. The forum's theme was "stronger medical technical cooperation and developing the health industry," and there were four meetings on infectious and non-infectious disease prevention and control, academic exchanges on traditional medicine, an international ophthalmology summit, and a Sino-Arab health industry exhibition (Feng 2015). The Second China–Arab Health Cooperation Forum was held in Beijing, August 16 to 18, 2019, and focused on health policies, investment in the fields of pharmaceutical industry, traditional medicine training of human cadres, managing hospitals, and manufacturing vaccines (Xinhua News Agency 2019a).

Promotion of the Health Silk Road during COVID-19: China's Giving

SEIZING OPPORTUNITIES TO HELP

Coming from Wuhan, a Chinese city, COVID-19 initially harmed China's reputation and its perceived capability of controlling the disease. Later, however, the pandemic was found to have presented an opportune moment for Beijing to promote its leadership in global health governance by providing direct and prompt medical help to those affected, given that the international spread of the pandemic created large gaps in the public health infrastructure of both developed and developing countries. The timing was particularly favorable to China since the Trump administration not only halted US funding to the WHO, which accounted for 29 percent of the organization's voluntary contributions, but decided to withdraw from the WHO altogether (Cao 2020, 27–28), accusing it of being manipulated by China (Rajah 2020, 13). In a telephone call with Italian prime minister Giuseppe Conte on March 16, 2020, President Xi brought the HSR proposal back to international attention by saying that China stood ready to increase anti-coronavirus cooperation with the rest of the world and contribute more to the construction of the HSR (Xinhua News Agency 2020a). Closer to home, Chinese foreign minister Wang Yi joined a virtual conference with his counterparts from Afghanistan, Nepal, and Pakistan in July 2020 to discuss plans to contain the COVID-19 pandemic (*Times of India* 2020).

Due to the coronavirus raging, the number of new contracts signed by Chinese contractors from January to August 2020 in 61 Belt-and-Road countries had contracted by 24.4 percent on a year-on-year basis (Construction Global 2020), and engineers and workers on existing BRI projects were largely quarantined. The pandemic also saw China fending off calls from indebted states to forgive some, or even all, of their loans disbursed by the state-owned China Exim Bank or China Development Bank, then announcing in April 2020 that it would freeze all debt repayments for the world's poorest countries until the end of the year. However, given that a crisis can always be an opportunity, China delivered medical support to partner countries using BRI ports, railways, and logistics hubs (Shepard 2020b). In other words, Beijing was trying its best to make up for the trade and investment setbacks of the BRI with its health and medical supplies.

SUPPLYING MEDICAL ASSISTANCE AND VACCINES

By March 2020, soon after COVID-19 started spreading worldwide, China was already providing assistance to over 80 countries as well as the WHO and African Union, and had sent medical teams to countries in need (Xinhua News Agency 2020b). More importantly, China's success in largely controlling the COVID-19 outbreak within its borders, at least for the time being, had reduced its need for vaccinations. As such, according to Huang Yanzhong, a global health expert at the US think tank Council on Foreign Relations, "China could use [its vaccines] to become the global leader in ensuring equitable access to vaccines, bridging the gap between the developed and developing world; certainly, this would help improve China's image and project soft power in those countries" (Lew, Zuo, and McCarthy 2021). Furthermore, China was winning purchase agreements in countries like Serbia, Brazil, Indonesia, Turkey, and the United Arab Emirates simply by being the only vaccine producer at the time able to produce and deliver in any large quantity (Mardell 2021).

At a WHO meeting in May 2020, Xi promised that China would provide $2 billion over two years to help other countries respond to the impact of the coronavirus pandemic (Cheng 2020). Saying that it considered the vaccine a "global public good," China, in a highly visible diplomatic move, later pledged roughly half a billion doses of its vaccines to more than 45 countries, claiming its vaccine makers would be able to produce at least 2.6 billion doses in 2021, particularly targeting the low- and middle-income countries largely left behind as rich nations grabbed most of the pricey vaccines produced by pharmaceutical firms like Pfizer and Moderna (Wu and Gelineau 2021). Unlike the ultra-cold storage needs of vaccines like Pfizer's, China's vaccines can be stored in standard refrigerators, which make them particularly attractive to tropical or subtropical countries, and are developed on a traditional and safe inactivated serum.

By June 2020, China had sent 29 medical teams to 27 countries; Jack Ma, co-founder and former executive chairman of Alibaba Group, had donated about 120 million face masks, 4 million testing kits, and 3,704 ventilators to over 150 countries; and Xiaomi, a Chinese electronics giant, had donated tens of thousands of face masks to Italy (Cao 2020, 29).

In a speech to ASEAN business leaders on November 27, 2020, Xi said that China would provide financial support to the COVID-19 ASEAN Response Fund (which ASEAN established in April 2020 to fund a strategic reserve of medical supplies for the pandemic), work with ASEAN to develop a regional reserve of medical supplies for public health emergencies and launch a liaison mechanism for public health emergencies, and act on the China-ASEAN human resources training program of the HSR (2020–2022) to train 1,000 administrative and specialized personnel in the health sector (MFA 2020). This training program was the continuation of a similar program from 2017, which was itself based on an earlier program in "China-ASEAN Talent Training in Public Health in 2015–2017" to train 100 public health talents for ASEAN countries (Ngeow 2020).

Although Chinese-made vaccines have, in general, lower efficacy rates—50.4 percent for the supposed privately-owned Sinovac and 79 percent for the government-run Sinopharm, compared to more than 90 percent for Pfizer and AstraZeneca vaccines—by February 15, 2021, China had shipped at least 46 million ready-made vaccines or their active ingredients around the world and pledged 10 million doses of its homegrown vaccines to the Covax Facility, the WHO-led initiative for equitable international vaccine access (Lew, Zuo, and McCarthy 2021). By March 2021, China had donated vaccines to 53 developing countries and exported them to 27 countries (*Global Times* 2021). According to Yin Weidong, chairman of Sinovac, his company was producing 6 million doses a day, with over 60 percent of the 260 million jabs supplied by the company by mid-April 2021 shipped overseas (McCarthy 2021). This demonstrates the importance the Chinese government attaches to its vaccine diplomacy.

Reception of the Health Silk Road during COVID-19: China's Taking

DISPENSING AND PURCHASING INFLUENCE

China has shown its readiness to use the opportunity provided by the pandemic to increase its influence inside the EU, with Italy as a tempting target. Italy was the first EU member state that officially joined China's BRI. Although Luigi Di Maio, foreign minister, claimed in early 2020 that despite Italy's request Europe had not offered assistance comparable to that of China, even so, personal protective equipment (PPE) sent by China (masks, ventilators, and other medical equipment) was part of a commercial deal with Italy, and only a small portion was donated (Tagliapietra 2020).

When the first medical supplies and health experts from China arrived in Serbia in March 2020, Serbia's president Aleksandar Vucic, who had complained of European tardiness in providing his country with medical aid to fight COVID-19, was on hand at Belgrade's airport to receive them and kiss the Chinese flag (Standish 2021a). Addressing an online gathering with 17 Central and Eastern European nations—the so-called 17 + 1 (China) forum—in February 2021, Xi said Chinese companies had already supplied a million doses of COVID-19 vaccines to Serbia (Ng and Lo 2021), about two-thirds of the amount ordered, making it the first country in Europe to start inoculating its population with China's vaccines, which constituted the

124 | China's Belt and Road Power Transition

majority of the country's supply (Wu and Galineau 2021). Hungary signed a deal with the Chinese pharmaceutical company for enough of its product to eventually treat 2.5 million people (Lew, Zuo, and McCarthy 2021).

Southeast Asia is a key target for Chinese vaccine diplomacy, accounting for 29 percent of China's total vaccine donations and 25.6 percent of its vaccine sales worldwide (Zaini 2021). In mainland Southeast Asia, Thailand is one of the countries grateful for China's support in its fight against COVID-19. In order to facilitate the cooperation, Thailand and China agreed to open a "fast lane" and a "green channel," respectively, for personal and good exchanges between the two countries (*Belt and Road News* 2020). Under these measures, medical personnel and medical goods were allowed to pass customs quickly and freely. A batch of 200,000 COVID-19 vaccines, the first shipment among 2 million doses Thailand ordered from China's Sinovac Biotech, was delivered by a Thai Airways International cargo flight from Beijing to Bangkok on February 24, 2021 (Xinhua News Agency 2021c). The prime minister of Thailand Prayut Chan-o-cha, the deputy prime minister and public health minister Anutin Charnvirakul, and Chinese Embassy officials were at the airport for the handover of the vaccines, with the prime minister expressing his thanks to the PRC and his hopes that the vaccine would contribute to the recovery of the tourism sector through easing restrictive measures.

In archipelagic Southeast Asia, Malaysia had received its first delivery of the Sinovac vaccine earlier, and Indonesia's president Joko Widodo, on January 13, 2021, rolled up his sleeves to receive his first shot of the Sinovac vaccine to kick off the nation's mass inoculation campaign (Xinhua News Agency 2021b), having ordered 140 million doses of the vaccine from China (Wu and Galineau 2021). Ever since the Delta variant surge in mid-2021, there has been some doubts among Indonesians regarding the effectiveness of Chinese vaccines, but these doubts are moot as Western vaccines have largely been hoarded by Western countries (Tani 2021). In the Philippines, where Beijing has donated 600,000 vaccines, PRC foreign minister Wang Yi was said to have given a subtle message to leaders to tone down public criticism of Chinese assertiveness in the disputed South China Sea, saying that he wanted "friendly exchanges in public, like controlling your megaphone diplomacy a little" (Wu and Galineau 2021). In any case, it is with Chinese vaccines that the Philippines was able to launch its mass vaccination campaign on March 1, 2021.

Elsewhere, as early as March 2020, China had provided a low-interest loan of $500 million over 10 years to Sri Lanka to combat COVID-19 (*Straits*

Times 2020) and sent 5.4 million face masks and more than a million test kits and thousands of protective suits to African countries (Mwangi 2020). By February 2021, Zimbabwe had received a donation of 200,000 doses of COVID-19 vaccines from China (Lew, Zuo, and McCarthy 2021), as did Kenya in September 2021 (Cheng 2022) with a further 10 million doses over the following 11 months (Xinhua News Agency 2022), and United Arab Emirates (UAE) has vaccinated millions of people using Sinopharm's vaccine (Mardell 2021).

By mid-May 2021, according to Beijing-based Bridge Consulting, China had sold a total of 651 million vaccine doses—far more than its donations of 17.4 million—with Latin America and the Asia-Pacific by far the biggest buyers, receiving 309 million and 248.46 million shots, respectively, and Europe accounting for 61.38 million. Africa bought 33 million doses, but it received only 5.45 million donated doses from China. China has pledged to donate vaccines to 35 African countries and the African Union Commission, and has donated the most of any country—10.5 million doses—to the Asia-Pacific region (Nyabiage 2021b).

Joint Medical Cooperation and Development of Vaccines

Chinese vaccine makers sought out international partnerships because of low infection rates at home, officially estimated at around 90,000 out of a population of about 1.4 billion in 2020 and 2021 (Worldometer 2021), which meant they had fewer people to test their vaccines on. The prime minister of Thailand, Prayut Chan-o-cha, said that his country hoped to increase cooperation with China on COVID-19 vaccine research and development (Lin 2020). Sinovac has partnered with the Buntantan Institute in Brazil, it has struck up agreements with institutions in Indonesia and Malaysia, and trials were also conducted in Turkey and Brazil (Wu and Galineau 2021). In Turkey, where Sinovac conducted part of its efficacy trials, officials said the vaccine was 91 percent effective. However, in Brazil, officials revised the efficacy rate in late-stage clinical trials from 78 percent to just over 50 percent after including mild infections, but according to a senior Chinese official, Brazil's efficacy rates were lower because its volunteers were healthcare workers who faced a higher risk of infection (Mardell 2021). For UAE, Sinopharm provided a relationship not offered by Western vaccine makers, namely, a full-scale transfer of medical technology, competencies, and the chance to manufacture a COVID-19 vaccine in UAE for regional distribution, for example, to the Seychelles, in pursuit of both UAE's and China's vaccine diplomacy (Mardell 2021). The joint venture between Sinopharm and the Abu Dhabi–based technological firm Group 42 is producing the vaccines at its manufacturing plant in Abu Dhabi with a planned capacity of about 200 million doses a year, and both pharmaceutical firms are working with a third one in the emirate of Ras el Khaimah to produce 2 million vaccine doses per month (Kok and Sim 2021). Likewise, an adequate supply of Chinese vaccines to Serbia have allowed its president to demonstrate both Serbia's and China's sway in the former Yugoslavia by both donating and selling AstraZeneca vaccines manufactured in India to neighboring Bosnia, Montenegro, and North Macedonia from March 2021 (Aljazeera 2021a).

Evolution of China's Health Silk Road Diplomacy

Although China revitalized the HSR to promote itself as an open-handed country and brush up its image, which was tarnished by being the originating country of COVID-19 and allowing it to spread abroad, international responses were polarized. Pro-China BRI countries and the WHO consider China's HSR beneficial to themselves and the world, while the US, which considers China a competitor if not a rival, and India, which has a border dispute with China that turned violent in 2020, hold opposite views. Through the HSR, China might have helped authoritarian governments in BRI countries enhance public health and security by exporting emerging technologies for supervising mass lockdowns, mandatory testing, and prompt delivery of medical supplies, which had so effectively and impressively stopped the spread of the coronavirus in China after the first two months. However, whether the end result was to promote good governance or stifle human rights is a matter of debate. QR health codes on WeChat and other Chinese smartphone apps, or paper versions of health travel certificates, required to gain entry to domestic transport and many public spaces in China have sparked privacy concerns and fears of expanded government surveillance (Aljazeera 2021b), especially if the system is copied throughout the world. Offers by Chinese 5G companies such as Huawei to store health data and hospital databases on their cloud systems have been spurned in Europe and other democratic countries as risky to privacy rights.

Beijing's impressive capacity to produce and deliver emergency medical items like face masks, ventilators, diagnostic kits, and protective gear has triggered growing anxiety in the West about the world's overdependence on China (Cao 2020, 25). In 2018 alone, over half of the EU's and 48 percent of America's imports of PPE came from China (25). China's immediate medical assistance did little to win Beijing many new friends, largely because while donating and selling medical supplies, Chinese diplomats and state media promoted conspiracy theories that the US military was responsible for spreading the pandemic, or that Italy was possibly the origin of the virus (Patey 2020). In 2020, reports of faulty medical equipment from China have led to their rejection from governments in Spain, Turkey, and the Netherlands, and Britain sourced millions of coronavirus testing kits from two Chinese firms, spending $20 million, only to find that they did not work (Serhan and Gilsinan 2020). To reduce medical supply-chain dependence on China, US lawmakers from both the Republican and Democratic parties have encouraged companies to make more medical supplies in the US as a matter of national security (Serhan and Gilsinan 2020). To prevent foreign penetration or acquisition of firms producing needed critical technologies such as biotechnology and medicine during the pandemic, Germany enhanced its foreign direct investment (FDI) screening process, France lowered its threshold for notification of FDI from 25 percent to 10 percent, and Spain introduced new restrictions on FDI (ICLG.com 2020). The last time China showed its readiness to help Italy, in the aftermath of the financial crisis, the People's Bank of China purchased shares worth more than $5 billion in the Italian stock market, acquiring holdings in important companies such as Unicredit, Eni, Enel, and Telecom Italia. To protect the country's strategic economic assets, the Italian government issued "golden power" measures in April 2020 to safeguard Italian assets, measures through which the government can oppose or require specific conditions for the purchase of shares of Italian firms by external buyers (Tagliapietra 2020). To support recovery from the COVID-19 pandemic, the EU has allocated EUR 750 billion for member states in its 2021–2027 budget plan (European Council 2020). Western democracies would be even more concerned if the Chinese government were to claim that the effective lockdown and quick testing of communities in China was the result of an integrated system of command, control, and monitoring that only a one-party state can carry out efficiently.

It is understandable that the Chinese would not, for the reason of "saving face," publicly acknowledge that the US sent 17.8 tons of medical equipment, the EU sent 50 tons of medical supplies, and the Japanese sent medical supplies and monetary contributions to China in the early weeks of the virus' spread (Verma 2020, 255–56). Nonetheless, the Chinese are proud, perhaps justifiably, to have met the demand of global emergency test kits, PPE, and vaccine supplies. This is all the more impressive considering that Chinese authorities were aiming to administer 100 million doses domestically by February 2021 but had only reached 40 million (Brown 2021). By the spring of 2021, as the virus metamorphosized into the Delta variant, a real shift had taken place to reduce logistical dependence on Chinese medical supplies and rebuild entire industries in the US, leading to widespread vaccine inoculations and declining prices for face masks and hygiene products with supplies from worldwide production. Already Chinese medical device manufacturers and pharmaceutical companies are moving or expanding outside China to places like Vietnam in search of greater market access and lower costs. However, China remains a significant market for medical services, for example the German pharmaceutical firm BioNTech's arrangement with Chinese drug maker Shanghai Fosun to supply China with 100 million doses of the COVID-19 vaccine after conducting tests there (Kansteiner 2020).

Notwithstanding criticisms of China, including its handling of the 2019 protests in Hong Kong and detention of Muslims in Xinjiang, both the West's and the developing world's dependence on Chinese medical supplies has meant allowing China to reposition itself as a responsible and altruistic global leader promoting economic recovery from the COVID-19 crisis. China's provision of vaccines to European countries such as Serbia and Hungary helped China to strengthen bilateral ties with Serbia's and Hungary's populist leaders, who are often critical of the EU. Chinese medical aid also allowed the Serbian president to play the China card in securing masks and other medical equipment from the EU as part of a $112 million aid package (Standish 2021a), which raises China's influence in Serbia and Europe. Although a study in July 2021 suggested that a Sinopharm vaccine offers poor protection from COVID-19 among the elderly (Wu and Spike 2021), forcing the Hungarian government to turn to the EU for Pfizer/BioNTech vaccines, Hungary still signed a letter of intent with Sinopharm to build a vaccine-producing facility (Reuters 2021). Iran, sanctioned by the US, provided a geopolitical opportunity for China to exploit, by donating over 400,000 masks, a waste disposal facility worth EUR 1 million, and medical experts to Tehran (Ghauttam, Singh, and Kaur 2020), winning praises from Iranians and Shiite Muslims. In late 2021, China pledged and delivered $31 million (RMB 200 million) worth of aid to the Taliban interim government of Afghanistan, including food supplies and three million doses of Sinopharm vaccines, for which Taliban officials have described China as Afghanistan's "most important partner" (BBC 2021). China's "giving" of medical supplies and vaccines is shrewdly balanced by its "taking" of diplomatic and prestige gains.

As China is the only national economy of any size to show expansion, not shrinkage, in 2020, and its foreign exchange reserves have held steady around $3,100 billion since March 2019 (Xiao 2020), China can again be the economic growth engine of many countries in the post-COVID world. Even in the thick of the pandemic, the China-led AIIB created a $5 billion crisis recovery fund to support the member nations and businesses (Hossain 2021, 607). Debt deferment, renegotiation of terms, or downsizing of projects will do little to discourage Chinese lending activities in BRI countries, given the political importance of the initiative as the capstone foreign policy enterprise for Xi and the current Chinese leadership. Disruptive though the pandemic was to the world economy, China's unexpectedly fast though temporary economic recovery in 2021 meant that supply chains would not yet be relocated. A post-COVID BRI is likely to see the Chinese government prioritizing more socially inclusive areas of cooperation, such as information technology, clean energy generation, and medicine to combat other diseases and viruses over hard infrastructure projects.

The Delta and subsequent Omicron outbreaks in China, which spread to more than half the country's provinces and prompted local lockdowns, sowed doubts on the effectiveness and durability of Chinese-made vaccines, especially on the young and the elderly, as Sinovac and Sinopharm use an inactivated virus rather than the genetic code in BioNTech/Pfizer's and Moderna's mRNA vaccines (*Financial Times* 2021). In December 2021, the health authorities of Singapore said that people who received two doses of the Sinovac or Sinopharm vaccine would need a third dose to be considered "fully vaccinated" (*Financial Times* 2021). Thailand has employed mix-and-match strategies with Western jabs to bolster the efficacy of Chinese vaccines, but still, to a great extent, as recognized by the WHO and supported by research studies since 2021, both vaccines significantly reduce the severity and fatality of a COVID-19 infection (McGregor 2021). Hence China's vaccines are rightly credited for providing some level of protection to billions worldwide in places that might not otherwise have access to vaccines. In early 2022, with Chinese leaders supporting traditional Chinese medicine and COVID-19 treatments included in national guidelines, China started selling Chinese medicines made from traditional formulas and herbal ingredients, such as *Lianhua Qingwen*, that are said to be effective against the

COVID-19 virus to its close friends Cambodia and Pakistan, although health experts in China and abroad have warned of a lack of proof of their effectiveness or possible cardiovascular side effects (Zhang 2020).

All this means that countries in the West or elsewhere not willing to participate in authoritarian China's HSR, the functioning of which will outlast the pandemic as an arm of the strategic BRI, will have to provide for their own health and medical care. To this end, the Philippines has worked with India to secure 8 million doses of the Covaxin vaccine, developed by India's Bharat Biotech, and 30 million doses of the Covovax vaccine, developed by the US company Novovax and manufactured by the Serum Institute of India by the second half of 2021 (Robles 2021). Leaders in the US, Australia, India, and Japan have also pledged, at their first Quad summit in March 2021, to boost India's vaccine production capacity by enabling it to produce at least 1 billion doses of vaccines for Asian countries, but only by the end of 2022 (Liu 2021). China is still very much in the act of vaccine diplomacy. Just hours after the White House announced on July 4, 2021, that the US would send 1.5 million Moderna vaccines to El Salvador, following an earlier pledge of 4 million doses of Moderna vaccines to Indonesia, Beijing proclaimed it would also dispatch 1.5 million Sinovac doses to El Salvador (Zhou 2021). By the end of 2021, China had delivered almost twice the number of vaccines as the US via Covax (*Financial Times* 2021). However, for all of China's generosity, only 7 percent of its vaccines sent abroad were donations; the rest were exported commercial goods (Shepard 2020b).

Chapter 5

China's Evolving Belt-and-Road Initiative

The imposition of trade tariffs and technological sanctions by the US against Chinese companies beginning in 2018 was not merely an attempt to cure the US' trade deficit with China or prevent China's 5G technology from dominating the US and world markets. Equally important, it should be understood as an attempt by the Trump administration to deprive China of its ability to make enough earnings from trade and technological deals with the US and other Western countries to finance its BRI ventures and promote Chinese interests and influence abroad. For China, the BRI has become a flanking action to the US-China trade "war," technology rivalry, and Free and Open Indo-Pacific initiative announced in July 2018, and ultimately their victim. Even though the BRI has been placed on the backburner since the COVID-19 virus, which arrived in China and worldwide in early 2020, it is far from inactive.

A Bid for World Leadership

As Yan Xuetong of Tsinghua University wrote, "China believes that its rise to great-power status entitles it to a new role in world affairs—one that cannot be reconciled with unquestioned US dominance" (Rachman 2021). China is reclaiming its historic position of leadership and centrality on the global stage. As China became the world's factory by the turn of the 21st century, it voraciously imported agricultural and animal products, raw materials, and minerals to produce capital equipment, electronic goods, household manufactures, and foodstuffs for export. However, Chinese wages were rising;

traditional markets in North America, Western Europe, and Japan were getting saturated; and construction materials such as cement and steel were piling up at home due to excess production. It was becoming imperative for the Chinese leadership to explore and develop new overseas markets, production platforms, and infrastructure investments to reach unexploited or underexploited natural resources. This was the immediate logic behind the Xi's push for the BRI, principally in Asia, Africa, and Europe, with the establishment of an accompanying AIIB as its financing arm. However, a longer-term strategic rationale to the initiative cannot be precluded. The Chinese leadership understands that, as of the 2010s and 2020s, China is not yet in the position to mount a full-frontal assault on American predominance in the world but believes that it is possible and worthwhile to pursue a course of flanking or outflanking the US in the conduct of international politics and economics. In any case, Belt-and-Road agreements are negotiated bilaterally between China and the countries concerned, which usually works in Beijing's favor as the stronger party economically and politically.

As pointed out, around the time of the global financial crisis in 2008, to upgrade the country's technological and industrial base China's authorities redoubled efforts to recruit world-class scientists, engineers, entrepreneurs, and financial experts from overseas working in high technology by offering them lucrative (by Western standards) research funds and relocation subsidies as part of its Thousand Talents Program. Additionally, in 2015, a Made in China 2025 strategic plan was unveiled by the PRC's State Council to raise domestic development and production and thereby reduce reliance on foreign supplies of core components and materials in robotics, communications technology, and advanced machine tools. The Made in China 2025 strategy was developed by Xi to further the country's civilian and military technological foundation by acquiring and facilitating the transfer of foreign technology and related intellectual property rights, with the Chinese government placing students and researchers from China in sensitive areas of academic research in the US (Akan 2018). In the PRC's 13th Five-Year Plan (2016–2020), Beijing identified the country's most critical technology priorities as clean energy, aerospace and deep-sea research, information technology, and manufacturing (Political Transcript Wire 2018). These priorities have been continued under the 14th Five-Year Plan (2021–2025), which stressed the development of digital technology. To reduce Western and American suspicions, China no longer mentions the Thousand Talents Program or Made in China 2025 in public; however, as the Xi leadership's

China's Evolving Belt-and-Road Initiative | 133

aim is still to attain world-leading production and technological status for China, neither the program nor the plan has been phased out.

By 2017, with Donald Trump as president, the US' trade deficit with China was already $375.6 billion, increasing to $419.2 billion in 2018, with US imports from China dominated by household electronics, apparel, and footwear (Amadeo 2021). The Trump administration grew increasingly convinced that China was underpricing its exports, not buying enough from the US, and pressuring US companies to transfer technology to gain access to the Chinese market. After imposing tariffs and quotas on solar panels and washing machines, the US imposed tariffs on steel and aluminum, all of which are major imports from China. In retaliation, China canceled all contracts on soybeans and agricultural products. After arduous negotiations, a trade deal between China and the US was signed in January 2020, but with the spread of the COVID-19 virus from China's Wuhan city to the first locations in the US only weeks away, Sino-US relations did not return to the pre-Trump era.

While the US-China trade conflict was taking place, Beijing was facing diminished foreign reserves, debt-distressed borrowers, a growing list of troubled projects worldwide and domestically, increasing domestic and overseas public scrutiny of opaque BRI lending, and domestic demands for financial de-risking. By late 2019, as the importance of allocating Chinese investment to other countries had weakened substantially, concern grew that the expected returns on such investments would decline (Park 2019). Authorities then throttled official overseas lending, which plummeted from $76 billion in 2016 to only $4 billion in 2019, but by then official loans from China in 52 BRI economies had doubled to $102 billion, accounting for 62 percent of what BRI countries owed to all official bilateral lenders, compared with $49 billion in 2014 (Arase 2021). In the first half of 2020, even with the COVID-19 pandemic, the BRI remained significant for China, as 30 percent of its total trade volume came from countries who had signed on to the initiative (Devonshire-Ellis 2020).

As of mid-2020, although around 20 percent of China's BRI projects had been significantly and adversely affected by the pandemic and 40 percent were slightly affected, according to Wang Xiaolong, director general of the PRC Foreign Ministry's International Economic Affairs Department (Crossley 2020), more than 2,600 projects valued at $3.7 trillion could be linked to the BRI (Siow 2021). Despite the intense trade and technological disputes and the ravages of the coronavirus, in 2021 China's economy recovered and grew at a rate faster than anyone expected, including the Chinese. Hence the Chinese government still had the resources to drive the BRI as fervently as before. According to the Asian Development Bank, Asia alone would need to invest $1.7 trillion per year in infrastructure until 2030 to maintain its growth momentum, tackle poverty, and respond to climate change (Siow 2021). As such, something like the BRI is a material necessity for many countries. The tepid response by Muslim majority countries, such as Egypt, Turkey, Iran, Saudi Arabia, Oman, United Arab Emirates, Pakistan, Maldives, Malaysia, and Indonesia, to the alleged human rights violations of the Uyghur Muslim minority in China's Xinjiang is a prominent example of the deference shown to China over its rising wealth and power, the benefits of which are demonstrated by the BRI.

It is hard to deny that even in 2022, nine years after the initiative was announced, the BRI is an archipelago of projects united more by a brand than an institution, although these projects are carried out somewhat under the purview of a central coordinating agency or according to a BRI directive. Descriptions of BRI projects by the Chinese state often seem to be invented after the fact to justify deals struck by various PRC state or state-backed entities in BRI member states. This is because Xi's aim for the BRI was always more than just building infrastructure or promoting trade throughout the world, despite the claims of China's propaganda machines (e.g., this rap-inspired music video featuring young singers extolling the economic virtues of the Belt-and-Road, produced by Xinhua News Agency, https://www.youtube.com/watch?v=98RNh7rwyf8). Rather, infrastructure and trade are the means to a new Chinese sphere of political and economic influence, involving the reorientation of networks of Afro-Asian trade and commerce from the West to China. Grouping disparate projects in different countries under the same label allows the BRI to be billed as a strategy to advance global benefits with China, much like Reform and Opening, which began under Deng Xiaoping in 1979. The post-COVID geopolitical environment, with its heightened rifts between China and the "West," makes BRI's expansion into countries like Australia, India, or Italy look less sustainable, but this only increases the salience and urgency for Beijing to forge new relationships with emerging markets in regions beyond its traditional targets of Southeast Asia, Central Asia, and Africa (Crabtree 2020).

In essence, therefore, the BRI operates as a "spokes-and-hub" strategy with China at the core, in the sense that China relates to Country A, Country B, or Country C separately. There is no relationship envisaged or operationalized between countries A and B, countries B and C, countries A and C, or among the three countries within the rubric of the BRI, despite its multilateral rhetoric. This is a deliberate setup by China to make sure that countries involved in the BRI cannot constitute a pressure group against Beijing.

Security concern was paramount for the governments of countries like Pakistan, Cambodia, or Myanmar when they signed on to China's BRI, for they are facing what they respectively consider to be deadly opponents like India, troublesome neighbors like Vietnam, or sanctions from Western countries, which had threatened or could threaten the survival of their countries or regimes. Siding with China to balance against such real or perceived existential threats would be natural for these countries. Additionally, a state is likely to embrace the BRI when close cooperation with China on infrastructure or connectivity development boosts growth-based performance (Kuik 2021, 261). While the survival of a state in the international system is often not at stake, the political survival of state leaders and elites usually is (Barnett and Levy 1991). If and when forging closer ties with China opens the ruling elites' pathways to legitimation and survival, then the state is likely to downplay apprehensions and embrace power-backed ventures like the BRI (Kuik 2021, 258).

Given these security and economic reasons, it might reasonably be assumed that debtor countries seeking to renegotiate terms with Chinese financial institutions risk negotiating from a position of weakness. Yet a number of debtor countries have been able to reschedule debt or even convert debt to grant aid. This demonstrates that although the activation of "debt traps" is possible for China, at least in theory, it would never be easy for China to seize assets or demand territorial concessions from debtor countries as they are sovereign, independent states, in the event that agreements are reneged upon by succeeding governments who are not parties to the initial borrowing. "Mutual gains" are, of course, China's stated goals in its deals with BRI partners, but in the event that the material benefits are less than expected, China could still gain diplomatic rewards or public relations victories, which China can reap with the provision of "public collective goods" at its own expense. As such, on a geostrategic level, the BRI's basic aim can be expected to remain the same for the foreseeable future, namely, to ensure that new networks of natural resources, trade and investments, and global value chains and economic security ties that connect them flow between China and its partner countries, rather than between Asia and the economically dominant nations of North America and Europe. Any progress on the BRI, no matter how small, would place China one step closer to achieving a power transition against the US sooner rather than later.

To the extent that supply chains and product quality control mechanisms are bilateral between China and a recipient country within the BRI framework, the arbitration processes are bilateral as well. To hear disputes arising from the BRI, the PRC's Supreme Court in June 2018 constituted the International Commercial Court of China, which would deal only with cases involving at least RMB 300 million where parties have resolved to bring their disputes to China's Supreme Court (HWF Briefing 2022), or as stipulated in the contracts of projects signed between China and BRI countries, such as Kenya. However, in accordance with Chinese law, no foreign judges can sit on legal benches in mainland China, so this means China plays the roles of both coach and referee, so to speak. As such, PRC's Hong Kong Special Administrative Region is trying to sell itself as having an independent court system as well as the Hong Kong International Arbitration Centre, but for legal judgments to be enforceable, disputants will have to be signatories to the New York Convention on the Recognition and Enforcement of Arbitral Awards 1958, of which the following countries involved in BRI projects are not signatories: Ethiopia, Iraq, Maldives, Timor-Leste, Turkmenistan, and Yemen. With state-owned corporations and sovereign entities, enforcement of mediation or arbitration measures could be problematic.

It has been suggested that the BRI is primarily a campaign to restore an ancient model in which emissaries from foreign countries would travel to China's capital city and pay tribute by prostrating themselves at the feet of the Chinese emperor, offering gifts in exchange for political patronage (Freymann 2021). Such a "tribute-patronage" relationship has not yet returned, if it ever will. Indeed, it is China that is presently lavishing on these countries to purchase their goodwill, for China has still to become the preeminent world power. However, the ultimate purpose of the BRI might well be to set such a relationship in place, should America decide or have to step aside. Hence, we are witnessing the expansion of the initiative to the South Pacific and Western Hemisphere, the Arctic, and even the digital world. With very few exceptions, political elites of recipient countries are more or less receptive to the material propositions provided by Chinese money under the initiative. Indeed, leaders of many developing countries are receptive to the Chinese political model perceived by some as strong and efficient. Failures of BRI megaprojects in these countries will be more than compensated for by diplomatic gratitude to China, which is harder to repay than the loans themselves.

BRI Geographically Extended

As the BRI develops, new states that were not a priori destined to join the revived ancient continental and maritime silk roads, such as some countries in West Africa, the island states in the Pacific Ocean and those in South America and the Caribbean, have also expressed their willingness to join the Chinese program. China is of course more than pleased to embrace their participation. This would not only make the initiative a global one but allow China to dispense more aid and offer more trade to small countries to increase its influence among them. It bears pointing out, though, that many projects already underway before the BRI have been framed under it, so it is not altogether clear-cut what constitutes a BRI project, unless or until the Chinese government says it is.

West Africa

China's BRI in Africa has been extending westward. By 2022, 52 of the 55 members of the African Union have signed memorandums of understanding to participate in the BRI. However, most of these memorandums are as yet just signatures on paper, as the Chinese have been very selective and strategic with their large infrastructure projects outside the historic maritime trade routes. The most notable of these other projects are in Gabon, Nigeria, and Senegal.

The 95-kilometer Port-Gentil-Omboué coastal road and the massive Booué Bridge in Gabon, completed in 2021, link Port-Gentil, the second-largest city and center of the petroleum industry in this Central African country, with its capital, Libreville, and was carried out by the China Bridge and Road Corp. with financing from Exim Bank (CR 2021). The Abuja–Kaduna railway line in the Gulf of Guinea state of Nigeria began commercial operation on July 27, 2016, after construction was completed by the China Civil Engineering Construction Company. As one of the first standard gauge railroad modernization projects in Nigeria, this railway line is the first of two phases of the Lagos–Kano standard metrics Nigeria Railway Modernization Project, which will connect the business centers of Nigeria with the economic activity centers of the northwestern part of the country (Saliu 2019). In Senegal, construction of the Foundiougne Bridge, the longest bridge in West Africa, has proceeded despite the pandemic. Constructed by the China Great Wall Industry Corp. and China Henan

International Corp., the 1,300-meter bridge will shorten the distance to neighboring Gambia and the Casamance region of Senegal (Mutethya 2022). Another salient BRI project, also in Senegal, is the four-lane 114-kilometer Thiès–Touba Toll Expressway, contracted by China Road and Bridge Corp., which connects Touba, Senegal's second-largest city, with the existing highway network in Thiès, on the outskirts of Dakar, the country's capital and dominant urban area (Lewis 2019). Huawei has been commissioned by Senegal to build the Diamniadio National Data Center with an $18.2 million loan (Eguegu 2022).

It is no coincidence that with China's involvement Gabon and Nigeria are major producers of oil and exporters of the commodity to China. Nigeria is the biggest country in Africa in terms of population, and Senegal is literally the beachhead of Chinese influence and interest in former French West Africa. By 2022, China had become the largest source of development finance in Africa, making up roughly 20 percent of all lending to the continent (Umbach 2022). In early 2024, Chinese state-owned and private consortiums joined Anglo-Australian company Rio Tinto to excavate two huge high-grade iron ore mines in Guinea's Simandou mountains and build a railway from the mines to a port, which would also be developed by the partners (Wilson 2024). Guinea had signed on to the BRI in 2018. The westward expansion of the BRI in Africa is a definite indication that China intends to extend its economic interests and diplomatic influence to the Atlantic Ocean, notwithstanding the fact that it has never been part of China's historical MSR.

South Pacific

China has become the second-largest aid donor in the South Pacific region, promising both infrastructure development and employment opportunities to BRI signatories such as New Zealand and its associated territories of Cook Islands and Niue, Fiji, Kiribati, Samoa, Solomon Islands, and Vanuatu. China often characterizes aid to lower- or middle-income Pacific Island nations as a part of "South-South cooperation" (Pan, Clarke, and Loy-Wilson 2019, 389). In fact, 97 percent of China's official aid to the Pacific Island states has been in the form of concessional loans from its Exim Bank, with standard concessional loans denominated in renminbi with an interest rate of 2 percent, a 5-to-7-year grace period, and a 15-to-20-year maturity. Between 2011 and 2017, China's commitment to loan projects in the South Pacific was worth a total value of about $1.7 billion (Rajah, Dayant, and Pryke 2019).

China's Evolving Belt-and-Road Initiative | 139

Specifically, China established a strategic partnership with Papua New Guinea (PNG) in 2014, and PNG has picked China's Huawei Technologies to build its internet infrastructure. In addition to approaching Australia, PNG is also looking to China to secure sizable general budget financing support (ABC News 2019). Kiribati and the Solomon Islands both broke diplomatic ties with Taipei in September 2019 to recognize the PRC, in hopes that China's larger budget and lack of an open approval process would make it easier for Beijing to give more development aid than Taipei can offer. New Zealand has a double tax agreement and a free trade agreement with China. China has paid the governments of the Cook Islands and Micronesia fishing license fees for blue and yellow fin tuna. Chinese investment in Fiji is expected to boost local tourism and the hotel industry. Samoa receives grants from China, and Tonga and Vanuatu owe debts to China. Tonga has deferred debt repayments to China several times, and Vanuatu has constructed a new wharf at Luganville with Chinese concessional loans. Kiribati offers a base for China's large fishing fleets in the South Pacific.

China's attempt to increase its influence over the South Pacific extends beyond squeezing Taiwan's diplomatic space, as 3 of the remaining 12 states (including the Holy See, as of June 2024) that have diplomatic relations with Taiwan as the Republic of China are the Marshall Islands, Palau, and Tuvalu. Three Pacific Island nations, PNG, Kiribati, and Vanuatu, have switched once before from the PRC to the ROC, before switching back to the PRC. China also wishes to resist the application of the US-led Indo-Pacific Strategy, part of which means bringing Western allies together to contain China's maritime expansion in the South Pacific. China may try to use its leverage through diplomacy, debt, trade, or elite capture to establish a military base somewhere in the South Pacific. In the aftermath of looting and rioting in the Chinatown of the Solomon Islands in November 2021, while the country's prime minister, Manasseh Sogavare, blamed the unrest on intervention by Taiwanese agents, its opposition leader accused him of using funds from the Chinese to prop up his government and allowing them to strip the country of its natural assets in return (*France 24* 2021). In April 2022, Sogavare's government signed a security agreement with China that would allow Chinese security forces to be deployed "to protect the safety of Chinese personnel and major projects in Solomon Islands" and to "make ship visits to, carry out logistical replenishment in, and have stopover and transition in Solomon Islands" (*Guardian* 2022). This move, on the coattails of BRI infrastructure spending on building a sports stadium and opening a gold mine, and $11.3 million in development funds promised in 2021 (Siow 2022), would allow China to expand its influence in the Southwest

Pacific, a longtime preserve of Australian and US interests. As such, the value to China of the Solomon Islands, as with Djibouti in the Horn of Africa, is primarily strategic and demonstrates that the BRI is more about power than about just economics. However, when PRC foreign minister Wang Yi tried to sell a similar security deal to its other 10 Pacific Island partner countries in Fiji during the China-Pacific Islands Forum summit in May 2022, no other country apart from Solomon Islands would sign on.

Australia and New Zealand have long considered the Pacific Island nations as part of their spheres of influence. As China's growing presence in the South Pacific means that Australia has far less leverage in the region, the BRI has compelled Australia to come up with its own "step-up" strategy in late 2018, in promising Pacific Islands up to $2.03 billion (AUS 3 billion) in cheap loans and grants (Veramu 2021). If Australia and the US are able to cooperate with China, they would be able to maximize the benefits of Pacific Island countries by making Chinese lending practices more transparent. However, Australia no longer seems interested in the BRI, and the US never wanted to be a part of it and was never invited by China to join.

Latin America and the Caribbean

In May 2017, China officially extended the BRI to Latin America (Sacks 2021), with President Xi calling the Latin American region "a natural extension of the 21st Century Maritime Silk Road" in a meeting with Argentine president Mauricio Macri in Beijing at the second biannual Belt-and-Road forum (Xinhua News Agency 2017). Since the early 21st century, Latin America has been an important source of mineral, meat, and agricultural imports for China. Aside from promoting trade and investment opportunities, bringing the BRI to Latin America and the Caribbean makes good geostrategic sense for China, as the region has always been considered the backyard of the US, and China is now making its influence felt in America's neighborhood. At the second ministerial meeting of the Forum of China and the Community of Latin American and Caribbean States, held in January 2018 in Santiago, Chile, three years after its first meeting, in Beijing, China invited 33 Latin American and Caribbean countries to join the BRI. For China, there is still the Taiwan factor to consider. In November 2017, Panama became the first Latin American country to officially endorse BRI, five months after switching diplomatic ties from Taiwan to China. However, there were still four countries left in Central America and another four countries in the Caribbean that recognized Taiwan, until Nicaragua switched diplomatic ties to Beijing in December 2021. As with elsewhere, the main allure of the BRI for Latin American and Caribbean states is expanded access to China as a growing export destination and source of external financing, not just for raw materials. Beijing has been looking to countries like Brazil and Argentina instead of traditional suppliers like the US and Australia to reduce overdependence on soybeans and corn imported for animal feed (Dace, Singh, and Hooper 2022). China is Latin America's second-largest trade partner, after the US. Closer ties with China through the BRI was supposed to bring finance for energy, roads, ports, and 5G infrastructure, among other benefits, but Chinese funds have declined over the past few years, particularly since the start of the "tariff war" with the US. Still, in 2021, China's official direct investments in Latin America exceeded $7.7 billion, more than in Europe and North America combined (Devonshire-Ellis 2021). Discouragingly for China though, Argentina, Brazil, Colombia, and Mexico—the four largest economies in the region that account for nearly 70 percent of its GDP—have yet to sign on to the BRI.

Of all the Latin American participants in the BRI, Venezuela and Ecuador have borrowed heavily from China by pledging their petroleum export. Venezuela has been particularly close to China since the left-wing Hugo Chavez presidency. Ecuador joined the BRI in 2018 and became the first Latin American member of the AIIB in early 2019. As early as October 2009, construction of the Coca Codo Sinclair hydroelectric dam project was awarded to a consortium led by Sinohydro (89 percent share) and a local Ecuadorian company Coandes (8 percent share), with $1.68 billion of the $2.6 billion being financed by the China Exim Bank, to be paid back in 15 years (Power Technology 2020). Aside from Venezuela and Ecuador, the key BRI states in Latin America are Peru, Bolivia, and Chile, together with Mexico. Peru and Chile are involved in several projects with China under the rubric of the BRI.

In Mexico, China's State Power Investment Corp bought the country's largest independent renewable energy company, Zuma Energia. Bolivia's 160-kilometer El Espino–Boyuibe Highway Project, which links the country's eastern departments of Santa Cruz, Chuquisaca, and Tarija with each other and with neighboring Paraguay and Argentina, is being built by China Railway Group Limited and considered a flagship BRI project in South America (Xinhua News Agency 2021a).

In Peru, China's state-owned enterprise giant China Three Gorges Corp acquired Sempra Energy's businesses for close to $3.6 billion. With China as the biggest buyer of Peruvian copper, China Ocean Shipping Company

142 | China's Belt and Road Power Transition

(COSCO) Shipping Ports Limited in May 2019 purchased a 60 percent controlling stake in the Chancay Port Terminal (67 kilometers north of Peruvian capital Lima) from the huge South American mining company Volcan (which previously held a 100 percent stake) for a sum of $225 million, and then inked a $3 billion deal with the Peruvian government to build two terminals: one for bulk, general, and rolling cargo with 4 berths and one container terminal of 11 berths. This is the first COSCO operation in Latin America. Phase 1 of construction of the port was contracted by COSCO to China Harbour Engineering Company (Labrut 2019).

The Amazon Waterway Project, also known as Amazon Hidrovia, is a $95 million project to dredge four important rivers in the Peruvian rainforest region and install advanced navigation systems. A consortium of Sinohydro Corp. and Peruvian construction firm Casa SA were awarded the project engineering contract in 2017, but the project was met with intense opposition by environmental and indigenous communities of Ucayali and Loreto (Angula 2020). Still, Peru's new left-wing president Pedro Castillo, inaugurated in July 2021, has been quick to extend a friendly hand to China, agreeing to be vaccinated by China's Sinopharm vaccine in August 2021 (Reuters 2021).

In Chile, the State Grid Corp. of China agreed to buy 57 percent of the Chilean electricity distributor CGE for $3 billion in 2020, just a few months after its $2 billion acquisition of Chilquinta energy company (*Belt and Road News* 2021). This purchase has led to concerns among Chilean legislators, who then pushed for stricter rules on foreign investment in sensitive projects to protect national sovereignty (Koop 2021). In March 2021, under the BRI framework, Chile unveiled 15 Chinese-made trains costing $87 million and handled by the CRRC Sifang (China)–Temoinsa (Chile) (Global Data 2019). China is also providing an underwater fiber-optic network linking the Chilean city of Valparaiso with Shanghai. This trans-Pacific fiber-optic cable demonstrates the importance and implementation of China's novel Digital Silk Road.

Digital Silk Road

LAYING A DIGITAL SILK ROAD

The acquisition, development, and sale of high-end digital technology for civilian and military purposes of automated task performance, manufacturing, communications, and surveillance are a salient component of China's BRI power transition effort. Under the Thousand Talents Program and Made in China 2025 initiative, encouraged and subsidized by various levels of Chinese central, provincial, and municipal governments, close partnerships between Chinese universities and firms with Western institutions and tech companies to bring about technology transfers have greatly increased China's potential in the development of various technologies, including artificial intelligence (AI), robotics, and semiconductors. With logistics infrastructures, payment and settlement services, and communications technologies established at home, China's domestic e-commerce network has been growing exponentially. A Digital Belt and Road (DBAR) program was initiated in 2016 by Chinese scientists in cooperation with experts from 19 countries and 7 international organizations, with the support of more than $32 million (RMB 200 million) from the Chinese Academy of Sciences to improve environmental monitoring, promote data sharing, and support policymaking by using big data, cloud computing, and remote sensing capabilities (Guo 2018). The launch of this DBAR was not an isolated event. China would very soon be the biggest manufacturer and exporter of solar panels and electric cars in the world. In the PRC's 13th Five-Year Plan (2016–2020), Beijing already identified its most critical technology priorities as clean energy, aerospace and deep-sea research, information technology, and manufacturing (US Senate 2018), which are very much related to the functions of the DBAR. The DBAR was later renamed Digital Silk Road (DSR).

Implementing the Digital Silk Road

The DSR has been promoted by China an extension of the BRI, which it said included 5G, quantum computing, nanotechnology, AI, big data, and cloud computing and involved helping other countries to build digital infrastructures, construct transnational platforms for e-commerce, generate QR codes, export promotion and financial services, and develop internet security, to bridge the "digital divide" between developed states with advanced information technologies and developing, information-poor countries. Between 2019 and 2020 alone, the value of global e-commerce soared from $38 billion to $62 billion and is projected to reach $172 billion by 2025 (Greene and Triolo 2020). Under the DSR, China's authorities, in partnership with Chinese technological companies such as Tencent, Alibaba, Huawei, and Didi, provide interested BRI nations with advanced IT infrastructures, including broadband, e-commerce hubs, and smart cities (Bora 2020). These companies host leading mobile payment systems such as Alipay, Baidu Wallet, and WeChat Pay in many of the BRI countries, where they also promote the use of the renminbi, with Chinese world mobile device manufacturers Oppo and Vivo constituting severe competition for other non-Chinese manufacturers (Hemmings 2020, 19).

The more advanced countries of Southeast Asia like Singapore, Malaysia, Thailand, and Indonesia are all very interested in developing smart cities. As an example, in November 2017, Alibaba established eHub, a hub for e-commerce in collaboration with the Malaysia Digital Economy Corp., a Malaysian state-owned company, which includes a regional logistics center near Kuala Lumpur International Airport and an accompanying electronic platform that will enable users—primarily small- and medium-sized enterprises—to conduct cross-border trade without cumbersome bureaucratic hurdles. Since 2017, Alipay has partnered with Malaysian banks to offer cashless payments, expanding its mobile e-wallet service to Malaysia via Touch 'n Go (Mochinaga 2020, 51).

By 2022, more than 120 countries along BRI have been covered by the 33-satellite Beidou Navigation Satellite System, including Pakistan, Laos, Thailand, and Indonesia (Lee 2021). Meant to offer a Chinese alternative to the US-led Global Positioning System (GPS), Beidou is used for purposes such as driving, monitoring traffic at ports, guiding rescue operations, and predicting the weather. As self-driving vehicle networks develop and become increasingly reliant on satellite navigation, the PRC's influence within these countries will grow with the adoption of Beidou. Chinese vendors, such as Baidu, can mass produce self-driving vehicles loaded with light detection and ranging (LiDAR) remote distance-sensing lasers and high-definition maps manufactured by the Chinese AI firm SenseTime (Ren and Liu 2023), thus driving down their costs versus that of Tesla, Honda, or other non-Chinese brands.

China's 2019 BRI forum incorporated, for the first time, a daylong business forum, attracting more than 850 private sector business executives from 80 countries (Zhang 2019), many from IT commercial enterprises. With the COVID-19 pandemic, many more people and companies were willing to do business online rather than in person. This provided an even greater opportunity for China to promote its information and communications technology (ICT), or digital technology, to BRI states. Some developing economies that have joined the BRI wish to develop their ICT industry, not least for online shopping and e-payment in an era of social distancing,

China's Evolving Belt-and-Road Initiative | 145

and would require initial expertise and infrastructure, which means that there is a lot of scope for further cooperation on ICT-related projects with China. Alibaba and Huawei constructed data centers for Saudi Arabia and Dubai, respectively, and SenseTime opened its Gulf regional headquarters in Abu Dhabi, whose Khalifa Port is home to the Abu Dhabi Terminal constructed by China's COSCO. Furthermore, China's Silk Road Fund bought 49 percent of Saudi Arabia's ACWA Power, a developer and operator of solar power generation and water desalination projects (Parikh 2019). In August 2022, the Solomon Islands, China's by-then security partner in the South Pacific, secured a $66 million 20-year loan from China's Exim Bank to fund Huawei's construction of 161 telecommunications towers across the archipelagic nation (SCMP 2022b). ICT is therefore key to increasing China's global influence in technology, industries, standards setting, and legal frameworks, and the DSR aims to realize the growth of China's ICT sector and digital infrastructure through international development. As Chinese companies build new telecom networks in BRI countries, China is making it more likely that its firms will continue to be selected for interoperable technologies in the future.

Of the five companies in the world offering complete 5G telecommunication systems, two are from China: ZTE and Huawei. Chinese companies using digital solutions to circumvent COVID-19 are already well established throughout the BRI with state-owned or state-supported telecom giants like China Mobile, China Telecom, and China Unicom, or ostensibly private companies such as Alibaba and Tencent. State-owned China Development Bank was reported to have extended around $100 billion to Huawei to assist its 5G expansion (Nakashima 2019). Huawei's main advantage is the ability to underprice its European competitors anywhere from 18 to 30 percent due to generous government subsidies, below-market interest rate loans from China Development Bank and other Chinese state-owned banks, and perhaps most importantly, a large and guaranteed market in China's domestic telecommunications industry to achieve economies of scale and provide complete mobile networks at low prices worldwide (Patey 2022, 135–36). Chinese firms have gone from participating in 7 percent of transnational undersea cable projects in 2012 to participating in 20 percent in 2019 (Lee 2017).

China also helped establish facial recognition technology, a heavy saturation of surveillance cameras, and geolocation devices on phones to collect huge databases on populations in real time, for monitoring and controlling purposes, in countries like Armenia, Azerbaijan, Kazakhstan, Kyrgyzstan,

Malaysia, Pakistan, Singapore, Sri Lanka, United Arab Emirates, Uzbekistan, and Zambia (Hemmings 2020, 16). ZTE has provided security cameras to Venezuela, Bolivia, and Argentina, with Huawei offering similar services to Ecuador (Malena 2021). Kragujevac, a city in central Serbia, signed an agreement in February 2020 for its local university to cooperate with the Chinese company Dahua Technology, which focuses on video surveillance technology (Standish, Cvetkovic, and Zivanovic 2021). For the technology, these countries will owe China a debt of gratitude, if not more.

GEOPOLITICAL IMPLICATIONS OF THE DIGITAL SILK ROAD

The DSR has deep global geopolitical implications, as building the foundation of communications infrastructure in BRI countries will allow the PRC to access, analyze, and exploit in real time the large data sets of recipient countries. The PRC implemented a comprehensive cybersecurity National Intelligence Law in 2017, which regulates critical infrastructure protection, requires the storage of data on Chinese businesses and citizens to be kept on servers inside China, and mandates network operators to support public and national security organizations, including allowing full access to data upon request. Revised in 2023, this law further authorizes Chinese security agencies to collect and process information by Chinese companies on foreign entities and individuals that they deal with, and Chinese tech companies, even private ones, could share data they collected overseas with the Chinese government. This cybersecurity legislation could be a model for developing countries that want to control data and internet use (Mochinaga 2020, 53). Furthermore, the BRI Connectivity and Standards Action Plan 2018–2020 was released by the Standardization Administration of China in the same year to promote uniform standards among BRI recipient states for technologies including 5G, AI, and satellite navigation systems (Chan 2019). The attractiveness of China's development model of top-down political authoritarianism and state-led capitalism would be greatly enhanced if cutting-edge digital connectiveness between foreign countries and China's giant high-technology companies were to multiply and become denser. Both the cybersecurity legislation and action plan have been met with acute suspicion and general repugnance from the Trump administration and the West, particularly with regard to its impact on privacy, security, and China's ability to promote an authoritarian internet model.

The marriage of ICT to infrastructure seems to have been a winning formula for China, in allowing Beijing to promote its own standards, companies, and digital currency and granting it the benefits of new captive markets for Chinese tech firms, rich sources of data for analysis, and tools for leverage over foreign political and business elites (Hemmings 2020). China's state-owned Hikvision company is well-known for manufacturing and supplying video surveillance equipment such as facial recognition, human movement detection, and thermal imaging cameras. However, as it is theoretically possible for the Chinese government to gather intelligence and information from Chinese monitoring devices set up in foreign countries even without the knowledge of their governments, not all countries are enamored with or have signed on to China's DSR, and some have only done so partially, following the US ban on Huawei as a national security risk.

As Google has banned its Android operating system for search engines from Chinese smartphones and other electronics, which severely impacted its sales in foreign markets, the French search engine Qwant and Huawei began their cooperation under the DSR in March 2020, with Qwant as the default browser in Huawei's P40 smartphones sold in Europe. However, in June 2021, Qwant was not able to gain enough funding from EU members to stave off bankruptcy after three years of consecutive losses (EUR 12 million in 2018, 23 million in 2019, and 13 million in 2020), and the company has asked Huawei for an EUR 8-million bailout, which may grant Huawei notable shares in Qwant and thus administrative power over the company (Braun 2021).

Under US pressure, the UK and Sweden became the only European countries to date to fully ban Huawei, but Poland, Czech Republic, Romania, and Estonia have planned to restrict Huawei's 5G operations conducted under the BRI's DSR. Germany and Italy have been on the fence about how to deal with Huawei's DSR projects in their countries, but as of May 2021, both countries have implemented stricter 5G security laws. Germany introduced the IT Security Law 2.0, under which Huawei and ZTE would be heavily monitored, and the German government has retained the right to cancel or block the two 5G providers upon any suspicious activity, much to China's chagrin, as Beijing is aware of the US' heavy lobbying to reduce Huawei's influence in Europe (Laurens 2021). Despite this, notable German companies, such as the popular Stocard e-wallet platform, are cooperating with Huawei on upgrading their online shopping apps, which have also introduced extra membership benefits for Huawei users. Still, in November 2022 concerns over national security and the flow of sensitive technological know-how to Beijing prompted the German government to block prospective Chinese investments in two domestic semiconductor producers, one of which is Silex, a Swedish company that is a subsidiary of the Chinese group Sai Microelectronics (Rinke and Murray 2022). Additionally, the Italian government has given telecommunications company Vodafone the right to use Huawei technology for its 5G radio access network, albeit on strict conditions (Pollina and Fonte 2021). In May 2022, Canada banned Huawei and CTE technologies from both 5G and 4G communications facilities operating in the country. In August 2022, Estonia and Latvia followed Lithuania in leaving the CEEC "16 + 1" group, reducing its membership to 14, plus China.

To maintain Vietnam's ICT independence, Vietnamese carriers selected Ericsson, Nokia, and Samsung to build the country's 5G infrastructure, without using equipment from Huawei (Boudreau and Uyen 2019). Archipelagic Southeast Asian states and Taiwan directly connect via cables to Japan to ensure their own cybersecurity (Mochinaga 2020, 57), and the Japan-Guam-Australia fiber-optic submarine cable system project in the Pacific Ocean connects institutions in these countries (Submarine Telecoms Forum 2019).

In Africa, Ethiopia's privatized telecom service license worth $850 million was awarded to a US-financed consortium, which includes Vodafone, Vodacom, Safaricom, and Sumitomo Corp., with the Chinese-financed South African MTN Group as the losing bidder. The low-interest loans from the US-led group come with a condition: the money cannot be used to buy telecom equipment from Huawei and ZTE (Somaliland Sun 2021). In the US-versus-China global tech contest, this was a definite though nonfatal setback for China.

Even though Huawei has been able to produce its own relatively advanced seven-nanometer chips (integrated circuits or semiconductor wafers for computer microprocessors) for its Mate60 Pro/Pro+ smartphones, it still depends on outside manufacturers to supply the technology and equipment for making them. In 2019 alone, China imported $300 billion worth of foreign-made chips, while homemade ones only met about 15 percent of market demand. The US also has curbed the supply of certain equipment, accessories, and raw materials that affect China's Semiconductor Manufacturing International Corp., the country's best hope for breaking its dependence on foreign suppliers (Bao and Liu 2020; Whalen 2020). However, the imperative of reducing China's reliance on imported tech products from the US and the West will only motivate Beijing to expedite plans to obtain technological self-sufficiency and supremacy in critical areas (Yang 2021, 141).

Paradoxically, over the course of 2021, Beijing clipped the wings of its once-high-flying technology giants, including internet conglomerates

Tencent and Alibaba, food delivery app Meituan, and ride-hailing app Didi. China's State Administration for Market Regulation took aggressive steps to rein in what it considered to be anticompetitive behavior by levying a record \$2.8 billion fine on Alibaba and a \$530 million fine on Meituan, and the Cyberspace Administration of China disrupted Didi's planned initial public offering in New York for failing to comply with a cybersecurity review for sensitive data (Liu and Leslie 2022). The crackdown, which saw massive fines levied on China's largest internet groups and the wiping of more than \$1 trillion from their collective market capitalization, falls under the ideological umbrella of "common prosperity" (*gong fu*), pushed by Xi to close the wealth gap in part by encouraging high-income individuals and businesses to "give back more to society." Further moves are afoot, beginning in late 2022, to merge these technological firms with China's state-owned enterprises to expand the party's control over them. It did not help matters that the assembly plant of Taiwanese firm Foxconn, in Zhengzhou, China's central Henan province, the world's largest manufacturing base for Apple's iPhone, was heavily disrupted by chronic COVID-19 lockdowns and worker unrest in 2022.

China has always depended on foreign companies for advanced technologies. Despite improving technological competitiveness and massive research and development spending that trails only the US, Chinese tech firms purchase much of their source material from the US or its friends and allies Japan, South Korea, the Netherlands, Germany, and Taiwan. China cannot yet match the US in core technologies and components of wireless modules, as most Chinese vendors still must rely on Qualcomm and Intel for module chips (Hong and Murmann 2022), the Taiwan Semiconductor Manufacturing Company for seven-nanometer semiconductors, or the Dutch multinational corporation ASML for photolithography machines used to produce computer chips. China's top memory chip maker, Yangtze Memory Technologies, was blacklisted by the US, such that Yangtze's chairman, Chen Nanxiang, complained that his company has been unable to get spare parts for equipment that it bought legally. Starting on July 22, 2023, under Japanese law, a license is required to export 23 types of semiconductor tools and materials, such as photoresists, to China, despite protestations from Beijing. Japan has been one of the biggest alternative suppliers for China's chip-making tools, with such imports from Japan growing 2.66 times since 2019 to \$4.8 billion in 2022 (Pan 2023).

The Biden administration has since its early days vowed to bring computer chip manufacturing supply chains back to the US (or relocate them to US-friendly countries such as Mexico, India, or countries in the Southeast

Asian region) to better prepare the country to compete technologically with China (Lee 2022). Both the merger and supply chain reorganization will have chilling effects on China's technological innovation and economic growth from this sector (Liu and Leslie 2022). In June 2021, the US Senate passed the US Innovation and Competition Act, which restricts scholars with ties to foreign (read: Chinese) talent programs from participating in US government-sponsored research, and in August 2022, President Biden signed into law a bipartisan bill that included more than $52 billion set aside for US companies producing semiconductors, as well as more than $44 billion in tax credits, to encourage investment in building local chip manufacturing plants (Breuninger 2022). Furthermore, in October 2022, the Biden administration published a sweeping set of export controls known as the foreign direct product rule to cut China off from advanced semiconductor chips made in foreign countries with US equipment, technology, and citizens, to slow Beijing's technological and military progress (Nellis, Freifeld, and Alper 2022).

With restrictions on high technology from the US and the West, China's technological exports might in time become less effective, attractive, or durable, especially for its infrastructure constructions, operations, and maintenance in BRI countries. However, for countries with rudimentary telecommunications infrastructure, inadequate mobile network coverage, or a desire to maintain national cyber sovereignty, China's DSR will remain an avenue to approach.

Arctic: The Next Silk Road?

The Arctic has become one of the latest locations to captivate China's BRI economic interest and power projection. China's active engagement in Arctic affairs started in 2013, when China became one of the 13 observer states of the Arctic Council and COSCO Shipping's Yong Sheng became the first Chinese cargo ship to sail from China to Europe via the polar "Northwest Passage" north of Alaska and Canada (Feng, Woodhouse, and Milne 2018). In 2018, China declared itself a "near Arctic state" and published a policy paper wherein it outlined three objectives: To understand, to develop and to participate in the governance of the Arctic. In the policy paper, while the Chinese government accepts that China, as a state outside the Arctic region, has no sovereignty over the Arctic, it asserts the rights of "scientific research, navigation, overflight, fishing, laying of submarine cables and pipelines in the high seas and other relevant sea areas in the Arctic Ocean, and rights to resource exploration and exploitation in the Area," pursuant to international treaties and international law for all states (State Council 2018). Global warming and the subsequent melting of ice caps has opened up a more viable route to Alaska, making the Arctic a fertile fishing ground, with the northwest migration of fish stocks, and a hard-to-ignore opportunity to gain access to precious resources, as the Arctic ice caps are believed by geologists to contain significant amounts of natural gas reserves. Furthermore, China greatly benefits from shipping northward to Europe through newly warmer Arctic waters, rather than the longer journey southward through the Malacca Strait choke point, past rival India and the volatile Middle East, and through the congested Suez Canal to the busy Mediterranean Sea. To this end, in June 2018, Beijing announced plans to build its first 30,000-ton nuclear icebreaker, making China the second country (after Russia) to possess nuclear icebreakers (Avdaliani 2021). In 2020, China announced plans to launch a new satellite that would track shipping routes in addition to monitoring changes in the Arctic region's sea ice. The satellite was set to be launched in 2022 (Wion 2021).

In the Chinese policy paper, China's objectives are tied with the BRI via the "Polar Silk Road," stating that Beijing will use BRI as a platform to increase cooperation with Arctic countries like Finland, Iceland, and Sweden to explore the Arctic. After the Western sanctions and the withdrawal of ExxonMobil and Eni from the liquefied natural gas project on Yamal peninsula in the tundra of northwestern Siberia, in which the Russian natural gas giant Novatek and China National Petroleum Corp. are already involved, the Chinese Silk Road Fund stepped in to purchase a 9.9 percent stake in the Yamal project in 2016, thus increasing the China-owned shares to 29.9 percent, and to provide an $813 million loan, with the Exim Bank of China and China Development Bank lending Russia another $11 billion (Wishnick 2021). China and Russia will construct a pipeline to transport the gas from Yamal to China via Mongolia. Since 2018, China has also made efforts to buy land in Iceland, airports in Greenland (which is an autonomous region of Denmark), and an old navy base in Sweden. Although unsuccessful in these land acquisitions, Chinese investment in Europe has been surging, especially in Sweden (Statista 2019) and Greenland (Clingendael Report 2020). Members of the political elite in Greenland favor independence from Denmark but resist taking the plunge because the island's economy is so dependent on Danish support; as such, the prospect of Chinese investment could change that (Anonymous 2018). By 2018, five projects with Chinese

152 | China's Belt and Road Power Transition

participation in raw materials and infrastructure were under development in Greenland (Biedermann 2020). Chinese tourism to Iceland had been increasing sharply before COVID-19.

Already in 2015, five Chinese warships were sailing along the Alaskan coast, and the US Coast Guard then named China as a threat to American interests in the Arctic (Biedermann 2020). In March 2021, a delegation of high-ranking diplomatic officials from the US and China, led on the Chinese side by Wang Yi, foreign minister, and Yang Jiechi, CCP politburo member and state councilor, met in Anchorage, Alaska, with the US secretary of state Anthony Blinken in the first face-to-face meeting of the Biden administration with China. This meeting was tense and no joint statement was issued afterward, but as it took place in Alaska, analysts commented that the US has become more wary of China's intentions in Alaska and the Arctic, worrying that China will use its economic and political clout to make land grabs and cause tensions, just like in the South China Sea. Partly to ward off such suspicions, China, together with Japan and South Korea, which are also observers in the Arctic Council, jointly initiated the Asian Forum for Polar Sciences, which is the only regional scientific cooperative organization in Asia on polar research management and use of natural resources, Arctic shipping and shipbuilding, and environmental protection (Biedermann 2020). Experts have nonetheless advised the US to be more active in the Arctic to counter China's moves (Magnier 2021).

The shortest land route from China to the Arctic would be, of course, by way of Russia's East Siberia and Far East, but ironically, this seems to be the biggest constraint to China's Polar Silk Road. China accounted for 73 percent of all foreign investments in the Russian Far East in 2021, including a 1.08-kilometer automobile bridge to connect the cities of Heihe and Blagoveshchensk and a 2.26-kilometer rail bridge joining Tongjiang and Nizhneleninskoye, both across the Heilongjiang/Amur River separating China from Russia (Simes and Simes 2021). However, most Chinese investment projects in the region remain committed rather than realized, as poor transportation infrastructure and difficult climate conditions hinder Chinese companies, and Russia is reluctant to allow foreign investors to control strategic resources or infrastructure such as ports (Simes and Simes 2021).

Chapter 6

Blowback to the Belt-and-Road Initiative Power Transition

Can and Will the West Strike Back?

China wants to change the rules of the game undergirding the present world order and the world order itself, and the US and the West are pushing back. According to US president Joe Biden, China wants to have the largest economy and military capacity in the world and is out to rewrite the rules of international relations, because, as Xi has told him, China was not there when those rules were written; however, he believes that Xi does not want war, conflict, or territorial expansion (CNN 2023).

Biden's predecessor as US president, Donald Trump, for all the controversies he was wont to court, saw through the trade, investment, and technological foundations of China's BRI power transition intentions. Trump's tariffs on Chinese goods (and retaliatory measures by Beijing that locked both sides into a trade war), together with his open support for Hong Kong's protestors in 2019, all reflected a wider bipartisan shift in American foreign policy thinking. To America's foreign-policy-making elite since 2017, China made big concessions to get into the WTO, but not only did it then not live up to its promises to open its vast government procurements to foreign companies, but it continued to shower subsidies on its state-owned technology sectors, it held foreign companies wishing to do business in China hostage to technology-sharing requirements, and it dragged its feet on granting US companies access to its market, equivalent to its companies' access to the US (Hout 2021). The previous American assumption, that China's increasing prosperity from its incorporation in

154 | China's Belt and Road Power Transition

the global trading system would eventually move it toward Western-style liberalism and democracy, was by 2017 basically gone. In its stead is a new consensus that China's model of governance, labeled as an autocracy by President Biden, was here to stay and strengthened by China's involvement in world markets, and would eventually lead it to challenge the existing world order led by the US (Chowdhury 2021, 9). By increasing China's global influence and turning the international order in China's favor, the BRI as an agent of global economic progress and political influence would, ideally for Beijing, also make US military alliances and alignments superfluous. With the BRI, in the words of political scientist John Mearsheimer, China would be, like America, secure in its own region and "free to roam" into other hemispheres (International Relations & Politics 2022).

Trump's import tariffs and high-technology embargo on China beginning in 2018 were the first moves to roll back Chinese interest and influence on the world stage spearheaded by and enmeshed in the BRI, which by then was perceived by American power elites to be burgeoning out of their control. One Chinese mid-level diplomat was so sure of the attractiveness and success of the BRI that he said, just before the 2019 BRI summit, that governments missing the summit would not be missed, as there was a long queue of countries that wanted to attend (Wong 2023, 232). When Australia in 2020 pushed for an international inquiry into the origins of COVID-19 in China, Beijing imposed severe trade restrictions on the import of Australian barley, iron ore, wine, and coal. This could be read as a demonstration to the world that since Australia was not a member of the BRI community of countries, China could easily shut it out of the large and lucrative Chinese market. However, by all indications Australia has found replacement destinations for most of the exports that it had hitherto sent to China. With the Chinese authorities perceived as concealing information regarding the coronavirus outbreak, confining Uyghurs in China's Xinjiang Autonomous Region to detention facilities indefinitely, bulldozing a widely scoped National Security Law on Hong Kong, and attacking Indian soldiers along a stretch of the disputed China-India border, China's relations with the West went into free fall. By February 2022, more out of economic constraints than reluctance, China had purchased only 57 percent of exports from the US that it was committed to under their 2020 bilateral agreement (India Briefing 2022). All this could have adverse financial impacts on the BRI if it makes countries less enthusiastic about engaging China and leads to alternative global infrastructure development plans, although by all accounts

China maintains substantive control over the projects in this "multilateral" Belt-and-Road engagement.

Challenges to the BRI: Foreign Initiatives

Since debt-infrastructure financing, awarding contracts without competitive bidding, and sole sourcing of materials have led to criticism of China for trapping borrower countries into debt and dependency, any competitive Western alternative to China's BRI will most likely have to be funded through a combination of interest-free loans and grants. However, the funds available for such an initiative are unlikely to rival those already committed by the BRI, at the very least for quite a few years, given the economic difficulties in the West. Furthermore, although Chinese projects can be criticized for top-down governmental imposition on local communities, with little or no record of inputs from nongovernmental consultative processes, many third world countries may not be keen to engage with the Western versions of the BRI if it means accepting rigid conditions, such as adhering to extensive societal consultation, human rights, and democracy.

Trump, as US president, attempted to set up an International Development Finance Corporation in 2017 with a $60 billion portfolio to provide and facilitate private financing for development projects in lower- and middle-income countries (Lo 2020). The Asia-Africa Growth Corridor was set up by India and Japan in 2018 to serve as a counterweight and more transparent balance to China's BRI (Taniguchi 2020). However, both apparent alternatives to China's BRI did not proceed as planned due to financial limitations in the organizing countries. Furthermore, America's trade deficit with China again rose after registering a decrease in 2019 as a result of US trade tariffs.

In March 2021, the French government approved a bill to increase France's foreign aid to 0.55 percent of GDP by 2022, focusing especially on aid to African countries, specifically to counter China's newfound influence in the continent due to BRI investments. A major focus of the G7 agenda for its June 2021 meeting was how to more effectively counter China's influence with its BRI and vaccine diplomacy. The G7 leaders proposed a plan to support lower- and middle-income countries in building better infrastructure to support Biden's Build Back Better World proposal, but the amount and timeframe for allocation was not announced. While some

156 | China's Belt and Road Power Transition

critics argue that the West is too late—China has already reached all the key regions of the world—others argue that China's failure in some places and growing complaints due to debt sustainability will offer a "second chance" for the West to take China's place as a key investor. If the G7's pledge to donate 1 billion shots worldwide materializes, it will outstrip the 742 million doses China sold and the 22 million doses it donated as of June 2021 (Zaini 2021). To underpin a post-COVID economic recovery through infrastructure investments, the EU launched the Global Gateway Initiative in December 2021 to mobilize EUR 300 billion between 2021 and 2027 (European Commission 2021). In June 2022, the G7 formally launched the Partnership for Global Infrastructure and Investment as an alternative to the BRI, to raise about $600 billion for global infrastructure projects in developing countries in the following five years (Tan 2022), from public and yet unspecified private sources. The US has promised $200 billion for the Partnership program, with highlighted initiatives including a solar-powered project in Angola, vaccine manufacturing facility in Senegal, and 1,609-kilometer submarine telecommunications cable connecting Singapore to France via Egypt and the Horn of Africa (BBC 2022). In August 2022, the Japanese pledged $30 billion to Africa in private and public financial contributions as development aid over a period of five years (Siow 2022). However, funds from the EU, US, or G7 are unlikely to replace funding from China, given its deep pockets, entrenched investments, and the BRI's political priority for PRC leadership. China's outward FDI from 2014 to 2020 was $1.6 trillion, most of it invested in BRI projects (Chen 2022). In March 2022, in the aftermath of Russia's invasion of Ukraine, the China-based AIIB suspended its projects in Russia and Belarus, as Western sanctions against the two nations could disrupt debt payments. Nonetheless, the bank has so far approved $800 million worth of investments and loans to Russia, and $222 billion (EUR 200 billion) worth of proposed projects in Belarus (Kawate 2022).

According to Biden's White House, "The president's vision for B3W [Build Back Better World] is to work with partners that share our democratic values to finance and develop infrastructure in a manner that is transparent, sustainable, adheres to high standards, and catalyzes the private sector where possible" (Widakuswara 2021). To this end, officials led by Daleep Singh, US deputy national security advisor, were in Colombia, Ecuador, and Panama, and later in Ghana and Senegal, to scout for infrastructure projects. "If the United States and its partners can mobilize investments from pension funds, life insurance companies and other institutional investors, B3W could be much larger than China's BRI," said Jonathan E. Hillman, Senior Fellow with the Center for Strategic and International Studies Economics Program (Widakuswara 2021). However, Biden's putatively expensive international endeavor could run into domestic difficulties, as it has encountered resistance from members of his own Democratic party. During his trip to Asia in May 2022, Biden pledged $40 billion for infrastructure construction to be divided among the 10 ASEAN nations; this contrasted miserably with China, which provided about $500 billion in donations and loans to the Philippines alone between 2016 and 2021 and spent around $6 billion on constructing the China–Laos high-speed railway (Janssen 2022). To blunt the advancement of China's Digital Silk Road, the US Senate passed the US Innovation and Competition Act in June 2021, which seeks to restrict scholars with ties to foreign talent programs from participating in US government-sponsored research, as well as increasing funding to boost American scientific and technological competitiveness vis-à-vis China. In August 2022, Biden also signed into law a bipartisan bill that includes more than $52 billion for US companies producing semiconductors, as well as more than $44 billion in tax credits to encourage investment in building chip manufacturing plants (Breuninger 2022).

Challenges to the BRI: Difficulties Arising from the Initiative Itself

Challenges from the competing initiatives aside, since 2020 China has been encountering difficulties even in the traditional aspects of the BRI, which was sold to the world, and especially developing countries, as a global development enterprise of win-win cooperative interdependence. Although membership in the AIIB, the BRI's multilateral financing arm where China is the largest shareholder and appoints its president, has increased to 105 countries, lending to the private sector has been increasing at the expense of government infrastructure projects (CRS 2022). Bilaterally, according to the PRC's Ministry of Foreign Affairs, by July 2022 the Chinese government has spent $1 trillion on the BRI, signed BRI "cooperation documents" with 149 countries and 32 international organizations, took on 3,000 infrastructure projects, established scientific and technological cooperation relations with 84 countries, backed 1,118 joint research projects, and launched 53 laboratories covering agriculture, energy, and health (Jennings 2022). However, some African countries like Zambia and Uganda have defaulted on Chinese investment projects. China has emerged as Zambia's biggest creditor over the last decade by offering an estimated $6 billion in loans as the African country embarked on ambitious infrastructure projects, but since Zambia had to default due to its economic slowdown during the pandemic, in July 2022 its finance ministry announced the cancellation of $2 billion in yet to be disbursed Chinese loans (Coterill and Wheatley 2022). Facing countries that are unable or unwilling to repay their debts, China agreed to forgive 23 interest-free loans for 17 African countries that had matured by the end of 2021, announced by China's foreign minister Wang Yi in August 2022 (Backhouse 2022).

As in Kenya, there have been public allegations in Nepal that parts of BRI agreements have not been made public (Kathju 2024). The money pit that Sri Lanka has become in 2022 and the fall of its pro-China Rajapaksa dynasty also lessened China's influence in Sri Lanka's political landscape as it turned to India and the IMF for urgently needed financial assistance. India promptly provided about $5 billion for food, fuel, and medical and cash aid, of which $3.5 billion was for 2022 alone, and in return successfully demanded that Sri Lanka prevent a Chinese research vessel, Yuan Wang 5, from docking at the China-built Hambantota port for a few days, on grounds that it could trace intelligence signals and track missiles (Lo 2022). It seems that debt could trap not just the debtor nations of the BRI but also the creditor country as well. The BRI could also be a death trap for some, as when a terrorist attack in March 2024 in the form of an explosive-laden car killed five Chinese engineers and their local driver working on the large-scale Chinese-funded CPEC Dasu Dam project on the Indus River in Pakistan (Gul 2024).

China's attempt to create a bloc of "China-Pacific Island" countries, during Wang Yi's eight-nation Pacific tour in May 2022, was a sign of Beijing's ambition to redraw the region's geopolitical map to its own advantage. However, although a dozen bilateral agreements, focusing on economy, health, disaster response, and technology, were signed with Pacific Island countries during Wang's trip as part of China's existing BRI, Pacific states were wary enough of US and Australian concerns to turn down a sweeping regional economic and security pact with China. Under separate agreements reached in 2022 and 2023, US Coast Guard officials gained the right to board foreign vessels in the exclusive economic zones of the Federated States of Micronesia and Papua New Guinea, respectively, without the presence of a local national personnel. By August 2023, although no official apology from Australia was forthcoming regarding its demand to investigate the origin of

COVID-19, which had so angered the Chinese leadership, China had (in response to its own demand) dropped anti-dumping import tariffs against Australia on barley, timber, and coal. Still, Nauru's switching of diplomatic relations from Taiwan to China in January 2024 and signing on to the BRI demonstrate the vulnerability of developing nations to China's offers of hefty financial inducements (AP 2024).

The SREB railway system from China to Europe could also face disruption should relations between China and Lithuania, or Belarus and Poland, deteriorate. The risk of Western sanctions as a result of Russia's attack on Ukraine has prompted hundreds of businesses to suspend ties with Russia, with firms like Cargotor, Maersk, and Mediterranean Shipping Company halting rail freight services through Russia as "a sign of solidarity with Ukraine" (Wong 2022). To avoid sanctions from the West, Sinopec has suspended talks with Russia for a gas chemical plant worth up to $500 million, and at least five Chinese companies stopped work on Russia's Arctic LNG 2 project in northern Siberia at the end of May 2022 (Wong 2022). Perhaps to avoid over-antagonizing the West, which was already irked by China's refusal to condemn Russia for its attack on Ukraine, China has not pushed for the construction for the ports, railroads, or tunnels envisaged in its Polar Silk Road for Russia and other circumpolar states. However, China's crude oil import from Russia increased by 55 percent from a year earlier to displace Saudi Arabia as China's top supplier in May 2022, according to the PRC's General Administration of Custom (*Straits Times* 2022).

In Southeast Asia, China's vaccine diplomacy has yet to generate strategic trust. Vietnam has steadfastly refused to source Chinese vaccines due to its South China Sea conflict with China, and Japan has remained the largest FDI in Southeast Asia as of 2021 (Rusli and Masri 2021, 194). Furthermore, Beijing's assertion of hard naval power in the South China Sea led to the 2021 AUKUS security pact between Australia, the UK, and the US to help Australia secure a fleet of nuclear-powered submarines from the US; naval vessels from Germany, the Netherlands, and Britain sailing through the South China Sea; and Japanese and US warships conducting their first ever anti-submarine warfare exercise in the contested waters. In August 2022, for the first time, warships from Germany joined a multinational naval exercise in the Asia-Pacific, off the coast of Australia. Throughout 2023, naval vessels of the Philippines, under President Marcos Jr., experienced a series of skirmishes with Chinese coast guard ships in the South China Sea near Palawan. As such, there are opportunities for the US, Japan, and countries in the West to exploit weaknesses where China believes

160 | China's Belt and Road Power Transition

that it already has influence. However, it would be next to impossible to dislodge China's sway over its neighbors, especially Central and Southeast Asia, where its economic and other interests are firmly entrenched. On June 8, 2022, Cambodia broke ground on Ream naval base, located on the Gulf of Thailand, which was bankrolled by China for its use as a port of call for its naval vessels such as frigates and destroyers and to monitor radar and signal intelligence, allowing China to project influence, if not force, into the heart of Southeast Asia (Yong 2022). Ream has been leased to China for 30 years, and China is Cambodia's only arms supplier (Abuza and Watson 2022). Although Thailand is a US ally, China has replaced the US as the top arms supplier to the country, and fighter jets, bombers, and early warning aircrafts from both the Chinese and Thai air forces held an 11-day Falcon Strike exercise in August 2022 at an air force base in Udon Thani, in northern Thailand (Liu 2022).

Confucius Institutes, although not strictly part of the BRI, are intended to bolster China's soft power by promoting knowledge of Chinese language and serving as tools of cultural diplomacy abroad. However, as they are typically attached to foreign universities and run classes under the Office of Chinese Language Council International or "Hanban," which has close ties to party and ministerial personnel and is funded by China's Ministry of Education, Confucius Institutes have fallen under suspicion and been criticized for presenting versions of Chinese history approved by the CCP and having implicit rules against discussing issues such as Tibet's Dalai Lama, Taiwan's independence, the Tiananmen Massacre, and Falun Gong. As a result, since 2013, several universities in countries such as Canada, the US, France, Germany, and Sweden have removed Confucius Institutes from their campuses.

Whether as a sign of China's diminished ambitions for the BRI or diminished interest in the initiative from other parties amid growing China-US tensions, recent international popular opinion polls have revealed record low levels of trust in the Chinese leadership and in Xi Jinping himself (Tiezzi 2022). The third Belt-and-Road forum, held on June 23, 2021, was, compared to the first two, a slimmed down affair: virtual, instead of in-person, and at the ministerial rather than head of state or government level, with only Columbia represented by its president. The meeting, involving 29 countries and parties, was hosted by Wang Yi, Chinese foreign minister, instead of President Xi as in the past.

The two main themes emphasized at the meeting were the equitable and affordable distribution of COVID-19 vaccines, especially in developing countries, and ensuring climate-friendly, low-carbon sustainable development in the post-pandemic era, including a pledge to strengthen environmental risk assessments for related projects based on "internationally recognized standards and best practices" (Tiezzi 2021). These are major aspects of Chinese BRI relations today. However, since the middle of 2021, highly transmissible coronavirus variants such as Delta and Omicron, and mutations of these strains, have been challenging the effectiveness of China's more draconian lockdown and testing measures of China's "zero-Covid" strategy, casting doubts on the efficiency of its vaccines and disrupting global supply chains centered on production in the major cities such as Shanghai or Zhengzhou, where citywide lockdowns in 2022 practically paralyzed the Volkswagen car plant and Apple Foxconn semiconductor production facilities, respectively. This erodes China's leadership in the world's fight against COVID-19 and damages confidence in its reliability to manufacture and supply goods to foreign countries. As for green projects, China's state-run Silk Road Fund has committed to financing them since 2015, so the forum was but an occasion to reiterate that commitment. Even so, China's priorities would remain attractive to many BRI countries, as vaccine supplies and pollution control remain as some of their major concerns.

As a hedge against deteriorating relations with West, China has been increasing its investments, particularly in the hydrocarbon, transportation, and AI sectors, of major Middle Eastern countries such as Saudi Arabia, United Arab Emirates, Oman, Iraq, and Iran, for which China is the top trader. According to Chinese official figures released in 2024, debts owed to the Exim Bank of China alone by BRI countries has reached more than $300 billion, out of China's total investment of about $600 billion in construction contracts and $420 billion in nonfinancial investments over the past 10 years (GIS 2024). Still, as long as China continues to be a huge market for foreign products and a major innovator of technological items such as solar panels, electric vehicles, smartphones, and even passenger aircrafts, the appeal of the BRI, though diminished, would endure.

Repackaging the BRI: The Global Development Initiative and Global Security Initiative

In light of the toll of the COVID-19 pandemic on debt-laden borrowers, shrinking credit from China, and the negative publicity the BRI has accumulated over the years, Xi launched a "new" global development initiative (GDI). Inaugurated against a backdrop of heightened great power competition, this GDI seeks once again to advance Chinese interests by building on existing Chinese strengths and capabilities as an international development provider, particularly to the Global South, this time with more funding for environmental protection, poverty reduction, and food security. Projects officially designated under the GDI are to be funded by the China International Development Cooperation Agency, established in 2018 as a vice-ministerial-level agency under the State Council, with $1 billion earmarked for South-South development (Chen 2023). By seeming to move away from a bilateral aid model to multilateral development institutions and funds, Xi wants his country to be the leading voice for multipolar global governance, in which smaller countries would gain a stronger voice (Lemoine and Gaffa 2022) that in turn would reinforce Chinese influence. The BRI summit scheduled for October 2023 was held, but the tired workhorse did not feature any spectacular new initiatives, and major Western state leaders did not attend. Whether promoting the BRI or GDI, China still supports a state-centric approach to development and considers economic development itself as a human right that precedes all other rights.

In tandem with the GDI, Beijing seeks to normalize a role for itself as a source of global security. China's foreign ministry issued a "concept paper" on a global security initiative (GSI) on February 21, 2023 (MFA 2023), after President Xi debuted both the GDI and GSI concepts in April 2022 without elaborating. The GSI emphasized familiar Chinese foreign policy concepts like "non-interference in internal affairs," which aims to delegitimize criticisms of domestic human rights, and "sovereign equality" under international law, which implies opposition to Western hegemony, the outsized influence of rich countries, and the US' role in Asia. The concept paper called for supporting "a bigger UN role in security affairs," which befits China's influence in the world body as a permanent Security Council member and promotes "more exchanges and cooperation among military and police academies," and pledged 5,000 training opportunities for developing countries over the next five years "to train professionals for addressing global security issues."

The GDI and GSI concepts are still being worked out. Whether as a restatement of or replacement for the BRI, they may matter more in form than in result, for even absent clear policy outcomes, engaging countries in vague diplomatic initiatives can cultivate a network of friendly international relationships. The ultimate objective is to build a global economic and security architecture to serve initially as an alternative to, and later as a rival of, the US-led system of treaties, economic institutions, and security alliances.

Conclusion

By the start of third decade of the 21st century, the rise of China had become a major structural challenge to the US-led international order. China has a resilient cultural, sociopolitical, and strategic tradition that is perhaps the only qualified match by any country alone to Western civilization, offers a huge and attractive market to foreign traders and investors, and is controlled by an authoritarian party that refuses to accept widely, if not universally, shared democratic values and human rights standards (Lai 2016). China, the rising power, had to put up with US, the system leader, on many issues when the former was much weaker and, for its economic development, needed the latter to look the other way. However, China has accumulated power and is pushing back, with Xi telling his country that restoring China's rightful place in the world is within their reach (Lai 2016), as "the East is rising while the West is declining" (Friedberg 2022, 155), and China's rightful place is to be the world's "Central Nation." Xi, as expected, sought and secured a third term as CCP secretary general at the party's 20th national congress in October 2022. On concluding a three-day visit to Russia in March 2023, Xi pointedly told Putin that the world was undergoing changes, "the likes of which we have not seen for 100 years, and we are the ones driving these changes together" (Jett 2023), with China in the lead and Russia, badly weakened by its war with Ukraine, following.

At the Asia-Pacific Economic Cooperation leaders' meeting in Bangkok, Thailand, in November 2022, French president Emmanuel Macron publicly called for an end to the "intensifying confrontation" and struggle for supremacy" between the US and China, which is forcing other countries to take sides, thus alluding to the fact that a power transition is underway (Sim 2022). Power transition theory therefore offers valuable insight into the current power competition: China is a great power, dissatisfied with the

164 | China's Belt and Road Power Transition

American-led status quo, with the ambition and demonstrated ability to alter regional and global power balances in its favor. A country's economic size is a basic measurement of its power, and calculated in terms of US dollars, China's economy was only 25 percent of the size of America's in 2007, but by 2021, it was at least 73.5 percent of the US economy (*Statistics Times* 2021). By 2022, in terms of purchasing power parity, China's economy had surpassed that of the US in size, although China still lags in dollar terms (World Bank 2022; CIA 2022). In terms of GDP growth rate, a crucial determinant of power differential between states, China had been ahead of the US for about three decades, until 2022. Although the RMB still accounts for only about 3 percent of global currency payments in the early 2020s, compared to around 50 percent for the US dollar as a fully convertible currency, settlements in RMB between China and BRI countries have been increasing.

In a survey conducted in June 2022 of 19 countries in North America, Europe, and the Western Pacific, the Pew Research Center found that, although the US is generally seen more positively than China and views of Biden remain much more positive than views of Xi, for 17 of the countries surveyed, significantly, 66 percent say China's influence on the world stage is getting stronger, while just 32 percent say the same about America (Pew Research Center 2022). According to a Pew Research Center report released in August 2023, although China's international behavior has not won it additional favors in North America, Europe, and Asia, in Africa and Latin America countries such as South Africa, Kenya, Nigeria, Argentina, and Mexico are very enthusiastic about Chinese investments (Ghosh 2023). In other words, irrespective of China's domestic politics or leadership, global (and particularly third world) perception of China's rise continues, and the BRI contributes to this in no small measure.

At least until Beijing's BRI push, US policy toward China was aimed at its beneficial integration into the world's markets. However, there has been a sea change since then. Domestically, China abolished its presidential term limits for Xi Jinping by 2018, and Xi has arrested political rivals on corruption and other charges. Detention of Uyghur minorities in western China and social control through technology and social credit systems are affronts to Western notions of freedom and democracy. US naval movement in waters claimed by China has become routine and characteristic of their geopolitical competition. Given the interconnected web of interests created by transnationalism and globalization, a conflict between the world's dominant and challenging powers, if it comes to that, would shake the beneficiaries and institutions of this interdependence to the core.

Visits to Beijing by US secretary of state Anthony Blinken, treasury secretary Janet Yellen, and climate envoy John Kerry in July 2023 have been widely criticized by Republicans in the US House of Representatives, who question whether these talks or continued US engagement with China have had any deliverables or serve US interests (Yong 2023). Such skepticism could be chalked up to political posturing in the lead-up to the November 2024 elections, not just for the presidency but also for the House and a portion of the Senate. It could also signify the fraying of an otherwise solid bipartisanship over China issues, demonstrated in the aftermath of at least one Chinese military balloon flight over US airspace in February 2023. In any case, simple resumption of high-level dialogues will not fundamentally change China's belief that the US is determined to block China's rise, nor will it change America's perception that China is determined to usurp the current world order (Yong 2023), and internal politics may reach a point where neither superpower sees engagement with the other as useful.

Notwithstanding these dialogues, since August 1, 2023, in response to Western restrictions on advanced equipment for the Chinese technology industry in the latest salvo of the US-China "chip war," China effectively banned, through export licenses, overseas sale of gallium and germanium, two necessary ingredients for the manufacture of semiconductors, on national security grounds. On August 9, 2023, President Biden signed an executive order, on grounds of protecting the nation's strategic interest, to restrict investment in China on technology that enables production or improvement of advanced integrated circuits (e.g., Nvidia's advanced A100 and H100 chips); production of quantum computers, sensors, and systems; and development of software for AI or robotic systems (Cheng 2023). President Biden and his commerce secretary Gina Raimondo subsequently warned of Chinese electric cars posing risks to US national security, as these vehicles could collect sensitive data about US citizens, infrastructure, driving routes, and biometric information for China's government (Sevastopulo and Leahy 2024). In May 2024, the US announced a 100 percent tariff on electric vehicles imported from China and a 25 percent import tariff on its lithium-ion batteries, which had the effect of galvanizing Turkey to add 40 percent tariffs on all vehicles and the EU to impose up to 38 percent tariffs on electric vehicles imported from China from July 2024 onward, on grounds of unfair subsidies (Bartlett-Imadegawa and de Beaurepaire 2024).

166 | China's Belt and Road Power Transition

More likely, it could be the result of massive price-cutting measures to boost sales in foreign markets due to the deterioration in the employment situation and purchasing power of China's population since the spread of COVID-19's highly contagious Omicron variant at the beginning of 2022 that led to frequent lockdowns and quarantines in many parts of China. In any case, the cutthroat competition between China and the US to develop militarily and economically strategic advanced digital technologies and set global industrial standards can be expected to continue for years to come, irrespective of which party captures the US presidency in 2024.

This book begins with a quote from Singapore's former leader Lee Kuan Yew, who was widely revered for, among other things, his acute observations on Chinese affairs. He was also quoted as saying that "the Chinese have also figured out that if they stay with 'peaceful rise' and just contest for first position economically and technologically, they cannot lose," but "to (directly) challenge a stronger and technologically superior power like the United States will abort their peaceful rise" (Pillsbury 2016, 229–30). In hindsight, these sounded like wise words. However, it has seemed, in the words of an Indian newscaster, that "Xi Jinping does not want China to play bigger role on the global stage; he wants to change the stage itself . . . ensuring that China bows to no one in world affairs" (Sharma 2021b). The BRI and its associated AIIB and Silk Road Fund are constructed around the personality of Xi Jinping and his control of the CCP and its domestic political and foreign policy. With the exhaustion of Russia as a result of its drawn out and fruitless war with Ukraine, China has practically emerged as the all-round number two world power. However, declining property prices due to excess supply since 2021 have been throttling revenues to provincial and municipal government coffers and hence the funds for foreign investments of state-owned enterprises under them. Furthermore, by mid-2023, China's local government debts registered $11,200 billion (RMB 80,000 billion), and central government debt $2,800 billion (RMB 20,000 billion) (Wang, Shiban, and Cheng 2023). To make matters worse, foreign investment in China decreased for six consecutive quarters since mid-2022. Besides, domestic consumption has greatly weakened, and exports have decreased, with shipping containers piling up in Chinese ports due to sluggish international trade after three years of the COVID-19 pandemic. On the other hand, since at least 2021 the Xi regime has been soliciting donations and levying surtaxes on the rich and their companies in China, which, if they do not flee the country or collapse, could provide more finances for government agencies to engage in more and larger BRI projects. In the longer term,

China's falling birth rate and rapidly aging population is having a negative impact on its economic growth by lowering its labor supply while raising the cost of elder care and retirement benefits.

The PRC, in weaving together the BRI to create its own bloc of states that are aligned with or beholden to it, under the direction of a leader who wants to be remembered for making his country the worthy rival of the US or even take over world leadership, might have overplayed its hand and invited an Anglo-American or Western backlash. Power transition theory discusses the transition of hegemony from Spain to the Netherlands to Britain and then to the US, and whether the wrestling of supremacy led to war, but those are the successful examples. There are also cases of unsuccessful challenges against the reigning hegemon, such as Napoleonic France, Nazi Germany, and the Soviet Union, attempts that resulted in great costs to themselves and others. The US operates more than 280 military bases or facilities in the territories of its friends and allies around the globe, possesses the most technologically advanced weapons in the world, and continues to dominate the high seas on which China is dependent both for importing energy and exporting products. Notwithstanding earnest efforts to achieve self-reliance, China is finding it extremely hard to escape the choking effect of Western technology embargoes due to its continued dependence on the West for high-end semiconductors and other cutting-edge technologies. If there is any issue that unites the Democrats and Republicans in the US, it is to prevent China from catching up with America technologically, and hence strategically. Some narrowing of the power gap between China and the US does not imply that it is now Beijing's time to present itself as an alternative to US world dominance. Believing otherwise would not bode well for China or the future of the BRI, whose shine has tarnished compared to its early years, but it is most unlikely that China, at least under Xi, will be dissuaded from promoting its Sinosphere-building initiative as the greatest roadshow on earth.

Notes

Introduction

1. The last case is often famously referred to as the "Thucydides trap," whereby in describing the Peloponnesian War in Greece in the fifth century BC, the contemporaneous Athenian historian Thucydides reasoned, in his book *History of The Peloponnesian War*, that "the real cause for this war was the growth of the Athenian power and the fear generated in the minds of the Spartans that made the war inevitable." It should be noted that the war involved not just Athens and Sparta but the respective alliances led by them.

2. All currency throughout the book is in USD unless otherwise noted.

Chapter 1

1. ASEAN is an intergovernmental organization of ten Southeast Asian countries: Brunei, Cambodia, Indonesia, Laos, Malaysia, Myanmar, the Philippines, Singapore, Thailand, and Vietnam. Timor Leste is only an observer member of ASEAN, but given its tiny land area, population, and economy vis-à-vis the other Southeast Asian countries combined, the terms "Southeast Asia" and ASEAN will be used interchangeably in this book.

2. East Asia Summit is an intergovernmental organization consisting of the ten ASEAN countries plus China, Japan, South Korea, India, Australia, New Zealand, the US, and Russia.

3. The thesis that China will continue to pursue a strategy of "peaceful rise" has been supported by Buzan but opposed by Mearsheimer. See Barry Buzan, "China in International Society: Is 'Peaceful Rise' Possible?," *Chinese Journal of International Politics* 3 (2010): 5–36; John J. Mearsheimer, "The Gathering Storm: China's Challenge to US Power in Asia," *Chinese Journal of International Politics* 3 (2010): 381–96.

Chapter 3

1. Interview with Dr. Kuik Cheng-chwee, associate professor at the School of History, Politics and Strategy of the National University of Malaysia, in Kuala Lumpur, Malaysia, on August 4, 2016.

2. Parthasarathy was the former Indian high commissioner to Pakistan.

3. Data is from a study by the Advisory Council of the Belt and Road Forum, created in 2018 as a nonprofit international policy advisory body to provide intellectual support to the BRI, whose membership includes former government ministers, academics, and experts from global organizations including the World Bank.

Chapter 4

1. COVID-19 (a disease caused by the SARS-CoV-2 virus or novel coronavirus) was declared a global pandemic by the World Health Organization on March 11, 2020.

References

ABC News. 2019. "Papua New Guinea Asks China for Help with $11.8b National Debt." Aug. 7, 2019. https://www.abc.net.au/news/2019-08-07/png-to-ask-china-for-help-refinancing-national-debt/11391186.

Abdollohian, Mark, Carole Alsharabati, Brian Efird, Jacek Kugler, Douglas Lemke, Allan C. Stam III, Ronald L. Tammen, and A. F. K Organski. 2000. *Power Transitions: Strategies for the 21st Century.* Thousand Oaks, CA: Sage.

Abera, Birhanu. 2020. "Ethiopian Officially Receives ETRSS-1 from China." Walta Media and Communication Corporate S.C., Dec. 3, 2020. https://waltainfo.com/ethiopian-officially-receives-etrss-1-from-china/.

Abuza, Zachary, and Cynthia Watson. 2022. "Learned Helplessness China's Military Instrument and Southeast Asian Security." National Bureau of Asian Research, Aug. 27, 2022. https://www.nbr.org/publication/learned-helplessness-chinas-military-instrument-and-southeast-asian-security/.

Ahamed, Rumman Udin. 2016. "Great Opportunity for Bangladesh." *Financial Express* (Dhaka), Oct. 9, 2016. https://today.thefinancialexpress.com.bd/public/views-opinion/great-opportunity-for-bangladesh.

Ahmed, Z. S. 2019. "Impact of the China–Pakistan Economic Corridor on Nation-Building in Pakistan." *Journal of Contemporary China* 28 (117): 400–14.

Ahn, Nguyen Thi Thuy, and Zhang Jianhua. 2015. "Transport Connectivity with China to Help Speed Up Vietnam's Economic Development." *Shanghai Daily*, Apr. 13, 2015. http://infotruck.blogspot.hk/2015/04/infrastructures-china-vietnam-modern.html.

Aizat, Shailoobek Kyzy. 2021a. "What a Kyrgyzstan Oil Refinery Reveals about China's Belt and Road Initiative." *Global Voices*, June 9, 2021. https://globalvoices.org/2021/06/09/what-a-kyrgyzstan-oil-refinery-tells-us-or-doesnt-tell-us-about-chinas-bri/.

———. 2021b. "In Kyrgyzstan, an Ultranationalist Group Thrives on Rising anti-Chinese Sentiment." *Global Voices*, June 16, 2021. https://globalvoices.org/2021/06/16/in-kyrgyzstan-an-ultranationalist-group-thrives-on-rising-anti-chinese-sentiment/.

172 | References

Akan, Emel. 2018. "China Fighting 'Real War' to Steal US Innovation: Openness Facilitates Cheating as China Seeks to Dominate World Economy." *Epoch Times*, July 23, 2018. https://www.theepochtimes.com/china-fighting-real-war-to-steal-us-innovation_2600736.html.

Akita, Hiroyuki. 2019. "Russia and China Romance Runs into Friction in Central Asia." *Nikkei Review*, July 29, 2019. https://asia.nikkei.com/Spotlight/Comment/Russia-and-China-romance-runs-into-friction-in-Central-Asia.

Alemdaroglu, A., and S. Tepe. 2020. "Erdogan Is Turning Turkey into a Chinese Client State." *Foreign Policy*, Sept. 16, 2020. https://foreignpolicy.com/2020/09/16/erdogan-is-turning-turkey-into-a-chinese-client-state/.

Aljazeera. 2021a. "Bosnia Receives Jabs from Serbia amid COVAX Dispute." Mar. 2, 2021. https://www.aljazeera.com/news/2021/3/2/bosnia-receives-jabs-from-serbia-amid-covax-dispute.

———. 2021b. "China Launches 'Virus Passport.'" Mar. 9, 2021. https://www.aljazeera.com/news/2021/3/9/china-launches-worlds-first-virus-passport.

Allam, Hannah. 2013. "Obama Searching for the Right Tone in Executing 'Asia Pivot.'" *St. Paul Pioneer Press*, Jan. 25, 2013. https://www.twincities.com/2013/01/25/obama-searching-for-right-tone-in-executing-asia-pivot/.

Ali, G. 2013. "China's Strategic Interests in Pakistan's Port at Gwadar." *East AsiaForum*, Mar. 24, 2013. http://www.eastasiaforum.org/2013/03/24/chinas-strategic-interests-in-pakistans-port-at-gwadar/.

Allison, Graham, Robert D. Blackwell, and Ali Wyne. 2013. *Lee Kuan Yew: The Grand Master's Insights on China, the United States, and the World.* Cambridge, MA: MIT Press.

Amadeo, Kimberly. 2021. "U.S. Trade Deficit with China and Why It's So High." The Balance, Oct. 25, 2021. https://www.thebalancemoney.com/u-s-china-trade-deficit-causes-effects-and-solutions-3306277.

Ambani, Mildred M. 2017. *GIS Assessment of Environmental Footprints of the Standard Gauge Railway (SGR) on Nairobi National Park, Kenya.* University of Nairobi. http://erepository.uonbi.ac.ke/bitstream/handle/11295/101271/Mildred%20Ambani_Final%20Project.pdf?sequence=1&isAllowed=y.

Angular, E. G. 2020. "The Chinese Amazon Waterway Project Threatens the Survival of Indigenous Communities in Peru." *Gran Angular*, Oct. 23, 2020. http://elgranangular.com/blog/reportaje/the-chinese-amazon-waterway-project-threatens-the-survival-of-indigenous-communities-in-peru/.

Anonymous. 2013a. "Debating America's Pivot." *Wilson Quarterly* 37 (1): 84–87.

Anonymous. 2013b. "The Problem with the Pivot." *Wilson Quarterly* 37 (3): 105–8.

Anonymous. 2018. "A Silk Road through Ice: China Wants to be a Polar Power." *Economist* (Apr. 14): 52–53.

Arase, David. 2021. "The Belt and Road Initiative Enters a Second Phase." *Asia Global Online*, Apr. 15, 2021. https://www.asiaglobalonline.hku.hk/belt-and-road-initiative-enters-second-phase.

References | 173

Arifeen, Mohammed. 2016. "Pakistan and China Share a Great History of Brotherly and Time-Tested Relations." *Financial Daily* (Karachi), May 21, 2016.

Asia News Monitor (Bangkok). 2017. "China: China's Xi Warns of Dangers of Trade War." Jan. 19, 2017.

Asian Infrastructure Investment Bank (AIIB). 2015. "Purpose, Functions and Membership." https://www.aiib.org/en/about-aiib/basic-documents/_download/articles-of-agreement/basic_document_english-bank_articles_of_agreement.pdf.

Asia-Pacific Broadcasting Union (APBU). 2012. "Sri Lanka, China Ink Deal to Build Communications Tower." Mar. 1, 2012. https://www.abu.org.my/2012/01/03/sri-lanka-china-ink-deal-to-build-communications-tower-2/#:~:text=Sri%20Lanka%20will%20sign%20an,through%20its%20official%20news%20portal.

Associated Press (AP). 2021. "Laos Opens Railway to China as Debt to Beijing Rises." *Voice of America (VOA)*, Dec. 4, 2021. https://www.voanews.com/a/laos-opens-railway-to-china-as-debt-to-beijing-rises/6339499.html.

———. 2024. "China Formally Restores Diplomatic Relations with Nauru after Pacific Island Nation Cut Taiwan Ties." Jan. 24, 2024. https://apnews.com/article/china-nauru-taiwan-diplomatic-recognition-23fd9cdd0210a2340b5ae2092d2a85d1.

Athwal, A. 2008. *China-India Relations: Contemporary Dynamics*. London: Routledge.

Auslin, Michael. 2014. "The New Normal in Asia: Beijing Will Continue Asserting Itself in Disputed Territories: Its Neighbors Will Continue to Do Little to Challenge It." *Wall Street Journal*, Aug. 12, 2014. https://www.wsj.com/articles/auslin-the-new-normal-in-asia-1407862416.

Avdaliani, Emil. 2021. "China Seeks to Boost Its Role in the Arctic." *Choice*, May 24, 2021. https://chinaobservers.eu/china-seeks-to-boost-its-role-in-the-arctic/.

Ayemba, Dennis. 2021a. "Egypt's New Administrative Capital Project Timeline and What You Need to Know." *Construction Review Online*, July 15, 2021. https://constructionreviewonline.com/project-timelines/egypts-new-administrative-capital-project-timeline-and-what-you-need-to-know/.

———. 2021b. "Tanzania SGR Project Timeline and All You Need to Know." *Construction Review Online*, July 15, 2021. https://constructionreviewonline.com/project-timelines/tanzania-sgr-project-timeline-and-all-you-need-to-know/.

Ayres, Alyssa. 2017. "India Objects to China's Belt and Road Initiative and It Has a Point." *Council on Foreign Relations*, May 17, 2017. https://www.cfr.org/blog/india-objects-chinas-belt-and-road-initiative-and-it-has-point.

Backhouse, Andrew. 2022. "China Forgives Debt for 17 African Nations." *News.com.au*, Aug. 22, 2022. https://www.news.com.au/finance/economy/china-forgives-debt-for-17-african-nations/news-story/28ab7f45440142634ff8efd0360b2fec.

Bajpai, Kanti, Huang Jing, and Kishore Mahbubani. 2016. *China-India Relations: Cooperation and Conflict*. London: Routledge.

Bangkok Post. 2012. "Clinton Urges ASEAN Unity over Islands." July 13, 2012. https://www.bangkokpost.com/world/302200/clinton-urges-asean-unity-over-islands.

174 | References

Bao, Anniek, and Liu Peilin. 2020. "China's Stumbling Sprint to Semiconductor Self-Sufficiency." *Caixin*, Nov. 20, 2022. https://www.caixinglobal.com/2020-11-20/chinas-stumbling-sprint-to-semiconductor-self-sufficiency-101630701.html.

Baqai, H. 2015. "CPEC: All to Benefit." *Pakistan Observer*, June 10, 2015, 5.

Barnes, Julian. E., and B. Spegele. 2012. "Panetta Calls for Calm in China–Japan Dispute." *Wall Street Journal*, Sept. 17, 2012. https://www.wsj.com/articles/SB10000872396390444450004578002004238703178.

Barnett, Michael N., and Jack S. Levy. 1991. "Domestic Sources of Alliances and Alignments: The Case of Egypt, 1962–73." *International Organization* 45 (3): 369–95.

Baron, Kevin. 2011. "Can the U.S. Afford the Asia 'Pivot'?" *National Journal Daily A.M.*, Dec. 11, 2011.

Bartlett, Kate. 2022. "After Anti-China Campaign, Kenya's Ruto Does About-Face." *Voice of America (VOA)*, Sept. 29, 2022. https://www.voanews.com/a/after-anti-china-campaign-kenya-s-ruto-does-about-face/6769282.html.

Bartlett, Paul. 2021. "Kazakh Ban on Foreign Farmland Sales Fails to Quell China Distrust." *Nikkei Asia*, May 14, 2021. https://asia.nikkei.com/Politics/Kazakh-ban-on-foreign-farmland-sales-fails-to-quell-China-distrust.

Bartlett-Imadegawa, Rhyannon, and Catherine de Beaurepaire. 2024. "EU Slaps Additional Duties of up to 38% on Chinese EVs." *Nikkei Asia*, June 12, 2024. https://asia.nikkei.com/Economy/Trade-war/EU-slaps-additional-duties-of-up-to-38-on-Chinese-EVs.

BBC Monitoring (South Asia). 2017. "Sri Lanka Backs China's Regional Economic Projects." Feb. 8, 2017.

Beattie, Victor. 2014. "United States/China: US Says China, Not Washington, Responsible for South China Sea Tensions." *Voice of America (VOA)*, Aug. 14, 2014. https://www.voanews.com/a/us-says-china-not-washington-responsible-for-south-china-sea-tensions/2410530.html.

Beijing Review. 2015. "Visions of the Maritime Silk Road." Feb. 5, 2015. http://www.bjreview.com.cn/world/txt/2015-02/02/content_666898.htm.

Belokrenitsky, V. Y. 2007. "South-Western Extension of Greater China." *Pakistan Horizon* 60, no. 3 (July): 83–98.

Belt and Road News. 2020. "China & Thailand to Open Green Channel." Oct. 17, 2020. https://www.beltandroad.news/2020/10/16/China-Thailand-to-Open-Green-Channel/.

———. 2021. "What Does China's Belt & Road Initiative Mean for Latin America?" Apr. 8, 2021. https://www.beltandroad.news/what-does-chinas-belt-road-initiative-mean-for-latin-america/.

Bermingham, Finbarr. 2021a. "Angry Birds Mogul Aims to Tunnel through Baltic Anti-China Sentiments." *South China Morning Post*, Apr. 4, 2021, 4.

———. 2021b. "EU Says It Won't Pay Off Montenegro's Billion-Dollar Highway Debt to China." *South China Morning Post*, Apr. 13, 2021. https://www.scmp.

com/news/china/diplomacy/article/3129263/eu-says-it-wont-pay-montenegros-billion-dollar-highway-debt.

Bhaumik, Subir. 2013. "China and India Use Buddha for Regional Karma." Aljazeera, Jan. 12, 2013. https://www.aljazeera.com/indepth/features/2013/01/2013171148400871.html.

Biedermann, Reinhard. 2020. "The Polar Silk Road: China's Multilevel Arctic Strategy to Globalize the Far North." *Contemporary Chinese Political Economy and Strategic Relations; Kaohsiung* 6, no. 2 (Aug./Sept.): 571–615.

Bloomberg. 2019. "South Sudan Will Provide a Sixth of Its Oil Output to China to Fund Road Projects." *South China Morning Post*, Apr. 6, 2019. https://www.scmp.com/print/news/china/diplomacy/article/3004962/south-sudan-will-provide-sixth-its-oil-output-china-fund-road.

Bokhari, F., A. Kazmin, and J. Kynge. 2017. "How China Rules the Waves: FT BIG NAVAL POWER." *Financial Times* (London), Jan. 13, 2017, 11.

Bora, L. Y. 2020. "Challenge and Perspective for Digital Silk Road." *Cogent Business & Management* 7 (1). https://www.tandfonline.com/doi/full/10.1080/23311975.2020.1804180.

Boudreau, John, and Nguyen Dieu Tu Uyen. 2019. "Vietnam Prefers Its Mobile Networks to Be Free of Huawei." *Bloomberg*, Aug. 26, 2019. https://www.bloomberg.com/news/articles/2019-08-26/vietnam-prefers-its-mobile-networks-to-be-free-of-huawei.

Boyle, Joe. 2012. "Tanzania's Invisible Web Revolution." BBC, Oct. 2, 2012. https://www.bbc.com/news/world-africa-19451044.

Brautigam, Deborah. 2011. "Aid 'with Chinese Characteristics': Chinese Foreign Aid and Development Finance Meet the OECD-DAC Aid Regime." *Journal of International Development* 23 (5): 752–64.

Braun, Elisa. 2021. "French Search Firm Qwant Seeks €8M Huawei Bailout Loan." *Politico*, June 12, 2021. https://www.politico.eu/article/french-search-engine-qwant-huawei-bailout-loan/.

Breslin, Shaun. 2012. "Paradigm(s) Shifting? Responding to China's Response to the Global Financial Crisis." In *The Consequences of the Global Financial Crisis: The Rhetoric of Reform and Regulation*, eds. Wyn Grant and Graham K. Wilson. Oxford Scholarship Online. https://oxford.universitypressscholarship.com/view/10.1093/acprof:oso/9780199641987.001.0001/acprof-9780199641987-chapter-12.

Breuninger, Kevin. 2022. "Biden Signs China Competition Bill to Boost U.S. Chipmakers." CNBC, Aug. 9, 2022. https://www.cnbc.com/2022/08/09/biden-to-sign-chips-act-china-competition-bill.html.

Brînză, Andreea. 2021. "Where China Went Wrong in Central and Eastern Europe." *South China Morning Post*. June 10, 2021. https://www.scmp.com/comment/opinion/article/3136630/where-china-went-wrong-central-and-eastern-europe.

176 | References

British Broadcasting Corporation (BBC). 2016. "Tanzania Bridge 'Liberates Commuters' in Dar es Salaam." Apr. 19, 2016. https://www.bbc.com/news/world-africa-36080577.

———. 2018. "Kenya Fraud Charges over Chinese-Funded $3bn Railway." Aug. 13, 2018. https://www.bbc.com/news/world-africa-45169690.

———. 2021. "China Offers $31m in Emergency Aid to Afghanistan." Sept. 9, 2021. https://www.bbc.com/news/world-asia-china-58496867.

———. 2022. "G7 Summit: Leaders Detail $600bn Plan to Rival China's Belt and Road Initiative." June 27, 2022. https://www.bbc.com/news/world-asia-61947325.

Brown, Tanner. 2021. "China Stumbles in the Vaccine Race: How It's Ramping Up Production, Inoculations After Shortfall." *Dow Jones*, Feb. 13, 2021.

Brunnersum, Sou-Jie van. 2022. "Nepal: What Happened to China's 'Belt and Road' Projects?" *DW*, May 20, 2022. https://www.dw.com/en/nepal-what-happened-to-chinas-belt-and-road-projects/a-61941737.

Bush, Richard C. III. 2012. "The Response of China's Neighbors to the U.S. 'Pivot' to Asia." *Brookings*, Jan. 31, 2012. https://www.brookings.edu/on-the-record/the-response-of-chinas-neighbors-to-the-u-s-pivot-to-asia/.

Business Wire (New York). 2016. "Naval Superpowers Increase Patrols in Indian Ocean, IHS Markit Says." Dec. 15, 2016. http://asia.nikkei.com/Viewpoints/Raj-Kumar-Sharma/Iran-port-tie-up-marks-strategic-milestone-for-India-and-Japan.

Cable News Network (CNN). 2023. "Fareed Zakaria Sits Down with President Joe Biden." July 10, 2023. https://www.youtube.com/watch?v=-SKC_rvEXrY.

Cai, Peter. 2016. "Why India Is Wary of China's Silk Road Initiative." *Huffington Post*, Sept. 2, 2016. http://www.huffingtonpost.com/peter-cai/india-china-silk-road-initiative_b_11894038.html.

Cao, Jiahan. 2020. "Toward a Health Silk Road: China's Proposal for Global Health Cooperation." *China Quarterly of International Strategic Studies* 6 (1): 19–35.

Carter, Ashton B. 2013. "The U.S. Defense Rebalance to Asia." Speech by US deputy secretary of defense delivered at the Center for Strategic and International Studies. Washington, DC, Apr. 8, 2013.

Central Intelligence Agency (CIA). 2022. "Country Comparisons—Real GDP (Purchasing Power Parity)." *The World Factbook*, United States. https://www.cia.gov/the-world-factbook/field/real-gdp-purchasing-power-parity/country-comparison/.

Chakrabarty, Malancha. 2016. "Ethiopia-China Economic Relations: A Classic Win-Win Situation?" *World Review of Political Economy* 7 (2): 226–48.

Chan, Jiahao. 2019. "China's Digital Silk Road and Stopping Divergent Technology Standards." Lowy Institute, May 21, 2019. https://www.lowyinstitute.org/the-interpreter/china-s-digital-silk-road-and-stopping-divergent-technology-standards.

Chan, Minnie. 2017. "China Has the World's Biggest Military Force. Now Xi Jinping Wants It to Be the Best." *South China Morning Post*, Oct. 19, 2017. http://www.scmp.com/news/china/diplomacy-defence/article/2115968/xi-orders-massive-military-shake-meet-threats-worlds.

Chan, Kai Yee. 2015. "One Belt, One Road Joint Construction for Prosperity: Speeding Up the Construction of Pan-Asian Railway for Connection of 'One Belt, One Road.'" China Central Television (CCTV), Apr. 28, 2015.

Chan, Robin. 2013. "US Presence 'Crucial for Asian Growth.'" *Straits Times*, July 28, 2013, 6.

Chand, Naresh. 2014. "China's Maritime Strategy for South Asia." *SP's Naval Forces*, no. 4. https://www.spsnavalforces.com/story/?id=332.

Chandran, N. 2016. "Modi's Focus Shifts from Investment to Foreign Policy Amid Kashmir, Balochistan Troubles." CNBC, Sept. 12, 2016. http://www.cnbc.com/2016/09/12/modis-focus-shifts-from-investment-to-foreign-policy-amid-kashmir-balochistan-troubles.html.

Chaudhury, Dipanjan Roy. 2022. "India-Russia-China Explore Alternative to SWIFT Payment Mechanism. *Economic Times*, Feb. 8, 2022. https://economictimes.indiatimes.com/news/economy/foreign-trade/india-russia-china-explore-alternative-to-swift-payment-mechanism/articleshow/72048472.cms.

Chaziza, Mordechai. 2023. "The Global Security Initiative: China's New Security Architecture for the Gulf." *The Diplomat*, May 5, 2023. https://thediplomat.com/2023/05/the-global-security-initiative-chinas-new-security-architecture-for-the-gulf/.

Chellaney, Brahma. 2017. "China's Debt-Trap Diplomacy." *Project Syndicate*, Jan. 23, 2017. https://www.project-syndicate.org/commentary/china-one-belt-one-road-loans-debt-by-brahma-chellaney-2017-01?barrier=accesspaylog.

Chen, Frank. 2018. "Region's Top Militaries Meet in SCO Anti-Terrorism Drill." *Asia Times*, Aug. 23, 2018. https://www.asiatimes.com/2018/08/article/regions-top-militaries-meet-in-sco-anti-terrorism-drill/.

Chen, Lijun. 2015. "Communist Party of China Embraces Virtues of Religion in Diplomacy." *Global Times*, May 4, 2015. https://www.globaltimes.cn/content/920035.shtml.

Chen, Liubing. 2018. "China, Africa Trade Volume Rises 14% to $170b." *China Daily*, Aug. 29, 2018. http://www.chinadaily.com.cn/a/201808/29/WS5b86536ea310add14f388762.html.

Chen, Xi. 2018. "Why Fears of China's Neocolonialism in Africa Ring False in the Face of Numbers That Tell a Different Tale." *South China Morning Post*, Sept. 25, 2018. https://www.scmp.com/print/comment/insight-opinion/united-states/article/2165489/why-fears-chinas-neocolonialism-africa-ring.

Chen, Xulong. 2015. "Developing Major-Country Diplomacy with Chinese Characteristics." *China Today*, Mar. 3, 2015. http://www.chinatoday.com.cn/english/columns/2015-03/03/content_672077.htm.

178 | References

Chen, Yunnan. 2023. "China's Global Development Initiative Is Not the BRI Reborn." *Nikkei Asia*, Mar. 8, 2023. https://asia.nikkei.com/Opinion/China-s-Global-Development-Initiative-is-not-the-BRI-reborn.

Chen, Zhao. 2022. "China's Wealth Dilemma." *South China Morning Post*, Mar. 26, 2022, B5.

Cheng, Evelyn. 2020. "China's Xi Pledges $2 Billion to Help Fight Coronavirus." CNBC, May 18, 2020. https://www.cnbc.com/2020/05/18/chinas-xi-pledges-2-billion-to-help-fight-corona-virus-at-who-meeting.html.

———. 2023. "What Biden's Executive Order Means for U.S. Investments in China." CNBC *News*, Aug. 10, 2023. https://www.cnbc.com/2023/08/11/what-bidens-executive-order-means-for-us-investors-in-china-.html.

Cheng, Kang-chun. 2022. "Africans' Reactions Mixed to Chinese Presence on Continent." *Voice of America* (*VOA*), Jan. 5, 2022. https://www.voanews.com/a/africans-reactions-mixed-to-chinese-presence-on-continent/6383863.html#:~:text=A%20recent%20survey%20conducted%20by,external%20influence%20on%20the%20continent.&text=China's%20presence%20can%20be%20seen%20throughout%20Nairobi.

Chin, Curtis. 2012. "America Needs a Business Pivot Toward Asia." *Wall Street Journal*, Aug. 9, 2012, A9.

China Briefing Team. 2021. "China and Central Asia: Bilateral Trade Relationships and Future Outlook." *China Briefing*, May 20, 2021. https://www.china-briefing.com/news/china-and-central-asia-bilateral-trade-relatisonships-and-future-outlook/.

China Daily. 2017. "Beijing Communiqué of the Belt and Road Health Cooperation & Health Silk Road." Aug. 18, 2017. http://subsites.chinadaily.com.cn/ministries/health/2017-08/18/c_110402.htm.

China Development Forum (CDF). 2019. *The Silk Road Fund*. https://cdf-en.cdrf.org.cn/cdf2019en/jgjs/7316.jhtml#content.

China Global Television Network. 2018. "Xi Urges More Security Cooperation Among SCO Members." Apr. 24, 2018. https://news.cgtn.com/news/3d3d414d3555444d77457a6333566d54/share_p.html.

China-CEE Fund. 2018. "The Establishment of China-Central and Eastern European Cooperation Fund II." Feb. 22, 2018. http://china-ceefund.com/Template/news.aspx?page=ContentPage&nodeid=12&contentid=165.

———. 2022. "China-Central and Eastern Europe Investment Cooperation Fund." Mar. 27, 2022. http://china-ceefund.com/Template/Condition_2.html.

China-US Focus. 2015. "China's Silky Indian Ocean Plans." May 11, 2015. http://www.chinausfocus.com/finance-economy/chinas-silky-indian-ocean-plans.

ChinaPower. 2020. "How Will the Belt and Road Initiative Advance China's Interests?" Center for Strategic and International Studies (CSIS), Aug. 26, 2020. https://chinapower.csis.org/china-belt-and-road-initiative/.

References | 179

Chow, Jermyn. 2012. "Beijing Unfazed by US' Asia Pivot." *Straits Times*, June 4, 2012, 1.

Chowdhury, I. A. 2015. "Pakistan in China's Eyes: Pawn, Pivot or a Pointer to Its World View?" Singapore: Institute of South Asian Studies (ISAS), Special Report no. 23, May 6, 2015.

———. 2016. "Xi Jinping in Dhaka: Implications for South Asian Politics." Singapore: Institute of South Asian Studies (ISAS), Special Report no. 355, Oct. 18, 2016.

Chowdhury, Denbasish Roy. 2021. "The Battle for Democracy." This Week in Asia, *South China Morning Post*, Aug. 8–14, 8–11. https://www.silkroadbriefing.com/news/2020/07/22/digital-yuan-bsn-track-replace-us-dollar-china-trade/.

Chua, Chin Hon. 2011. "Pivot and Push in Asia: How Will China React to the New US Strategic Focus on Asia-Pacific." *Straits Times*, Nov. 19, 2011, 2.

Chung, Chien-peng, and Thomas J. Voon. 2017. "China's Maritime Silk Road Initiative: Political-Economic Calculations of Southeast Asian States." *Asian Survey* 57 (3): 416–49.

Clingendael Report. 2020. "Greenland: What Is China Doing There and Why?" https://www.clingendael.org/pub/2020/presence-before-power/4-greenland-what-is-china-doing-there-and-why/.

Clover, Charles, and Luna Lin. 2016. "China Foreign Policy: Throwing Out the Rule Book." *Financial Times*, Sept. 1, 2016. https://www.ft.com/content/810b4510-6ea4-11e6-9ac1-1055824ca907.

Colby, Elbridge, and Ely Ratner. 2014. "Roiling the Waters." *Foreign Policy*, Jan. 21, 2014, 10–13.

Congressional Research Service (CRS). 2022. "Asian Infrastructure Investment Bank." Mar. 17, 2022. https://crsreports.congress.gov/product/pdf/IF/IF10154.

Conley, Heather A., Jonathan E. Hillman, Donatienne Ruy, and Maesea McCalpin. 2020. "China's 'Hub-and-Spoke' Strategy in the Balkans." Center for Strategic and International Studies (CSIS), Apr. 27, 2020. https://www.csis.org/analysis/chinas-hub-and-spoke-strategy-balkans.

Construction Global. 2020. "China Belt and Road Initiative Spending Hit by Pandemic." Nov. 4, 2020. https://www.constructionglobal.com/construction-projects/china-belt-and-road-initiative-spending-hit-pandemic.

Construction Review Online (CR). 2021. "Port-Gentil-Omboué Road Construction in Gabon Ready for Use." Aug. 17, 2021. https://constructionreviewonline.com/news/port-gentil-omboue-road-construction-in-gabon-ready-for-use/.

Copeland, Dale C. 2000. *The Origins of Major War*. Ithaca, NY: Cornell University Press.

Coterill, Joseph, and Jonathan Wheatley. 2022. "China Agrees Landmark Debt Relief Deal for Zambia." *Financial Times* (London), July 30, 2022. https://www.ft.com/content/45521cfc-0eb3-4f11-be31-4ac08ac98a8c.

180 | References

CPEC (China-Pakistan Economic Corridor). 2020. "CPEC Projects Progress Update." http://cpec.gov.pk/progress-update.

———. 2022. "720MW Karot Hydropower Project, AJK/Punjab." http://cpec.gov.pk/project-details/16.

CPEC-Gwadar. 2022. "Gwadar Projects Under CPEC." http://cpec.gov.pk/gwadar.

Crabtree, James. 2020. "The Third Phase of China's Belt and Road." HKUST IEMS Policy Briefs no. 1. Hong Kong University of Science and Technology. https://iems.ust.hk/publications/policy-briefs/the-third-phase-of-china-s-belt-and-road-initiative-by-james-crabtree.

Crossley, Gabriel. 2020. "China Says One-Fifth of Belt and Road Projects 'Seriously Affected' by Pandemic." Reuters, June 19, 2020. https://www.reuters.com/article/us-health-coronavirus-china-silkroad-idUSKBN23Q0I1.

Dace, Hermione, Ariana Kiran Singh, and Karen Hooper. 2022. "Are We Ready for a Chinese Reshaping of the Global Agrifood System?" Tony Blair Institute for Global Change, Mar. 28, 2022. https://institute.global/policy/are-we-ready-chinese-reshaping-global-agrifood-system.

Daily News (Colombo). 2017. "52 Arrested, 21 Remanded After Hambantota Clash." Jan. 7, 2017. http://www.dailynews.lk/2017/01/08/local/104093/52-arrested-21-remanded-after-hambantota-clash.

Devonshire-Ellis, Chris. 2020. "The Digital Yuan & BSN Are On Track to Replace the US Dollar in China Trade." *Silk Road Briefing*, July 22, 2020.

———. 2021. "Chinese Companies Hunting in Latin America for Belt and Road M&A." *Silk Road Briefing*, June 10, 2021. https://www.silkroadbriefing.com/news/2020/12/30/chinese-companies-hunting-in-latin-america-for-belt-and-road-ma/.

Darabshaw, Sohrab. 2021. "Wind Farm to Come Online in Kazakhstan." *Metal Miner*, June 18, 2021. https://agmetalminer.com/2021/06/18/massive-wind-farm-part-of-chinas-belt-and-road-to-come-online-in-kazakhstan/.

Dasgupta, Saibal. 2015. "China's Ambitious 'Silk Road' Plan Faces Hurdles." *Voice of America (VOA)*, Apr. 15, 2015. http://www.voanews.com/content/chinas-ambitious-silk-road-plan-faces-hurdles/2719660.html.

Delaney, Robert. 2023. "'I Wouldn't Say I'm Optimistic' About State of China Relations, Says US Ambassador to Beijing Nicholas Burns." *South China Morning Post*, Dec. 16, 2023. https://www.scmp.com/news/china/diplomacy/article/3245299/i-wouldnt-say-im-optimistic-about-state-us-china-relations-says-ambassador-beijing-nicholas-burns.

Devaranade, Jaya. 2017. "Buddhism: A New Frontier in the China-India Rivalry." *Carnegie India*, Mar. 17, 2017.

Dodwell, David. 2022. "Bulwark in Unsafe World." *South China Morning Post*, Apr. 2, 2022, B4.

Donnellon-May, Genevieve, and Zhang Hongzhou. 2022. "Recipe for Disaster?: Implications of the Ukraine-Russia War on China's Food Security."

AsiaGlobal Online, Mar. 24, 2022. https://www.asiaglobalonline.hku.hk/recipe-disaster-implications-ukraine-russia-war-chinas-food-security.

Dorjee, Rinzin. 2018. "The Dalai Lama and China's Quest for Buddhist Soft Power." *The Diplomat*, Oct. 29, 2018. https://thediplomat.com/2018/10/the-dalai-lama-and-chinas-quest-for-buddhist-soft-power/.

Dorsey, J. M. 2017. "Why Saudi Arabia, China and Islamic State Are Courting the Maldives." This Week in Asia, *South China Morning Post*, Mar. 12, 2017, 17.

Doshi, Rush. 2021. "The Long Game: China's Grand Strategy to Displace American Order." *Brookings*, Aug. 2, 2021. https://www.brookings.edu/essay/the-long-game-chinas-grand-strategy-to-displace-american-order/.

Economics Relations Division (ERD), Government of the People's Republic of Bangladesh. 2016. *Flow of External Resources into Bangladesh 2014–15*. Dhaka: ERD.

Economist. 2010a. "Asia: Testing the Waters; Strategic Jousting Between China and America." July 31, 2010, 32.

———. 2010b. "The Start of Something Big? Asian Defence Ministers Meet in Hanoi." Oct. 12, 2010. https://www.economist.com/banyan/2010/10/12/the-start-of-something-big.

———. 2013. "Spin and Substance: Japan and America." Mar. 2, 2013, 39–40.

———. 2014. "So Long, and Thanks for All the Naval Bases: Barack Obama's Asian Tour." Apr. 28, 2014. https://www.economist.com/banyan/2014/04/28/so-long-and-thanks-for-all-the-naval-bases.

Eguegu, Ovigwe. 2022. "The Digital Silk Road: Connecting Africa with New Norms of Digital Development." *Asia Policy* 17, no. 3 (July): 33.

Elmer, Keegan. 2019. "China and Russia Plan to Boost Cooperation in Science and Innovation." *South China Morning Post*, Dec. 29, 2019, 1.

Eurasianet. 2022. "Russia's Ukraine Invasion Is Bad News for China's Belt and Road Ambitions." Mar. 12, 2022. https://oilprice.com/Energy/Energy-General/Russias-Ukraine-Invasion-Is-Bad-News-For-Chinas-Belt-And-Road-Ambitions.html.

Euronews and AFP. 2021. "Hungary's PM Viktor Orbán Vaccinated Against COVID with Chinese Sinopharm Vaccine." *Euronews*, Feb. 28, 2021. https://www.euronews.com/2021/02/28/hungary-s-pm-viktor-orban-vaccinated-against-covid-with-chinese-sinopharm-vaccine.

European Commission. 2021. "Global Gateway: Up to €300 Billion for the European Union's Strategy to Boost Sustainable Links Around the World." Dec. 1, 2021. https://ec.europa.eu/commission/presscorner/detail/en/ip_21_6433.

European Council, Council of the European Union. 2020. "Long-Term EU Budget 2021–2027 and Recovery Package." https://www.consilium.europa.eu/en/policies/the-eu-budget/long-term-eu-budget-2021-2027/.

European Parliament. 2018. *Briefing: China, the 16+1 Format and the EU*. Sept. 2018, 7.

182 | References

Feng, Emily, Alice Woodhouse, and Richard Milne. 2018. "China Reveals Arctic Ambitions with Plan for 'Polar Silk Road.'" *FT.com* (*Financial Times*), Jan. 26, 2018. https://www.ft.com/content/c7bd5258-0293-11e8-9650-9c0ad2d7c5b5.

Feng, Hui. 2015. "China-Arab States Health Cooperation Forum Declaration." People's Republic of China National Health and Family Planning Commission, Sept. 18, 2015. http://en.nhc.gov.cn/2015-09/18/c_45733.htm.

Ferguson, Niall. 2012. "All the Asian Rage: It's Not Just the Middle East; China's on the March." *Newsweek*, Oct. 1, 2012, 20.

Filippov, Andrey. 2018. "Shanghai Cooperation Organization 2018: Economic Prospects." DOC Research Institute, June 15, 2018. https://doc-research.org/2018/06/65128/.

Financial Express (Dhaka). 2016a. "China-Bangla Economic Cooperation: Current Trends and Future Prospects." Oct. 11, 2016. https://thefinancial express.com.bd/views/opinions/china-bangla-economic-cooperation-current-trends-and-future-prospects.

———. 2016b. "Manna from China: Investment Proposals Aplenty." Nov. 5, 2016. https://bdnews24.com/opinion/comment/manna-from-china-investment-proposals-aplenty.

———. 2016c. "Wheel within Wheels: China vs India." June 13, 2016. https://mail.thefinancialexpress.com.bd/views/wheel-within-wheels-china-vs-india.

Financial Express (New Delhi). 2016d. "Narendra Modi Changed India's 'Attitude' Towards MSR: Chinese Daily." July 4, 2016. http://www.financialexpress.com/india-news/narendra-modi-changed-indias-attitude-towards-msr-chinese-daily/305917/.

Financial Post (Karachi). 2016. "CPEC Is Progressing Rapidly: Chinese Officials." Oct. 14, 2016. https://archive.pakistantoday.com.pk/2016/10/13/cpec-progressing-rapidly-chinese-officials/.

Financial Times. 2021. "Doubts Over Efficacy of Chinese Vaccines Stoke Anxiety at Home and Abroad." Dec. 7, 2021. https://www.ft.com/content/c57028b4-573e-4ca4-8266-4d7c0ab72492.

France 24. 2021. "Pro-Beijing Solomon Islands PM Survives Confidence Vote, Blames Crisis on 'Taiwan Agents.'" Dec. 6, 2021. https://www.france24.com/en/asia-pacific/20211206-pro-beijing-solomon-islands-pm-survives-confidence-vote-blames-crisis-on-taiwan-agents.

Friedberg, Aaron L. 2022. *Getting China Wrong*. Cambridge: Polity Press.

Fu, Ying. 2015. "China's New Silk Road Promises Prosperity Across Eurasia." *Huffington Post*, July 31, 2015. http://www.huffingtonpost.com/fu-ying/china-silk-road-eurasia_b_7899236.html.

Fukushima, Glen S. 2012. "Japan's Role in America's Asia Pivot." *Washington Post*, Dec. 21, 2012, A27.

Freymann, Eyck. 2020. "One Belt One Road: Chinese Power Meets the World." In *Harvard East Asian Monographs no. 439*. Cambridge, MA: Harvard University Asia Center.

Gabuev, Alexander. 2017. "Bigger, Not Better: Russia Makes the SCO a Useless Club." Carnegie Endowment for International Peace, June 23, 2017. https://carnegie.ru/commentary/71350.

Gady, F.-S. 2016. "China to Supply Pakistan with 8 New Stealth Attack Submarines by 2018." *The Diplomat*, Aug. 30, 2016. https://thediplomat.com/2016/08/china-to-supply-pakistan-with-8-new-stealth-attack-submarines-by-2028/.

Ghauttam, Priya, Bawa Singh, and Jaspal Kaur. 2020. "COVID-19 and Chinese Global Health Diplomacy: Geopolitical Opportunity for China's Hegemony?" *Millennial Asia*, Oct. 12, 2020. https://journals.sagepub.com/doi/full/10.1177/0976399620959771?utm_source=summon&utm_medium=discovery-provider.

Ghosh, Nirma. 2023. "China Foreign Policy Not Winning Fans, but Its Africa Investment Is." *Straits Times*, July 28, 2023, A10.

Gilpin, Robert. 1983. *War and Change in World Politics*. Cambridge: Cambridge University Press.

Global Capital (London). 2015. "The Potential of One Belt, One Road." Nov. 30, 2015. https://www.globalcapital.com/asia/article/28mxzhx7fnfxq45kuqp6o/emerging-markets/asia/the-potential-of-one-belt-one-road.

Global Data. 2019. "Chile's Government Launches Its Biggest Railway Investment Programme in History." *Railway Technology*, Sept. 23, 2019. https://www.railway-technology.com/comment/chiles-government-launches-its-biggest-railway-investment-programme-in-history/#:%7E:text=The%20plan%2C%20which%20is%20the,tons%20a%20year%20by%202027.

Global Intelligence Services (GIS). 2024. "What Is the Future of China's Belt and Road Initiative?" Feb. 19, 2024. https://www.gisreportsonline.com/r/what-is-the-future-of-chinas-belt-and-road-initiative/

Global Times. 2021a. "ASEAN Becomes China's Largest Trading Partner in 2020, with 7% Growth." Jan. 14, 2021. https://www.globaltimes.cn/page/202101/1212785.shtml.

———. 2021b. "Update: Chinese Vaccines Donated to 53 Developing Countries, Exported to 27 Nations." Mar. 6, 2021. https://www.globaltimes.cn/page/202103/1216920.shtml.

Gong, Xue. 2020. "China's Belt and Road Initiative Financing in Southeast Asia." In *Southeast Asian Affairs 2020*, eds. Malcolm Cook and Daljit Singh, 77–95. Singapore: ISEAS.

Green Belt and Road Initiative Center. 2021. *Countries of the Belt and Road Initiative (BRI)*. https://green-bri.org/countries-of-the-belt-and-road-initiative-bri/.

Greene, Robert, and Paul Triolo. 2020. "Will China Control the Global Internet Via Its Digital Silk Road?" Carnegie Endowment for International Peace, May 8, 2020. https://carnegieendowment.org/2020/05/08/will-china-control-global-internet-via-its-digital-silk-road-pub-81857.

Guardian. 2022. "US Warns Solomon Islands Against China Military Base as Australian MPs Trade Blame." Apr. 23, 2022. https://www.theguardian.com/

184 | References

world/2022/apr/23/us-warns-solomon-islands-against-china-military-base-as-australian-mps-trade-blame.

Gul, Ayaz. 2024. "China Says 'Deeply Rooted' Ties with Pakistan Unaffected by Terror Attack." *Voice of America (VOA)*, Mar. 27, 2024. https://www.voanews.com/a/china-says-deeply-rooted-ties-with-pakistan-unaffected-by-terror-attack/7545833.html.

Guo, Huadong. 2018. "Steps to the Digital Silk Road." *Nature* 554, no. 7690 (Feb. 1): 25–27.

Guo, Yuan. 2014. "Japan's South China Sea Policy in 2013: Retrospect and Assessment." *New Orient* 3, 14–20.

Guerreiro, Phillip. 2021. "What Chinese Dams in Laos Tell Us About the Belt and Road Initiative." *The Diplomat*, Dec. 31, 2021. https://thediplomat.com/2021/12/what-chinese-dams-in-laos-tell-us-about-the-belt-and-road-initiative/.

Hart, Michael. 2021. "From Bangkok to Nong Khai: China's Thai Railway Vision Edges Forward." *Geopolitical Monitor*, Apr. 26, 2021. https://www.geopoliticalmonitor.com/from-bangkok-to-nong-khai-chinas-thai-railway-vision-edges-forward/.

Hashimova, Umida. 2021. "Official Hints at Challenges for Chinese Businesses in Uzbekistan." *The Diplomat*, May 25, 2021. https://thediplomat.com/2021/05/official-hints-at-challenges-for-chinese-businesses-in-uzbekistan/.

Heever, Claire van den. 2017. "Confucius Institutes across Africa are Nurturing Generations of Pro-China Mandarin Speakers." *Quartz*, Nov. 3, 2017. https://qz.com/1113559/confucius-institutes-in-africa-are-nurturing-mandarin-speakers-with-pro-china-views/.

Hemmings, John. 2020. "Reconstructing Order: The Geopolitical Risks in China's Digital Silk Road." *Asia Policy* 15, no. 1 (Jan.): 5–21.

Heydarian, Richard. 2021. "Putin's Next Canon." *South China Morning Post*, July 24, 2021, A16.

Hiep, Le Hong. 2021. "In Vietnam's Power Plants, US Finds a Counter to China's Belt and Road." *South China Morning Post*, Feb. 5, 2021. https://www.scmp.com/week-asia/opinion/article/3120522/vietnams-power-plants-us-finds-counter-chinas-belt-and-road.

Hillman, Jonathan E., and Maesea McCalpin. *2019a*. "Watching Huawei's 'Safe Cities.'" Center for Strategic and International Studies (CSIS), Nov. 4, 2019. https://www.csis.org/analysis/watching-huaweis-safe-cities.

———. 2019b. "Will China's '16+1' Format Divide Europe?" Center for Strategic and International Studies (CSIS), Apr. 11, 2019. https://www.csis.org/analysis/will-chinas-161-format-divide-europe.

Hindustani Times. 2022. "Nepal PM Deuba Inaugurates Second International Airport Near Lumbini." May 16, 2022. https://www.hindustantimes.com/lifestyle/travel/nepal-pm-deuba-inaugurates-second-international-airport-near-lumbini-101652713209277.html.

Hoang, Thi Ha. 2023. "Why Is China's Global Development Initiative Well Received in Southeast Asia?" *ISEAS Perspectives, Sept. 2023.* https://www.iseas.edu.sg/articles-commentaries/iseas-perspective/2023-9-why-is-chinas-global-development-initiative-well-received-in-southeast-asia-by-hoang-thi-ha/.

Hong, Jiang, and Johann Peter Murmann. 2022. "The Rise of China's Digital Economy: An Overview." *Management and Organization Review* 18, no. 4 (Aug.): 797.

Hossain, Md. Farid. 2021. "Coronavirus (COVID-19) Pandemic: Pros and Cons of China's Soft Power Projection." *Asian Politics & Policy* 13, 597–620.

Hout, Thomas. 2021. "A New Approach to Rebalancing the U.S.-China Trade Deficit." *Harvard Business Review*, Dec. 20, 2021. https://hbr.org/2021/12/a-new-approach-to-rebalancing-the-u-s-china-trade-deficit.

Hu Jintao, H. E. 2005. "Build Towards a Harmonious World of Lasting Peace and Common Prosperity." Speech at the United Nations, Sept. 15, 2005. https://www.un.org/webcast/summit2005/statements15/china050915eng.pdf.

Hu, Yongqi. 2016. "New Financial Holding Company Set Up to Finance China-CEE Projects." *China Daily*, Nov. 6, 2016. https://www.chinadaily.com.cn/world/2016liattendsSCOCCEEC/2016-11/06/content_27286146.htm.

———. 2017. "Li Signs 11 Accords in Hungary State Visit." *China Daily*, Nov. 30, 2017. https://www.chinadaily.com.cn/china/2017-11/30/content_35129531.htm.

Huang, Cary. 2016. "Four Reasons Duterte Will Have to Change Tune on China and the U.S." *South China Morning Post*, Oct. 29, 2016. http://www.scmp.com/week-asia/opinion/article/2041077/four-reasons-duterte-will-have-change-tune-china-and-us.

Huang, Lingyan, and Zhong Jianshan. 2015. "Hong Kong Media: China's 'One-Belt One Road' Plan Southeast Asian Countries' Reactions Warm." *China Daily*, Apr. 28, 2015. http://caijing.chinadaily.com.cn/2015-05/12/content_20691422_3.htm.

Huang, Yukon. 2014. "Can a Chinese 'Maritime Silk Route' Cool Tensions in Asia?" *The Diplomat*, May 5, 2014. http://www.eastasiaforum.org/2014/05/05/can-a-chinese-maritime-silk-route-cool-tensions-in-asia.

Hussain, J., Z. Yuan, and G. Ali. 2016. "China Pakistan Economic Corridor." *Defence Journal* 19 (6): 13.

Hussain, Tom. 2021. "A Pandora's Box Opens in Afghanistan." This Week in Asia, *South China Morning Post*, July 4–10, 9–11.

Hussain, Z. Z. 2015. "The 'BCIM Regional Cooperation': An Emerging Multilateral Framework in Asia." *Geopolitics, History and International Relations* 7 (2): 173–89.

Hutton, H. I. 2020. "Satellite Images Show That Chinese Navy Is Expanding Overseas Base." *Forbes*, May 10, 2020. https://www.forbes.com/sites/hisutton/

186 | References

2020/05/10/satellite-images-show-chinese-navy-is-expanding-overseas-base/?sh=46b184636869.

Hutton, Jeffrey. 2018. "Chinese Catch-22 That Could Derail Widodo." *This Week in Asia, South China Morning Post*, May 13–19, 2018. https://www.scmp.com/week-asia/politics/article/2145806/catch-22-china-could-derail-indonesias-widodo.

HWF Briefing. 2022. "The-Belt-and-Road-Initiative: Dispute Resolution Along the Belt and Road." https://www.hfw.com/The-Belt-and-Road-Initiative-Dispute-Resolution-along-The-Belt-And-Road.

ICLG.com. 2020. "Foreign Direct Investment Regimes 2021." *Global Legal Group*, Nov. 5, 2020. https://www.alcadvogados.com/xms/files/v1/Publicacoes/2020/ICLG_to_Foreign_Direct_Investment_Regimes_2021_Angola.pdf.

Indeo, Fabio. 2019. "Regional Implications of China's Military Base in Tajikistan." NATO Defense College Foundation, Central Asia, Feb. 2019. https://www.nato foundation.org/wp-content/uploads/2020/02/NDCF-ST-CENTRAL-ASIA-Feb-2019.pdf.

India Briefing. 2022. "Wang Yi in Nepal: Progress Made on Free Trade, Infrastructure Projects, and Cross-Border Energy Networks." Mar. 28, 2022. https://www.india-briefing.com/news/wang-yi-in-nepal-progress-made-on-free-trade-infrastructure-projects-and-cross-border-energy-networks-24621.html/.

International Relations & Politics. 2022. "Complete Debate, Can China Rise Peacefully, John Mearsheimer vs Yan Xuetong." YouTube video. https://www.youtube.com/watch?v=07A0iD4ogaY.

Jamil, M. 2016. "India's Unwarranted Concerns over CPEC." *Pakistan Observer*, Aug. 16, 2016. http://www.Pakobserver.net/indias-unwarranted-concerns-over-cpec/.

Janssen, Cyrus. 2022. "Why Asia Pacific Chose China (You Won't Believe What America Did)." *Vlog*, May 29, 2022. https://www.youtube.com/watch?v=3GQiTe4BNQ0.

Japan Times (Tokyo). 2016. "Japan, India Likely to Ink Pivotal US-2 Aircraft Deal." Nov. 6, 2016. http://www.japantimes.co.jp/news/2016/11/06/national/japan-india-likely-ink-pivotal-us-2-aircraft-deal/#.WN9vktJ97IU.

Javaid, Umbreen. 2016. "Assessing CPEC: Potential Threats and Prospects." *Journal of the Research Society of Pakistan; Lahore* 53, no. 2 (Dec.): 254–69.

Jennings, Ralph. 2022. "Official Hits Out over 'Debt Trap Lie.'" *South China Morning Post*, Aug. 20, 2022, A5.

Jett, Jennifer. 2023. "Xi Leaves Russia with Putin Firmly in the Back Seat of China's Drive for a New Global Order." NBC News, Mar. 23, 2023. https://www.nbcnews.com/news/world/china-russia-xi-jinping-vladimir-putin-new-global-order-us-ukraine-rcna76268.

Jiji Press. 1996. "US Calls for Restraint in Senkaku Dispute." Sept. 24, 1996.

Johnson, Gareth. 2021. "New Siem Reap International Airport 42 Per Cent Complete." *Khmer Times* (Phnom Penh), May 14, 2021. https://www.khmertimeskh.com/50856711/new-siem-reap-international-airport-42-per-cent-complete/.

Johnson, Keith. 2015. "China, Sri Lanka, and the Maritime Great Game." *Foreign Policy*, Feb. 12, 2015. http://foreignpolicy.com/2015/02/12/china-sri-lanka-and-the-maritime-great-game-silk-road-xi-port/.

Johnston, Eric. 2012. "US Senate Passes Senkaku Backing." *Japan Times*, Dec. 1, 2012. https://www.japantimes.co.jp/news/2012/12/01/national/u-s-senate-passes-senkaku-backing/.

Kacungira, Nancy. 2017. "Will Kenya Get Value for Money from Its New Railway?" BBC, June 8, 2017. https://www.bbc.com/news/world-africa-40171095.

Kansteiner, Fraiser. 2020. "BioNTech, through Fosun Deal, Pledges 100M Coronavirus Vaccine Doses for China." *FiercePharma*, Dec. 16, 2020. https://www.fiercepharma.com/pharma/biontech-and-fosun-lock-down-100m-covid-19-vaccine-doses-for-china.

Kapoor, Kanupriya, and Linda Sieg. 2015. "Indonesian President Says China's Main Claim in South China Sea Has No Legal Basis." Reuters, Mar. 23, 2015. https://www.reuters.com/article/us-indonesia-china-southchinasea/indonesian-president-says-chinas-main-claim-in-south-china-sea-has-no-legal-basis-idUSKBN0MJ04320150323/.

Kasonta, Adriel. 2022. "Quest for New World Order." *South China Morning Post*, Oct. 2, 2022, A16.

Kasturi, C. S. 2017. "India Boycotts Xi's Road Summit." *Telegraph* (Calcutta), May 17, 2017. https://www.telegraphindia.com/1170514/jsp/frontpage/story_151557.jsp.

Kathju, Junald. 2024. "Amid China-India Rivalry, Nepal's Political Shift Tips Scales in Favour of Beijing." *South China Morning Post*, Mar. 23, 2024. https://www.scmp.com/week-asia/politics/article/3256390/amid-china-india-rivalry-nepals-political-shift-tips-scales-favour-beijing.

Kavalski, Emilian. 2019. "China's '16+1' Is Dead? Long Live the '17+1.'" *The Diplomat*, Mar. 29, 2019. https://thediplomat.com/2019/03/chinas-161-is-dead-long-live-the-171/.

Kawate, Iori. 2022. "China-Backed AIIB Freezes Lending to Russia and Belarus." *Nikkei Asia*, Mar. 4, 2022. https://asia.nikkei.com/Politics/Ukraine-war/China-backed-AIIB-freezes-lending-to-Russia-and-Belarus.

Kazungu, Kalume. 2018. "Kenyans to Wait Longer For First Berth at Lamu Port." *Daily Nation* (Nairobi), Oct. 1, 2018. https://www.nation.co.ke/news/Kenyans-to-wait-longer-for-port-berth/1056-4786110-y065hdz/index.html.

Kennedy, Scott, and David A. Parker. "Building China's 'One Belt, One Road'" Center for Strategic and International Studies." April. 3, 2015. https://www.csis.org/analysis/building-chinas-one-belt-one-road.

Keohane, Robert O. 1984. *After Hegemony: Cooperation and Discord in the World Political Economy*. Princeton, NJ: Princeton University Press.

———. 1993. "Institutional Theory and the Realist Challenge After the Cold War." In *Neorealism and Neoliberalism: The Contemporary Debate*, ed. David A. Baldwin, 269–300. New York: Columbia University Press.

Keohane, Robert O., and Joseph S. Nye. 1977. *Power and Interdependence: World Politics in Transition*. Boston: Little, Brown.

Khurana, Gurpreet S. 2015. "China's 'Maritime Silk Road': Beyond 'Economics.'" National Maritime Foundation, Apr. 16, 2015. http://www.maritimeindia.org/CommentryView.aspx?NMFCID=8495.

Kok, Xinghui, and Dewey Sim. 2021. "A Shot in the Arm." This Week in Asia, *South China Morning Post*, Apr. 11–17, 6–7.

Koop, F. 2021. "State Grid Grows Presence in Chile with CGE Purchase." *Dialogo Chino*, Feb. 23, 2021. https://dialogochino.net/en/climate-energy/39680-state-grid-grows-presence-in-chile-with-cge-purchase/.

Koswaraputra, Dandy. 2022. "Indonesia Wants Chinese Lender to Fund Overrun for High-Speed Rail Line." *Radio Free Asia*, Apr. 22, 2022. https://www.rfa.org/english/news/china/indonesia-railway-04222022095730.html.

Krishnan, Ananth. 2015. "An Asian Anchor: While the India-China Bilateral Relationship Carries Its Own Weight, Engaging with India Is Being Seen in the Context of China's Ongoing Great Game with the US." *India Today*, May 18, 2015, 3.

Kugler, Jacek, and Ronald L. Tammen, eds. 2012. *The Performance of Nations*. Washington, DC: Rowman and Littlefield.

Kuik, Cheng-Chwee. 2021. "Asymmetry and Authority: Theorizing Southeast Asian Responses to China's Belt and Road Initiative." *Asian Perspective* 45, no. 2 (Spring): 255–76.

Kwok, Kristine. 2013. "China's 'Maritime Silk Road' Linking Southeast Asia Faces a Rocky Birth." *South China Morning Post*, Oct. 19, 2013. http://www.scmp.com/news/china/article/1334803/chinas-maritime-silk-road-linking-southeast-asia-faces-rocky-birth.

Kynge, James. 2016. "China's Ambitions for Asia Show Through in 'Silk Road' Lending." *Financial Times* (London), Apr. 1, 2016. https://www.ft.com/content/8e1219d8-f7e3-11e5-803c-d27c7117d132.

Labott, Elise. 2010. "U.S. Walks Tightrope in China-Japan Dispute." *CNN*, Sept. 24, 2010. https://edition.cnn.com/2010/POLITICS/09/24/us.china.japan/index.html.

Labrut, M. 2019. "Cosco Shipping Ports Inks Deal to Build $3bn Port in Chancay, Peru." *Seatrade Maritime*, May 15, 2019. https://www.seatrade-maritime.com/americas/cosco-shipping-ports-inks-deal-build-3bn-port-chancay-peru.

Lai, David. 2016. "The US-China Transition: Stage II." *The Diplomat*, June 30, 2016. https://thediplomat.com/2016/07/the-us-china-power-transition-stage-ii/.

Lau, Stuart. 2021. "Lithuania Pulls Out of China's '17+1' Bloc in Eastern Europe." *Politico*, May 21, 2021. https://www.politico.eu/article/lithuania-pulls-out-china-17-1-bloc-eastern-central-europe-foreign-minister-gabrielius-landsbergis/#.

Laurens, Cerulus. 2021. "Germany Falls in Line with EU on Huawei." *Politico*, Apr. 23, 2021. https://www.politico.eu/article/germany-europe-huawei-5g-data-privacy-cybersecurity/.

Larson, Deborah Welch, and Alexei Shevchenko. 2019. *Quest for Status: Chinese and Russian Foreign Policy*. New Haven, CT: Yale University Press.

Lee, Seung-Joo. 2022. "The US-China Technology War and Korea's Strategy." *East Asia Foundation*, May 10, 2022. http://www.keaf.org/book/EAF_Policy_Debate_The_US-China_Technology_War_and_South_Koreas_Strategy_kr.

Lee, Stacia. 2017. "The Cybersecurity Implications of Chinese Undersea Cable Investment. University of Washington, Henry M. Jackson School of International Studies." Henry M. Jackson School of International Studies, Jan. 25, 2017. https://jsis.washington.edu/news/cybersecurity-implications-chinese-undersea-cable-investment.

Lee, Yen Nee. 2021. "China Races to Rival the U.S. with Its Own GPS System—but One Analyst Says It Won't Overtake the U.S. Yet." CNBC, May 31, 2021. https://www.cnbc.com/2021/06/01/tech-war-chinas-beidou-gains-market-share-challenges-us-gps.html.

Lemoine, Joseph, and Yomna Gaafa. 2022. "There's More to China's New Global Development Initiative Than Meets the Eye." *New Atlanticist*, Aug. 18, 2022. https://www.atlanticcouncil.org/blogs/new-atlanticist/theres-more-to-chinas-new-global-development-initiative-than-meets-the-eye/.

Lendon, Brad. 2020. "Philippines Says It Won't End US Military Access Agreement Amid South China Sea Tensions." CNN, June 4, 2020. https://edition.cnn.com/2020/06/03/asia/philippines-us-agreement-south-china-sea-intl-hnk/index.html.

Leng, Sidney. 2020. "Coronavirus: China's Belt And Road Partners Call for More Cooperation on Public Health." *South China Morning Post*, June 19, 2020. https://www.scmp.com/news/china/diplomacy/article/3089925/coronavirus-chinas-belt-and-road-partners-call-more.

Leng, Thearith. 2015. "Navigating the Maritime Silk Road: Cambodia's Foreign Policy Options with China." Policy Forum (May). http://www.policyforum.net/navigating-the-maritime-silk-road/#sthash.merGyNUJ.dpuf.

———. 2019. "Underlying Factors of Cambodia's Bandwagoning with China's Belt and Road Initiative." *East Asia* 36, 243–53.

Lew, Linda, Mandy Zuo, and Simone McCarthy. 2021. "China Tilts to Covid-19 Vaccine Diplomacy as Domestic Jab Programme Lags." *South China Morning Post*, Feb. 15, 2021. https://www.scmp.com/news/china/diplomacy/article/3121766/china-tilts-covid-19-vaccine-diplomacy-domestic-jab-programme.

Lewis, Scott. 2019. "Best Project, Road/Highway: Thies-Touba Toll Expressway Project." ENR (Engineering News Record), Sept. 25, 2019. https://www.enr.com/articles/47612-best-project-roadhighway-thies-touba-toll-expressway-project#:~:text=This%20114%2Dkm%20expressway%20connects,with%20French%20codes%20and%20standards.

Li, Z. 2013. "An Analysis of India's Monroe Doctrine." *YaFeiZongheng* 4, 15–21.

Li-Chen, Sim, and Farkhod Aminjonov. 2020. "Potholes and Bumps Along the Silk Road Economic Belt in Central Asia." *The Diplomat*, Feb. 1, 2020.

190 | References

https://thediplomat.com/2020/02/potholes-and-bumps-along-the-silk-road-economic-belt-in-central-asia/.

Liberty Times. 2022. "Sri Lanka Collapse a Wake-Up Call." *Taipei Times*, July 20, 2022, 8.

Liberty Times Net (Taipei). 2016. "India Prime Minister Visit to the US: India and the US Should Prevent China from Expanding Its Power in South China Sea." June 10, 2016. http://news.ltn.com.tw/news/world/paper/999199.

Liu, Brian, and Raquel Leslie. 2022. "China's Tech Crackdown: A Year-in-Review." *Lawfare*, Jan. 7, 2022. https://www.lawfareblog.com/chinas-tech-crackdown-year-review.

Liu, Caiyu. 2021. "Quad's Billion-Dose Vaccine Plan Merely Exchange of Interests: Analysts." *Global Times*, Mar. 14, 2021. https://www.globaltimes.cn/page/202103/1218327.shtml.

Liu, Jianchao. 2014. "China's Asian Security Concept." *China Today*, May 23, 2014. http://www.chinatoday.com.cn/english/news/2014-05/23/content_620550.htm.

Liu, Zhen. 2022. "PLA Drills with Thai Military Amid Tensions with US." *South China Morning Post*, Aug. 21, 2022, A6.

Lo, Alex. 2022. "Enter India as China Snubs Sri Lanka Call." *South China Morning Post*, Aug. 13, 2022, A2.

Lo, Kinling. 2020. "US International Development Finance Corporation Targets Asia as Washington Seeks to Offer Alternative to Chinese Cash." *South China Morning Post*, Jan. 12, 2020. https://www.scmp.com/news/china/diplomacy/article/3045686/us-international-development-finance-corporation-targets-asia?-campaign=3045686&module=perpetual_scroll_0&pgtype=article.

Lobe, Jim. 2013. "Intra-Asian Security Ties Good for U.S." *Global Information Network*, June 12, 2013, 17.

Lu, Yang. 2016. *China-India Relations in the Contemporary World: Dynamics of National Identity and Interest*. Abingdon, UK: Routledge.

Lyle, Amaani. 2013. "National Security Advisor Explains Asia-Pacific Pivot." *American Forces Press Service*, Mar. 12, 2013. http://www.defense.gov/News/newsarticle.aspx?ID=119505.

Macrae, Penny. 2021. "Deep Freeze, but No Cold Turkey." This Week in Asia, *South China Morning Post*, Sept. 19–25, 16–17.

Magnier, Mark. 2021. "A More Accessible Arctic Becomes Proving Ground for US-China Military Jockeying." *South China Morning Post*, May 3, 2021. https://www.scmp.com/news/china/diplomacy/article/3132125/more-accessible-arctic-becomes-proving-ground-us-china.

Mahbubani, Kishore. 2020. *Has China Won?* New York: Hachette Books.

Malena, Jorge. 2021. "The Extension of the Digital Silk Road to Latin America: Advantages and Potential Risks." Council on Foreign Relations and Brazilian Center for International Relations, Jan. 19, 2021, 11–12.

Maoz, Zeev. 2010. *Networks of Nations: The Evolution, Structure, and Impact of International Networks, 1816–2001*. Cambridge: Cambridge University Press.

Marantidou, V. 2014. "Revisiting China's 'String of Pearls' Strategy: Places 'with Chinese Characteristics' and their Security Implications." *Issues & Insights* 14, no. 7 (June). http://csisprod.s3.amazonaws.com/s3fspublic/legacy_files/files/publication/140624_issuesi nsights_vol14no7.pdf.

Marcus, Jonathan. 2019. "Turkey Defies US as Russian S-400 Missile Defence Arrives." BBC, July 12, 2019. https://www.bbc.com/news/world-europe-48962885.

Mardell, Jacob. 2017. "The 'Community of Common Destiny' in Xi Jinping's New Era." *The Diplomat*, Oct. 25, 2017. https://thediplomat.com/2017/10/the-community-of-common-destiny-in-xi-jinpings-new-era/.

———. 2021. "China's Coronavirus Vaccines: For Many Countries, It's Not Political, It's The Only Choice." *South China Morning Post*, Feb. 20, 2021. https://www.scmp.com/news/china/diplomacy/article/3121766/china-tilts-covid-19-vaccine-diplomacy-domestic-jab-programme.

Marks, Simon. 2020. "How an African State Learned to Play the West off China for Billions." *Politico*, Feb. 7, 2020. https://www.politico.com/news/2020/02/07/ethiopia-china-west-power-competition110766.

Masood, Salman. 2019. "Pakistan to Accept $6 Billion Bailout from I.M.F." *New York Times*, May 12, 2019. https://www.nytimes.com/2019/05/12/world/asia/pakistan-imf-bailout.html.

McCarthy, Simone. 2021. "Coronavirus: China and US Reach 200 Million Vaccine Shots but Beijing Up Against Tight Supply." *South China Morning Post*, Apr. 22, 2021. https://www.scmp.com/news/china/science/article/3130655/coronavirus-china-and-us-both-mark-200-million-vaccine-shots.

McCoy, Alfred W. 2015. "The Geopolitics of American Global Decline." *Huffington Post*, June 8, 2015. http://www.huffingtonpost.com/alfred-w-mccoy/the-geopolitics-of-american-global-decline_b_7534046.html.

Mcdonald, Joe, Munir Ahmed, and Sylivester Domasa. 2018. "China's New Silk Road Hits Political and Financial Potholes." AP, Jan. 11, 2018. https://apnews.com/ce03e625a5234bffae78f2bdec76e3f6.

McGregor, Grady. 2021. "How Do China's COVID Vaccines Fare Against the Delta Variant?" *Fortune*, Aug. 31, 2021. https://fortune.com/2021/08/31/china-covid-vaccine-sinovac-sinopharm-delta-variant-effective/.

Mead, Nick Van. 2018. "China in Africa: Win-Win Development, or a New Colonialism?" *Guardian*, July 31, 2018. https://www.theguardian.com/cities/2018/jul/31/china-in-africa-win-win-development-or-a-new-colonialism#img-1.

Mehdi, S. Z. 2021. "Iran, China Sign Deal on 'Belt and Road' Project." *Anadalou Agency*, Mar. 27, 2021. https://www.aa.com.tr/en/asia-pacific/iran-china-sign-deal-on-belt-and-road-project/2190154.

Metropol TV Kenya. 2022. "State Refuses to Make SGR Contract Public." Jan. 19, 2022. https://www.youtube.com/watch?v=NjEKGAGv0l0.

Miller, Meredith. 2015. "China's Relations with Southeast Asia: Testimony before the U.S.-China Economic and Security Review Commission." National Bureau of Asian Research, May 13, 2015. http://www.uscc.gov/sites/default/files/Miller_Written%20Testimony_5.13.2015%20Hearing.pdf.

Miller, Tom. 2017. *China's Asian Dream*. London: Zed Books.

Ministry of Defence (Mindef), Singapore. 2013. Joint declaration on the second ASEAN Defence Ministers' Meeting Plus, Aug. 29, 2013. https://www.mindef.gov.sg/web/portal/mindef/news-and-events/latest-releases/article-detail/2013/Aug./2013aug29-news-releases-01811/.

Ministry of Foreign Affairs (MOFA), Japan. 1976. *Treaty of Amity and Cooperation in Southeast Asia*. https://www.mofa.go.jp/region/asia-paci/asean/treaty.html.

Ministry of Foreign Affairs of the People's Republic of China (MFA). 2020. "Remarks by H. E. Xi Jinping, President of the People's Republic of China, at the Opening Ceremony of the 17th China-ASEAN Expo and China-ASEAN Business and Investment Summit." Nov. 27, 2020. https://www.fmprc.gov.cn/mfa_eng/zxxx_662805/t1836117.shtml.

———. 2023. *The Global Security Initiative Concept Paper*. Feb. 21, 2023. https://www.fmprc.gov.cn/mfa_eng/wjbxw/202302/t20230221_11028348.html.

Mobley, Terry. 2019. "The Belt and Road Initiative: Insights from China's Backyard." *Strategic Studies Quarterly* 13 (3): 52–72.

Mochinaga, Dai. 2020. "The Expansion of China's Digital Silk Road and Japan's Response." *Asia Policy* 15, no. 1 (Jan.): 41–60.

Mok, Winston. 2015. "China's New Silk Road Plan Should Focus on Strategic Links to Southeast Asia." *South China Morning Post*, May 11, 2015. http://www.scmp.com/comment/insight-opinion/article/1789322/chinas-new-silk-road-plan-should-focus-strategic-links.

Moody's. 2017. "Kenya, Government of." Oct. 2, 2017. https://www.moodys.com/credit-ratings/Kenya-Government-of-credit-rating-806356852.

Morlin-Yron, Sophie. 2016. "This Is What Africans Really Think of the Chinese." CNN, Nov. 6, 2016. http://edition.cnn.com/2016/11/03/africa/what-africans-really-think-of-china/index.html.

Motamedi, Maziar. 2023. "What's Behind Iran and Russia's Efforts to Link Banking Systems?" Aljazeera, Feb. 8, 2023. https://www.aljazeera.com/news/2023/2/8/whats-behind-iran-and-russias-efforts-to-link-banking-systems.

Mu, Yongpeng. 2015. "The 21st Century Maritime Silk Road." *Financial Daily* (Karachi), Mar. 27, 2015.

Mundy, Simon, and Kathrin Hille. 2019. "The Maldives Counts the Cost of Its Debts to China." *Financial Times*, Feb. 11, 2019. https://www.ft.com/content/c8da1c8a-2a19-11e9-88a4-c32129756dd8.

Murray, Michelle. 2019. *The Struggle for Recognition in International Relations: Status, Revisionism, and Rising Powers*. New York: Oxford University Press.

Mutethya, Edith. 2022. "BRI Projects Light Up Africa's Prospects." *China Daily*, Jan. 6, 2022. https://www.chinadailyhk.com/article/254798.

Mwakio, Philip. 2017. "Kenya Railways Takes Delivery of 160-Ton Capacity Crane from China Read." *Standard Digital*, Oct. 26, 2017. https://www.standardmedia.co.ke/business/article/2001258471/kenya-railways-receives-heavy-duty-recovery-crane.

Mwangi, Nyawira. 2020. "China's Aid to Africa in Fighting COVID-19." CGTN, June 18, 2020. https://africa.cgtn.com/2020/06/18/chinas-aid-to-africa-in-fighting-covid-19/.

Nakashima, Ellen. 2019. "U.S. Pushes Hard for a Ban on Huawei in Europe, but the Firm's 5G Prices Are Nearly Irresistible." *Washington Post*, May 29, 2019. https://www.washingtonpost.com/world/national-security/for-huawei-the-5g-play-is-in-europe—and-the-us-is-pushing-hard-for-a-ban-there/2019/05/28/582a8ff6-78d4-11e9-b7ae-390de4259661_story.html.

National Development and Reform Commission (NDRC), People's Republic of China. 2015. *Vision and Actions on Jointly Building the Silk Road Economic Belt and 21st Century Maritime Silk Road*, Mar. 28, 2015. https://www.belt-androad.gov.hk/visionandactions.html.

National Security Strategy (NSS). 2022. Washington, DC: White House, United States of America, Oct. 2022. https://www.whitehouse.gov/wp-content/uploads/2022/10/Biden-Harris-Administrations-National-Security-Strategy-10.2022.pdf.

Nellis, Stephen, Karen Freifeld, and Alexandra Alper. 2022. "U.S. Aims to Hobble China's Chip Industry with Sweeping New Export Rules. Reuters, Oct. 10, 2022. https://www.reuters.com/technology/us-aims-hobble-chinas-chip-industry-with-sweeping-new-export-rules-2022-10-07/.

New Indian Express (Chennai). 2017. "China Offers 100 Billion Yuan for New Silk Road Initiative." May 14, 2017. http://www.newindianexpress.com/world/2017/may/14/china-offers-100-billion-yuan-for-new-silk-road-initiative-1604758.html.

Ng, Teddy, and Kinling Lo. 2021. "Chinese President Xi Jinping Offers Covid-19 Vaccines and Trade Ties in Bid to Keep Central and Eastern Europe on Side." *South China Morning Post*, Feb. 9, 2021. https://www.scmp.com/news/china/diplomacy/article/3121185/chinese-president-xi-jinping-offers-covid-19-vaccines-and.

Ng, Terry. 2020. "China Promises to Boost Belt and Road Health Projects Amid Coronavirus Pandemic." *South China Morning Post*, May 24, 2020. https://www.scmp.com/news/china/diplomacy/article/3085849/china-promises-boost-belt-and-road-health-projects-amid.

Ngeow, Chow-Bing. 2020. "COVID-19, Belt and Road Initiative and the Health Silk Road: Implications for Southeast Asia." *Friedrich-Ebert-Stiftung*, Oct. 22, 2020. https://www.fes-asia.org/news/health-silk-road-pub/.

Nikkei Asian Review. 2019. "Pakistan Dam in Spotlight as Contract Goes to Former China Critic." Jan. 11, 2019. https://asia.nikkei.com/Spotlight/Belt-and-Road/Pakistan-dam-in-spotlight-as-contract-goes-to-former-China-critic.

194 | References

Nyabiage, Jevans. 2021a. "China Promotes Peace Conference for Horn Of Africa Nations." *South China Morning Post*, Jan. 8, 2021. https://www.scmp.com/news/china/diplomacy/article/3162440/china-promotes-peace-conference-horn-africa-nations.

———. 2021b. "Coronavirus: China Seeks to Boost Influence by Filling 'Vaccine Vacuum' in Poor Nations." *South China Morning Post*, May 14, 2021. https://www.scmp.com/news/china/diplomacy/article/3133563/coronavirus-china-seeks-boost-influence-filling-vaccine-vacuum.

———. 2022a. "Beijing Buckles Down with Suez Investments." *South China Morning Post*, Jan. 2, 2022, A7.

———. 2022b. "Beijing Opens School to Teach Its Political Model in Africa." *South China Morning Post*, Feb. 28, 2022, A7.

Nyakazeya, Paul. 2018. "China Sued Again by Dubai Based Firm Over Djibouti Port." *East African Business Week*, Nov. 6, 2018. https://www.busiweek.com/china-sued-again-by-dubai-based-firm-over-djibouti-port/.

Nye, Joseph S. 2004. "Soft Power: The Means to Success in World Politics." Washington, DC: Public Affairs Press.

———. 2011. "Obama's Pacific Pivot." *Daily News Egypt*, Dec. 12, 2011. https://dailynewsegypt.com/2011/12/12/obamas-pacific-pivot/.

———. 2015. "American Hegemony or American Primary." *Azernews*, Mar. 11, 2015. https://www.belfercenter.org/publication/american-hegemony-or-american-primacy.

Oirere, Shem. 2021. "Kenya Railways to End SGR Contract with Afristar." *International Railway Journal*, Mar. 12, 2021. https://www.railjournal.com/africa/kenya-railways-to-end-sgr-contract-with-afristar/#:~:text=Kenya%20Railways%20to%20end%20SGR%20contract%20with%20Afristar.

Onea, Tudor A. 2014. "Between Dominance and Decline: Status Anxiety and Great Power Rivalry." *Review of International Studies* 40 (01): 125–52.

Organski, A. F. K. 1968. *World Politics*. 2d ed. New York: Knopf.

Organski, A. F. K., and Jacek Kugler. 1980. *The War Ledger*. Chicago: University of Chicago Press.

Osborn, Ted. 2011. "Hidden Weakness in China's Banks." *Wall Street Journal*, May 27, 2011. http://online.wsj.com/article/SB100014240527023045208045763470208760629818.htm.

Oseledko, Vyacheslav. 2018. "Central Asia's Economic Evolution from Russia to China." *Stratfor*, Apr. 5, 2018. https://worldview.stratfor.com/article/central-asia-china-russia-trade-kyrgyzstan-kazakhstan-turkmenistan-tajikistan-uzbekistan.

Oxford Analytica Daily Brief Service. 2009. "US/Vietnam: China Concern Promotes Security Ties." Apr. 16, 2009. https://dailybrief.oxan.com/Analysis/DB150506/US-VIETNAM-China-concern-promotes-security-ties.

———. 2012. "U.S.-Asian 'Pivot' Strategy Faces New Challenges." June 18, 2012. https://dailybrief.oxan.com/Analysis/DB176384/US-Asian-pivot-strategy-faces-new-challenges.

References | 195

———. 2015. "INDIA: Delhi Has Pivotal Role in China-West Rivalry." Feb. 2, 2015. https://doi.org/10.1108/OXAN-DB197394.

———. 2016a. "ASIA: Geopolitics Will Heat Up in the Indian Ocean." Jan. 4, 2016. https://dailybrief.oxan.com/Analysis/DB207597/Geopolitics-will-heat-up-in-the-Indian-Ocean.

———. 2016b. "SOUTH ASIA: China Foray into South Asia Is Risky for Both Sides." Apr. 21, 2016. https://doi.org/10.1108/OXAN-DB210673.

Pan, Che. 2023. "Fight at the Silicon Curtain." *South China Morning Post*, July 22, 2023, B3.

Pan, Chengxin, Matthew Clarke, and Sophie Loy-Wilson. 2019. "Local Agency and Complex Power Shifts in the Era of Belt and Road: Perceptions of Chinese Aid in the South Pacific." *Journal of Contemporary China* 28 (117): 385–99.

Panda, Ankit. 2017. "As Somali Pirates Return, Chinese Navy Boasts of Anti-Piracy Operations." *The Diplomat*, Apr. 17, 2017. https://thediplomat.com/2017/04/as-somali-pirates-return-chinese-navy-boasts-of-anti-piracy-operations/.

Page, Jeremy. 2014. "China Sees Itself at Center of New Asian Order." *Wall Street Journal*, Nov. 9, 2014. http://www.wsj.com/articles/chinas-new-trade-routes-center-it-on-geopolitical-map-1415559290.

Parikh, Anjana. 2019. "Silk Road Fund Gets 49% Stake in Saudi Arabia's ACWA Power." *Mercom*, July 5, 2019. https://www.mercomindia.com/silk-road-fund-stake-acwa-power.

Park, Albert. 2019. "Which Countries Have Benefited the Most from China's Belt and Road Initiative?" HKUST IEMS Thought Leadership Briefs no. 32. https://iems.ust.hk/publications/thought-leadership-briefs/park-countries-benefit-from-belt-and-road-initiative-tlb32.

Parthasarathy, G. 2016. "The Hindu Business Line: Watch Out for China's Naval Aggression." *Newstex Global Business Blogs* (Chatham), Mar. 9, 2016. https://www.thehindubusinessline.com/opinion/columns/g-parthasarathy/watch-out-for-chinas-naval-aggression/article8332134.ece.

———. 2017. "The Hindu Business Line: A Chinese Chakravyuha in South Asia." *Newstex Global Business Blogs* (Chatham), Jan. 25, 2017. https://www.the hindubusinessline.com/opinion/columns/g-parthasarathy/a-chinese-chakravyuha-in-south-asia/article64537557.ece.

Pasricha, Anjana. 2017. "India Launches South Asia 'Diplomacy' Satellite for Communication Services." *Voice of America (VOA)* (Lanham, MD), May 5, 2017. https://www.voanews.com/a/india-launches-south-asia-diplomacy-satellite-commercial-services/3839366.html.

Patey, Luke. 2020. "COVID-19 Pandemic Is No Soft Power Victory for China." Danish Institute for International Studies, Apr. 23, 2020. https://www.diis.dk/en/research/covid-19-pandemic-is-no-soft-power-victory-china.

———. 2022. *How China Loses*. Oxford: Oxford University Press.

196 | References

Pautasso, Diego. 2016. "The Role of Africa in the New Maritime Silk Road." *Revista Brasileira de Estudos Africanos* [*Brazilian Journal of African Studies*] 1 (2): 118–30.

People's Daily. 2010. "China, 'Stabilizer' of World Economy." Feb. 2, 2010. http://english.people.com.cn/ 90001/90778/90862/6885538.html.

Perlez, Jane. 2013. "China Criticizes Clinton's Remarks About Dispute with Japan over Islands." *New York Times*, Jan. 20, 2013. http://www.nytimes.com/2013/01/21/world/asia/china-criticizes-clintons-remarks-about-dispute-with-japan-over-islands.html?_r=0.

Pew Research Center. 2022. "Across 19 Countries, More People See the U.S. than China Favorably, but More See China's Influence Growing." June 29, 2022. https://www.pewresearch.org/fact-tank/2022/06/29/across-19-countries-more-people-see-the-u-s-than-china-favorably-but-more-see-chinas-influence-growing/.

Phuong, Nguyen. 2016. "Vietnam and the Maritime Silk Road." *ASEANFocus* 3, 10.

Piekos, William, and Elizabeth C. Economy. 2015. "Risks and Rewards of SCO Expansion." Council on Foreign Relations, July 7, 2015. https://www.cfr.org/expert-brief/risks-and-rewards-sco-expansion.

Pillsbury, Michael. 2016. *The Hundred-Year Marathon*. New York: St. Martin's Griffin.

Political Transcript Wire (Lanham). 2013. *Secretary of Defense Chuck Hagel Remarks at Malaysia's Institute of Defence and Security*. United States Department of Defense, Aug. 25, 2013.

———. 2018. U.S. Senate Judiciary Committee. Border Security and Immigration Subcommittee Hearing on Student Visa Integrity, June 6, 2018. https://www.judiciary.senate.gov/committee-activity/hearings/a-thousand-talents-chinas-campaign-to-infiltrate-and-exploit-us-academia.

Pollina, Elvira, and Giuseppe Fonte. 2021. "Italy Gives Vodafone 5G Deal with Huawei Conditional Approval—Sources." Reuters, May 31, 2021. https://www.reuters.com/technology/italy-gives-vodafone-5g-deal-with-huawei-conditional-approval-sources-2021-05-31/.

Power Technology. 2020. "Coca Coda Sinclair Hydroelectric Project." Oct. 1, 2020. https://www.power-technology.com/projects/coca-codo-sinclair-hydroelectric-project/.

Press Trust of India. 2019. "SCO Summit: PM Modi Hits Out at Trade Protectionism, Calls for Rules-Based Trading System." *Livemint*, June 14, 2019. https://www.livemint.com/news/india/pm-modi-hits-out-at-trade-protectionism-calls-for-rules-based-trading-system-1560518980446.html.

PTI. 2018. "China Asks Its Citizens Not to Travel to Maldives." *National Herald* (India). Feb. 5, 2018. https://www.nationalheraldindia.com/international/china-asks-its-citizens-not-to-travel-to-maldives.

Putz, Catherine. 2020. "Kyrgyz-Chinese Joint Venture Scrapped After Protests." *The Diplomat*, Feb. 20, 2020. https://thediplomat.com/2020/02/kyrgyz-chinese-joint-venture-scrapped-after-protests/.

Qian, Gang. 2010. "How Should We Read China's 'Discourse of Greatness'?" *China Media Project*, Feb. 23, 2010.

Rachman, Gideon. 2013. "The Shadow of 1914 Falls Over the Pacific Ocean." *Financial Times*, Feb. 5, 2013, 9.

———. 2021. "Russia and China's Plans for a New World Order." *Financial Times*, Jan. 23, 2021. https://www.ft.com/content/d307ab6e-57b3-4007-9188-ec9717c60023.

Radio Free Asia (RFA). 2019. "Laos and Its Dams: Southeast Asia's Battery, Built by China." https://www.rfa.org/english/news/special/china-build-laos-dams/.

———. 2021a. "Lao Village Farmland, Paddies Destroyed by Work on Lao-China Railway Line." Jan. 30, 2021. https://www.rfa.org/english/news/laos/covered-01292021182459.html.

———. 2021b. "Jakarta in Balancing Act as Ties Deepen with Beijing, Analysts Say." June 18, 2021. https://www.rfa.org/english/news/china/ties-06182021171542.html.

Rafique, G. 2015. "Countering India's Geopolitical Ambitions." *Pakistan Observer*, Apr. 7, 2015, 4.

RailFreight.com. 2021. "Kazakhstan Stops Trucks to Free Up Space for China-Europe-Trains." Mar. 2, 2021. https://www.railfreight.com/beltandroad/2021/03/02/kazakhstan-stops-trucks-to-free-up-space-for-china-europe-trains/?gdpr=accept.

Rajah, Roland, Alexandre Dayant, and Jonathan Pryke. 2019. "Ocean of Debt? Belt and Road and Debt Diplomacy in The Pacific." Lowy Institute, Oct. 21, 2019. https://www.Lowyinstitute.org/Publications/Ocean-Debt-Belt-And-Road-And-Debt-Diplomacy-Pacific.

Ramon-Berjano, Carola. 2018. "The Belt and Road Initiative: Infrastructure, Investments and Opportunities for Latin America." *Megatrend Review* 15 (3): 173–92.

Ranade, J. 2017. "CPEC: How Pakistan Is Losing Out to China." *Rediff News* (India), Apr. 10, 2017. http://www.rediff.com/news/column/cpec-how-pakistans-losing-out-to-china/20170410.htm.

Ranaraja, Yasiru, and Maya Majueran. 2020. "Is the Health Silk Road a Debt Trap of China's BRI for Sri Lanka?" CGTN, Apr. 25, 2020. https://news.cgtn.com/news/2020-04-25/Is-the-Health-Silk-Road-a-debt-trap-of-China-s-BRI-for-Sri-Lanka--PXqPCPd7Ta/index.html.

Ren, Daniel, and Pearl Liu. 2023. "In Search of Perfection." *South China Morning Post*, May 29, 2023, B3.

Ren, Huai-Feng, and Fu-Kuo Liu. 2013. "Transitional Security Pattern in the South China Sea and the Involvement of External Parties." *Issues and Studies* 49 (2): 103–45.

Ren, Na, and Liu Hong. 2019. "Domesticating 'Transnational Cultural Capital': The Chinese State and Diasporic Technopreneur Returnees." *Journal of Ethnic and Migration Studies* 45 (13): 2308–27.

Reuters. 2017. "China's 'Silk Road' Push Stirs Resentment and Protest in Sri Lanka." Feb. 2, 2017. http://www.in.reuters.com/article/us-sri-lanka-china-tonight-id NKBN15G5UT.

198 | References

———. 2021a. "Hungary Signs Letter of Intent to Produce Chinese Sinopharm Shots." Sept. 10, 2021. https://www.reuters.com/business/healthcare-pharmaceuticals/hungary-signs-letter-intent-produce-chinese-sinopharm-shots-2021-09-10/.

———. 2021b. "Peru's President Pedro Castillo Prioritizes China Ties in First Days in Office." *South China Morning Post*, Aug. 6, 2021. https://www.scmp.com/news/world/americas/article/3144037/perus-president-pedro-castillo-prioritises-china-ties-first.

Richburg, Keith B. 2021. "U.S. Pivot to Asia Making China Nervous." *Washington Post*, Nov. 17, 2021, A9.

Rinke, Andreas, and Miranda Murray. 2022. "Germany Blocks Chinese Stake in Two Chipmakers over Security Concerns." Reuters, Nov. 10, 2022. https://www.reuters.com/markets/deals/germany-block-chinese-takeover-semiconductor-firm-ers-electronic-handelsblatt-2022-11-09/.

Robles, Alan. 2021. "Calling the Shots." This Week in Asia, *South China Morning Post*, Mar. 21–27, 6–7.

Robles, Raissa. 2021. "Duterte's US$24 bn Question." This Week in Asia, *South China Morning Post*, Aug. 15–21, 12–13.

Robson, Seth. 2013. "China's Aggressive Tactics Turning Off Asian Neighbors." *Stars and Stripes*, June 25, 2013. https://www.stripes.com/migration/china-s-aggressive-tactics-turning-off-asian-neighbors-1.226581.

Roche, Elizabeth. 2017a. "China May Invite India to 'One Belt One Road' Meet, but Delhi Wary." *Mint* (New Delhi), Jan. 6, 2017. http://www.livemint.com/Politics/iwSTA1EPSjrcnxba0HghTO/china-may-invite-india-to-one-belt-one-road-meet-but-Delhi.html.

———. 2017b. "India, Bangladesh Likely to Sign Pacts Worth over $9 Billion." *Mint* (New Delhi), Apr. 10, 2017. https://www.livemint.com/Politics/i6Xjz3AqSDmXI0CSixIrAM/India-Bangladesh-likely-to-sign-pacts-worth-over-9-billion.html.

Rocknifard, Julia. 2019. "Mahathir's Belt and Road Balancing Act Confirms Malaysia's 'Middle Power' Ambitions." *South China Morning Post*, Apr. 25, 2019. https://www.scmp.com/week-asia/opinion/article/3007569/mahathirs-belt-and-road-balancing-act-confirms-malaysias-middle.

Rolland, Nadege. 2015. "China's New Silk Road." National Bureau of Asian Research, Feb. 12, 2015. http://www.nbr.org/research/activity.aspx?id=531.

———. 2020. "China's Pandemic Power Play." *Journal of Democracy* 31 (3). https://www.journalofdemocracy.org/articles/chinas-pandemic-power-play-2/.

Rusli, Andi Ibnu Masri. 2021. "How COVID-19 Pandemic Bolsters China's Influence toward Hegemonic Race in ASEAN." *Nation State Journal of International Studies* 4 (2): 178–203.

Sacks, David. 2021. "Countries in China's Belt and Road Initiative: Who's In and Who's Out." Council on Foreign Relations, Mar. 24, 2021. https://www.cfr.org/blog/countries-chinas-belt-and-road-initiative-whos-and-whos-out.

Saliu, Olatunji. 2019. "Feature: Nigeria's First Standard Gauge Railway Marks 900 Days of Safe Operation-Belt and Road Portal." *China.org.cn*, Jan. 15, 2019. http://www.china.org.cn/world/Off_the_Wire/2019-01/13/content_74366803. htm.

Sauvage, Gregoire. 2021. "France Shifts Policy on Aid to Africa to Counter Rising Chinese Influence." *France 24*, Mar. 6, 2021. https://www.france24.com/en/africa/20210306-france-shifts-policy-on-aid-to-africa-to-counter-rising-chinese-influence.

Schweller, Randall L., and Xiaoyu Pu. 2011. "After Unipolarity: China's Vision of International Order in an Era of U.S. Decline." *International Security* 36 (3): 41–72.

Seiwert, Eva. 2019. "India-Pakistan Tensions Test the Shanghai Cooperation Organization's Mettle." *The Diplomat*, Mar. 23, 2019. https://thediplomat.com/2019/03/india-pakistan-tensions-test-the-shanghai-cooperation-organizations-mettle/.

Serhan, Yasmeen, and Kathy Gilsinan. 2020. "Can the West Actually Ditch China?" *Atlantic*, Apr. 24, 2020. https://www.theatlantic.com/politics/archive/2020/04/us-britain-dependence-china-trade/610615/.

Servant, Jean-Christophe. 2019. "Will a New Port Make Tanzania 'Africa's Dubai'?" *The Nation*, Feb. 19, 2019. https://www.thenation.com/article/tanzania-china-bagamoyo-port/.

Sevastopulo, Demetri, and Joe Leahy. 2024. "Joe Biden Says Chinese Smart Cars Could Pose US Security Threat." *Financial Times*, Feb. 29, 2024. https://www.ft.com/content/40003f25-23e9-433f-83a3-a2244fb8b942.

Shaahunaaz, F. 2016. "Maldives Pledges Full Support for China's New Silk Road." *Mihaaru.com*, Nov. 22, 2016. en.mihaaru.com.maldives-pledges-full-support-for-China's-new-silk-road/.

Shahla, Arsalan. 2021. "China Signs 25-Year Deal with Iran in Challenge to the U.S." *Bloomberg*, Mar. 27, 2021. https://www.bloomberg.com/news/articles/2021-03-27/china-signs-25-year-deal-with-iran-in-challenge-to-the-u-s.

Shanghai Cooperation Organization (SCO). n.d. "About SCO." Official website. Accessed Mar. 3, 2024. http://eng.sectsco.org/about_sco/.

———. n.d. "Documents." Official website. Accessed Mar. 3, 2024. http://eng.sectsco.org/documents/.

———. n.d. "Secretariat." Official website. Accessed Mar. 3, 2024. http://eng.sectsco.org/secretariat/.

———. 2018. "Presentation of China Development Bank and SCO Interbank Association at SCO Headquarters." Jan. 22, 2018. http://eng.sectsco.org/news/20180122/377285.html.

Sharma, Palki. 2021a. "Gravitas Plus: China Is Weaponising the Belt and Road Initiative." *Wion*, Dec. 18, 2021. https://www.youtube.com/watch?v=8FGM9 LpCOFE.

200 | References

———. 2021b. "Gravitas Plus: What Does Xi Jinping Want? Inside the Mind of Chinese President." *Wion*, Nov. 13, 2021. https://www.youtube.com/watch?v=c4fGwG9Ai28.

Shepard, Wade. 2020a. "How China's Belt and Road Became a 'Global Trail of Trouble.'" *Forbes*, Jan. 29, 2020. https://www.forbes.com/sites/wadeshepard/2020/01/29/how-chinas-belt-and-road-became-a-global-trail-of-trouble/#22ebce04443d.

———. 2020b. "China's 'Health Silk Road' Gets a Boost from COVID-19." *Forbes*, Mar. 27, 2020. https://www.forbes.com/sites/wadeshepard/2020/03/27/chinas-health-silk-road-gets-a-boost-from-covid-19/#43fa3a6c6043.

Shih, Gerry. 2019. "In Central Asia's Forbidding Highlands, a Quiet Newcomer: Chinese Troops." *Washington Post*, Feb. 19, 2019. https://www.washingtonpost.com/world/asia_pacific/in-central-asias-forbidding-highlands-a-quiet-newcomer-chinese-troops/2019/02/18/78d4a8d0-1e62-11e9-a759-2b8541bbbe20_story.html.

Shull, Benjamin. 2017. "The Hungry Dragon." *Wall Street Journal* (Eastern ed.), Feb. 27, 2017, A17.

Shrivastava, C. 2016. "China Expansionism Engulfs India." *Alive* (New Delhi), June 2016. https://link.gale.com.proxy.lnu.se/apps/doc/A454365530/STND?u=vax univ& sid=bookmark-STND&xid=8a4a776a.

Sim, Dewey. 2022. "Macron Issues Warning as US and China Battle for Influence." *South China Morning Post*, Nov. 19, 2022, 3.

Simes Dimitri Jr., and Tatiana Simes. 2021. "Lost Decade." This Week in Asia, *South China Morning Post*, Aug. 29–Sept. 6, 2021.

Siow, Maria. 2021. "Code Switch." This Week in Asia, *South China Morning Post*, Nov. 21–27, 6–7.

———. 2022a. "Japan Boost Ties in Pacific Amid China Concerns." *South China Morning Post*, May 8, 2022, A9.

———2022b. "Quality over Quantity." This Week in Asia, *South China Morning Post*, Oct. 2–8, 6.

Smith, Helena. 2017. "Greece Blocks EU's Criticism at UN of China's Human Rights Record." *Guardian*, June 18, 2017. https://www.theguardian.com/world/2017/jun/18/greece-eu-criticism-un-china-human-rights-record.

Solana, Javier. 2012. "America's Perilous Pivot." *Project Syndicate*, Nov. 26, 2012. https://www.project-syndicate.org/commentary/america-s-strategic-shift-from-the-middle-east-to-asia-by-javier-solana.

Solomon, Salem. 2018. "Chinese Officials Arrested for Bribery Amid Kenya's SGR Corruption Inquiry." *Voice of America (VOA)*, Nov. 26, 2018. www.voanews.com/a/china-kenya-bribery/4673798.html.

Somaliland Sun. 2021. "U.S.-China Tech Fight Opens New Front in Ethiopia." May 23, 2021. https://www.somalilandsun.com/u-s-china-tech-fight-opens-new-front-in-ethiopia/.

Song, Miou. 2015. "21st Century Maritime Silk Road Matches Very Well with Brunei's Economic Diversification Drive." Xinhua News Agency, May 23, 2015. http://news.xinhuanet.com/english/2015-05/23/c_134263515.htm.

South China Morning Post (SCMP). 2015. "PLA Ships to Hold Naval Drills with Malaysia." Sept. 13, 2015, 7.

———. 2020. "China's US$62 Billion Belt and Road Project in Pakistan Risks Becoming Corridor to Nowhere." Mar. 4, 2020. https://www.scmp.com/news/asia/south-asia/article/3064849/chinas-us62-billion-belt-and-road-project-pakistan-risks.

———. 2021. "Myanmar Sentences 28 People to 20 Years in Jail for Torching Chinese-Run Factories." Reuters, May 28, 2021. https://www.scmp.com/news/asia/southeast-asia/article/3135217/myanmar-sentences-28-people-20-years-jail-torching-chinese.

———. 2022a. "Treat China the Same as Any Creditor in Debt Talks." Apr. 24, 2022, A9.

———. 2022b. "US$66m Chinese Loan Secured to Install Huawei Towers." Aug. 20, A10.

Spetalnick, Matt. 2013. "Obama Urges De-Escalation, Dialogue in China–Japan Maritime Row." Reuters, June 8, 2013. https://www.reuters.com/article/usa-china-maritime-idUSL1N0EK0K420130608.

Standish, Reid. 2021a. "China's Strategic Vaccine Diplomacy Gains a Foothold in the Balkans." Radio Free Europe, Radio Liberty, Feb. 16, 2021. https://www.rferl.org/a/china-strategic-vaccine-diplomacy-gains-a-foothold-in-the-balkans/31106320.html.

———. 2021b. "How Will Kyrgyzstan Repay Its Huge Debts to China?" Radio Free Europe, Radio Liberty, Feb. 27, 2021. https://www.rferl.org/a/how-will-kyrgyzstan-repay-its-huge-debts-to-china-/31124848.html.

Standish, Reid, Ljudmila Cvetkovic, and Maja Zivanovic. 2021. "China Deepens Its Balkans Ties Using Serbian Universities." Radio Free Europe, Radio Liberty, May 11, 2021. https://www.rferl.org/a/china-balkans-ties-using-serbian-universities/31249503.html.

State Council Information Office of the People's Republic of China. 2018. "China's Arctic Policy." Jan. 26, 2018. http://english.www.gov.cn/archive/white_paper/2018/01/26/content_281476026660336.htm.

State Council of the People's Republic of China. 2006. "The National Medium-and-Long Term Programme for Science and Technology Development (2006–2010): An Outline." https://www.itu.int/en/ITU-D/Cybersecurity/Documents/National_Strategies_Repository/China_2006.pdf.

Statista. 2019. "Annual Flow of Foreign Direct Investments from China to Sweden between 2009 and 2019." https://www.statista.com/statistics/720599/china-outward-fdi-flows-to-sweden/.

202 | References

Statistics Times. 2021. "Projected GDP Ranking." Oct. 21, 2021. https://statistics-times.com/economy/projected-world-gdp-ranking.php.

Stearns, Scott. 2013. "How Would US Attack on Syria Affect Washington's Asia Pivot?" *Voice of America (VOA)*, Aug. 30, 2013. https://www.voanews.com/a/how-would-us-attack-on-syria-affect-washingtons-asia-pivot/1740077.html.

Stevens, Philip. 2013. "China has thrown down gauntlet to America." *Financial Times*, Nov. 29, 2013. https://www.ft.com/content/569ac0a8-5764-11e3-b615-00144feabdc0.

Straits Times. 2016. "Envoy Says China 'Will Not Sit Idly By' if Its Interests Are Infringed Upon." Feb. 3, 2016. https://www.straitstimes.com/world/envoy-says-china-will-not-sit-idly-by-if-its-interests-are-infringed-upon.

———. 2020. "Mask Diplomacy: China Tries to Rewrite Coronavirus Narrative." Mar. 20, 2020. https://www.straitstimes.com/asia/east-asia/mask-diplomacy-china-tries-to-rewrite-coronavirus-narrative.

———. 2022. "Putin Seeks Stronger Ties with Brics Nations Amid Sanctions." June 24, 2022, A6.

Strangio, Sebastian. 2020. "Laos Stumbles Under Rising Chinese Debt Burden." *The Diplomat*, Sept. 7, 2020. https://thediplomat.com/2020/09/laos-stumbles-under-rising-chinese-debt-burden/.

———. 2021. "In Rare Three-Party Conclave, Vietnam Pushes Back Against Growing Chinese Influence." *The Diplomat*, Sept. 28, 2021. https://thediplomat.com/2021/09/in-rare-three-party-conclave-vietnam-pushes-back-against-growing-chinese-influence/.

Su, Ken Moriya. 2021. "Tanzania to Revive $10bn Indian Ocean Port Project with China." *Nikkei Asia.* June 27, 2021. https://asia.nikkei.com/Politics/International-relations/Indo-Pacific/Tanzania-to-revive-10bn-Indian-Ocean-port-project-with-China.

Submarine Telecoms Forum. 2019. "Japan-Guam-Australia North Cable System Begins Installation." Sept. 12, 2019. https://subtelforum.com/jga-north-cable-system-begins-installation.

Sukhankin, Sergey. 2021. "Tracking the Digital Component of the BRI in Central Asia, Part One: Exporting 'Safe Cities' to Uzbekistan." Jamestown China Brief 21, no. 3. https://jamestown.org/program/tracking-the-digital-component-of-the-bri-in-central-asia-part-one-exporting-safe-cities-to-uzbekistan/.

Sunday Times (Colombo). 2017. "Clashes Erupt as Govt Launches Southern Development Projects." Jan. 8, 2017. http://www.sundaytimes.lk/170108/news/clashes-erupt-as-govt-launches-southern-development-projects-223369.html.

Suneja, Kirtika. 2016. "India Plans to Block Entry of Cheap Chinese Goods." *Economic Times (Times of India)* (Mumbai). Oct. 28, 2016. http://www.economictimes.indiatimes.com/news/economy/policy/india-looks-to-cut-tariff-concessions-on-chinese-goods/articleshow/55102373.cms.

Sweeney, Pete. 2022. "China's Belt and Road Strafed by Vladimir Putin." *Reuters*, Mar. 3, 2022. https://www.reuters.com/breakingviews/chinas-belt-road-strafed-by-vladimir-putin-2022-03-03/.

Tagliapietra, Alberto. 2020. "The European Union Won't Be Fooled by China's Health Silk Road." German Marshall Fund of the United States, Sept. 2, 2020. https://www.gmfus.org/blog/2020/09/02/european-union-wont-be-fooled-chinas-health-silk-road.

Taipei Times. 2012. "China Rebuffs Calls for Talks on S. China Sea." July 13, 2012, A1.

Tammen, Ronald L., Jacek Kugler, and Douglas Lemke. 2017. "Foundations of Power Transition Theory." *Oxford Research Encyclopedias*, Oct. 26, 2017. https://oxfordre.com/view/10.1093/acrefore/9780190228637.001.0001/acrefore-9780190228637-e-296.

Tan, Chee-Beng. 2022. "China and Chinese Overseas: A Softer Soft Power[?] Policy Needed?" *ISEAS Perspectives*, Mar. 7, 2022, 5.

Tan, Su-Lin. 2022. "G-7's Infrastructure Plan Offers an Alternative to China's Belt and Road Initiative in a 'Deliberate Way.'" CNBC, June 28, 2022. https://www.cnbc.com/2022/06/28/new-g-7-infrastructure-plan-offers-alternative-to-china-belt-road-.html.

Tan, Xiaodong, Xiangxiang Liu, and Haiyan Shao. 2017. "Healthy China 2030: A Vision for Health Care." *ScienceDirect* 12 (C), 112–14.

Tang, Siew Mun. 2013. "Give the 'Dragon' Space to Grow." *New Straits Times*, June 4, 2013.

*Tani, Shotaro. 2021. "*Chinese Vaccines: Sinovac Needs Outweigh Doubts in Indonesia." *Nikkei Asian Review, June 28, 2021.* https://asia.nikkei.com/Spotlight/Coronavirus/COVID-vaccines/Chinese-vaccines-Sinovac-needs-outweigh-doubts-in-Indonesia.

Taniguchi, Takuya. 2020. "Should We Forget about the Asia-Africa Growth Corridor?" *Lettre du Centre Asie* 87, Oct. 19, 2020. https://www.ifri.org/en/publications/editoriaux-de-lifri/lettre-centre-asie/should-we-forget-about-asia-africa-growth.

Tarrosy, Istvan, and Zoltan Vörös. 2018. "China and Ethiopia, Part 1: The Light Railway System." *The Diplomat*, Feb. 22, 2018. https://thediplomat.com/2018/02/china-and-ethiopia-part-1-the-light-railway-system/.

Tedros, Adhanom Ghebreyesus. 2017. "Towards a Health Silk Road." World Health Organization, Aug. 18, 2017. https://www.who.int/director-general/speeches/detail/towards-a-health-silk-road.

Telecom Egypt. 2018. "Telecom Egypt Obtains US$200 Million Long-Term Financing with Chinese Financial Institutions Facilitated by Huawei." May 30, 2018. https://ir.te.eg/en/CorporateNews/PressRelease/66/Telecom-Egypt-obtains-US-200-million-long-term-financing-with-Chinese-financial-institutions-facilitated-by-Huawei.

204 | References

The Hindu Business Line. 2016. "India, China Explore Opportunities in Green Energy." Oct. 11, 2016. http://www.thehindubusinessline.com/economy/India-chin-explore-opportunities-in-green-energy/article9208419.ece.

———. 2020. "Greater Male Connectivity Project (GMCP)." *Civilsdaily*, Oct. 13, 2020. https://www.civilsdaily.com/news/greater-male-connectivity-project-gmcp-2/#:%7E:text=The%20GMCP%20consists%20of%20a,for%20commercial%20and%20residential%20purposes.

The News International. 2020. "China, Pakistan to Boost Health Corridor Sharing Technology." Oct. 4, 2020. https://www.thenews.com.pk/print/724434-china-pakistan-to-boost-health-corridor-sharing-technology.

The Star. 2021. "Laos-China Expressway to Be Ready in 10 Years." June 24, 2021. https://www.thestar.com.my/aseanplus/aseanplus-news/2021/06/24/laos-china-expressway-to-be-ready-in-10-years.

Tiezzi, Shannon. 2021. "China Holds Slimmed-Down Belt and Road Conference." *The Diplomat*, June 25, 2021. https://thediplomat.com/2021/06/china-holds-slimmed-down-belt-and-road-conference/.

———. 2022. "Elizabeth Economy on 'The World According to China.'" *The Diplomat*, Jan. 4, 2022. https://thediplomat.com/2022/01/elizabeth-economy-on-the-world-according-to-china/.

Times of India. 2020. "China Holds First FMs Meeting with Pakistan, Nepal, Afghanistan on Covid-19, BRI." July 27, 2020. https://timesofindia.indiatimes.com/world/china/china-holds-first-fms-meeting-with-pakistan-nepal-afghanistan-on-covid-19-bri/articleshow/77205916.cms.

Umbach, Frank. 2022. "How China's Belt and Road Initiative Is Faring." *Geopolitical Intelligence Services* (*GIS*). Apr. 8, 2022. https://www.gisreportsonline.com/r/belt-road-initiative/.

"University of Shanghai Cooperation Organization (SCO University)." Accessed Mar. 3, 2024. https://urfu.ru/en/international/international-projects/sco-university/.

UNCTAD. 2015. "India Leads Regional Foreign Direct Investment as Inflows to South Asia Rise by 16 Per Cent in 2014." June 24, 2015. https://unctad.org/press-material/india-leads-regional-foreign-direct-investment-inflows-south-asia-rise-16-cent-2014.

US Department of State. 2012. Briefing by Clinton in Phnom Penh on trip to Asia, July 12, 2012. https://2009-2017.state.gov/secretary/20092013clinton/rm/2012/07/194909.htm.

US Senate Committee on Science, Space, and Technology. 2018. "House Science, Space & Technology Subcommittees Issues Testimony from U.S.-China Economic and Security Review Commission." Apr. 11, 2018. www.govinfo.gov/content/pkg/CHRG-115hhrg29781/pdf/CHRG-115hhrg29781.pdf.

USTR. 2021. "Association of Southeast Asian Nations (ASEAN)." Office of the United States Trade Representative. https://ustr.gov/countries-regions/southeast-asia-pacific/association-southeast-asian-nations-asean.

Valencia, Mark J. 2014. "The East China Sea Disputes: History, Status, and Ways Forward." *Asian Perspective* 38 (2): 183–218.

Varathan, Preeti. 2018. "The Recent History of the Global Economy, in One Chart." *Quartz*, Jan. 23, 2018. https://qz.com/1183308/the-economic-reversal-of-asia-and-africa-in-one-striking-chart/.

Veramu, Joseph. 2021. "The Belt & Road Initiative Is Not a Plan for World Domination through Global Trading Networks." *Fiji Sun*, June 19, 2021. https://fijisun.com.fj/2021/04/11/the-belt-road-initiative-is-not-a-plan-for-world-domination-through-global-trading-networks/.

Verlare, Jikkie, and Frans Paul van der Putten. 2015. "One Belt, One Road: An Opportunity for EUs Security Strategy." Clingendael Policy Brief. The Hague: Netherlands Institute of International Relations.

Verma, Raj. 2020. "China's Diplomacy and Changing the COVID-19 Narrative." *International Journal* 75 (2): 248–58.

Visham, M. 2014. "China's Xi Touts 'Maritime Silk Road' on South Asia Tour." AFP, Sept. 15, 2014. https://www.yahoo.com/news/chinas-xi-begins-south-asia-tour-maldives-215155367.html?ref=gs.

Viswanath, Anurag. 2016. "Reviving the Silk Route via One Belt, One Road." *Financial Express* (New Delhi), Feb. 29, 2016. https://www.financialexpress.com/opinion/reviving-the-silk-route-via-one-belt-one-road/217271/.

Wall Street Journal. 2011. "China Tests Buddha-Tooth Diplomacy in Myanmar." Nov. 24, 2011. https://blogs.wsj.com/chinarealtime/2011/11/24/china-tests-buddha-tooth-diplomacy-in-myanmar/.

———. 2012. "The Bully of the South China Sea." Aug. 14, 2012, 16.

Wang, Jisi. 2011. "China's Search for a Grand Strategy—A Rising Great Power Finds Its Way." *Foreign Affairs* 90 (3): 68–79.

Wang, Orange. 2022. "US and China 'Sorely Need' to Resume Trade Talks, with Pact Seen as Catalyst." *South China Morning Post*, Feb. 28, 2022, A3.

———. 2023. Beijing will Boost Ukraine Imports, Kyiv Negotiator Told." *South China Morning Post*, July 22, 2023, A3.

Wang, Songyu, Yang Jun, and Peng Mengyao. 2021. "Rail Transit Along the 'Belt and Road' Will Accelerate Its Development in 2021!" *China One Belt One Road Network*, Dec. 27, 2021. https://mp.weixin.qq.com/s/UYPLnsiasMefHMpZ8kirLA.

Wang, Yuan-kang. 2010. "China's Response to the Unipolar World: The Strategic Logic of Peaceful Development." *Journal of Asian and African Studies* 45 (3): 554–67.

Wen, Jiabao. 2009. "Special Message by H. E. Wen Jiabao." *World Economic Forum*, Jan. 28. http://www.fmprc.gov.cn/eng/wjdt/zyjh/ t536429.htm.

Whalen, Jeanne. 2020. "U.S. Considers Cutting Trade with China's Biggest Semiconductor Manufacturer." *Washington Post*, Sept. 5, 2020. https://www.washingtonpost.com/technology/2020/09/05/us-weighs-trade-ban-smic/.

206 | References

Wheeler, Andre. 2018. "How Negotiations Gave Myanmar and China Both a Better Deal In Joint Port Project." *South China Morning Post*, Aug. 2, 2018. https://www.scmp.com/comment/insight-opinion/asia/article/2157848/how-negotiations-gave-myanmar-and-china-both-better.

Widakuswara, Patsy. 2021. " 'Build Back Better World': Biden's Counter to China's Belt and Road." *Voice of America (VOA)*, Nov. 4, 2021. https://www.voanews.com/a/build-back-better-world-biden-s-counter-to-china-s-belt-and-road/6299568.html.

Wignaraja, Ganeshan, Dinusha Panditaratne, Pabasara Kannangara, and Divya Hundlani. 2020. *Chinese Investment and the BRI in Sri Lanka*. London: Chatham House, the Royal Institute of International Affairs. https://www.chathamhouse.org/sites/default/files/CHHJ8010-Sri-Lanka-RP-WEB-200319.pdf.

Wines, Michael, and Edward Wong. 2009. "An Unsure China Steps onto the Global Stage." *New York Times*, Apr. 1, 2009, 31.

Wion. 2021. China Pledges to Build Polar Silk Road by 2025 to Tap Natural Resources." Mar. 6, 2021. https://www.wionews.com/world/china-pledges-to-build-polar-silk-road-by-2025-to-tap-natural-resources-368390.

———. 2022. "Gravitas: What Will China Do if Russia Invades Ukraine?" YouTube video, Feb. 16, 2022. https://www.youtube.com/watch?v=uwEvyXsrY9w.

Wilson, Tom. 2024. "World's Biggest Mining Project to Start after 27 Years of Setbacks and Scandals." Jan. 7, 2024. https://www.ft.com/content/80f37963-c718-4f8b-8d77-0f0d5b1c99fe.

Wishnick, Elizabeth. 2021. "Will Russia Put China's Arctic Ambitions on Ice?" *The Diplomat*, June 5, 2021. https://thediplomat.com/2021/06/will-russia-put-chinas-arctic-ambitions-on-ice/.

Wong, Chun Han. 2023. *Party of One: The Rise of Xi Jinping and China's Superpower Future*. London: Corsair.

Wong, Edward. 2010. "Chinese Military Seeks to Extend Its Naval Power." *New York Times*, Apr. 23, 2010. https://www.nytimes.com/2010/04/24/world/asia/24navy.html.

Wong, Kandy. 2022. "Ukraine War Casts Shadow over China's Belt and Road Ties with Russia-Led Eurasian Trade Bloc. *South China Morning Post*, June 11, 2022. https://www.scmp.com/economy/global-economy/article/3181259/ukraine-war-casts-shadow-over-chinas-belt-and-road-ties?module=perpetual_scroll_0&pgtype=article&campaign=3181259.

World Bank. 2022. "GDP, PPP (Current International $)." https://data.worldbank.org/indicator/NY.GDP.MKTP.PP.CD.

Worldometer. 2021. "COVID-19 Coronavirus Pandemic." Mar. 9, 2021. https://www.worldometers.info/coronavirus/.

Writer, S. 2021. "Eyeing Chinese Investment, Turkey Kicks off Canal Istanbul Project." *Nikkei Asia*, June 27, 2021. https://asia.nikkei.com/Politics/International-relations/Eyeing-Chinese-investment-Turkey-kicks-off-Canal-Istanbul-project.

Wu, Gang, and Yan Shuang. 2012. "Xi Pledges 'Great Renewal of Chinese Nation.'" *Global Times*, Nov. 30, 2012. https://www.globaltimes.cn/content/747443.shtml.

Wu, Huizhong, and Justin Spike. 2021. "Study: Chinese COVID Shot May Offer Elderly Poor Protection." AP, July 23, 2021. https://apnews.com/article/europe-middle-east-business-science-health-4b770731d5995e3bb49a1d8ec63febbd.

Wu, Huizhong, and Kristen Gelineau. 2021. "Chinese Vaccines Sweep Much of the World, Despite Concerns." AP, Mar. 2, 2021. https://apnews.com/article/china-vaccines-worldwide-0382aefa52c75b834fbaf6d869808f51.

Wu, Lunting. 2023. "China's Transition from the Belt and Road to the Global Development Initiative." *The Diplomat*, July 11, 2023. https://thediplomat.com/2023/07/chinas-switch-from-the-belt-and-road-to-the-global-development-initiative/.

Xiao, Anthony. 2020. "China's Belt and Road Initiative in a Post-Pandemic World." *Invesco Limited*, June 15, 2020. https://www.invesco.com/invest-china/en/institutional/insights/chinas-belt-and-road-initiative-in-a-post-pandemic-world.html.

Xinhua News Agency. 2011. "Chinese Buddha Sacred Tooth Relic Conveyed to Pagoda in Myanmar." Dec. 8, 2011. http://en.people.cn/90782/7670648.html.

———. 2013. "China Vows to Build Community of Common Destiny with ASEAN." Oct. 3, 2013. http://news.xinhuanet.com/english/china/2013-10/03/c_132770494.htm.

———. 2016a. "Economic Cooperation between China, CEE on Fast Track. *China Daily*, Nov. 7, 2016. http://www.chinadaily.com.cn/world/2016liattends SCOCCEEC/2016-11/07/content_27301528_2.htm.

———. 2016b. "Chinese-Built Broadband Gives Tanzania Premium Speed: Official." Dec. 3, 2016. http://www.xinhuanet.com/english/2016-12/03/c_135878368.htm.

———. 2017a. "Chinese-Funded Silkroad International Bank Opens in Djibouti." *China Daily*, Jan. 19, 2017. http://www.chinadaily.com.cn/business/2017-01/19/content_27999949.htm.

———. 2017b. "'Belt and Road'" Incorporated into CPC Constitution." Oct. 24, 2017. http://www.xinhuanet.com/english/2017-10/24/c_136702025.htm.

———. 2017c. "Constructive Role in 16+1, SCO Show China as Responsible Power." *Beijing Review*, Nov. 5, 2017. http://www.bjreview.com/Latest_Headlines/201712/t20171206_800111564.html.

———. 2018. "Feature: Ethiopia-Djibouti Railway Winning Hearts of Passengers." Mar. 25, 2018. http://www.xinhuanet.com/english/2018-03/25/c_137064573.htm.

———. 2019a. "China-Arab Health Forum Opportunity for Fruitful Dialogue: Arab League." Feb. 22, 2019. http://www.xinhuanet.com/english/2019-08/23/c_138330081.htm.

———. 2019b. "Belt of Security and 'Road' to Development for SCO in Challenging Times." *China Daily*, June 13, 2019. https://www.chinadailyhk.com/articles/236/176/172/1560408041975.html.

208 | References

———. 2020a. "Xi Says China to Send More Medical Experts to Italy." Mar. 17, 2020. http://www.xinhuanet.com/english/2020-03/17/c 138884664.htm.

———. 2020b. "Commentary: Let the Community with Shared Future Vision Shine Brighter." Mar. 24, 2020. http:// www.xinhuanet.com/english/2020-03/24/c_138912849.htm.

———. 2021a. "Commentary: Bolivian Highway Project, a Vivid Symbol of China; LatAm Win-Win Cooperation." Feb. 6, 2021. http://www.xinhuanet.com/english/2020-02/07/c_138763739.htm.

———. 2021b. "More Southeast Asian Nations Embrace Chinese Vaccines to Fight COVID-19." Feb. 28, 2021. https://www.globaltimes.cn/page/202102/1216753.shtml.

———. 2021c. "Thailand Signs Three Contracts for Thai-Chinese High-Speed Railway." Mar. 29, 2021. http://www.xinhuanet.com/english/2021-03/29/c_139844694.htm.

———. 2022. "Zimbabwean President Thanks China for Additional Donation of 10 mln COVID-19 Vaccines." Jan. 13, 2022. http://www.xinhuanet.com/english/20220113/18e70a79b156495c861dbd0d9c7f300e/c.html.

Xinhuanet. 2018a. "Commentary: The 'Shanghai Spirit' Shows Its Strength." May 30, 2018. http://www.xinhuanet.com/english/2018-05/30/c_137217942.htm.

Xinhuanet. 2018b. "SCO Economic Cooperation Sees Remarkable Progress." May 31, 2018. http://www.xinhuanet.com/english/2018-05/31/c_137220715.htm.

———. 2021. "Thailand Receives 1st Batch of COVID-19 Vaccines from China's Sinovac." Feb. 24, 2021. http://www.xinhuanet.com/english/2021-02/24/c_1397 63953.htm.

Xu, Keyue, and Cao Siqi. 2021. "Xi Chairs China-CEEC Summit, Charts Course for Post-Pandemic Cooperation." *Global Times*, Feb. 10, 2021. https://www.globaltimes.cn/page/202102/1215475.shtml.

Yamei. 2018. "Commentary: The 'Shanghai Spirit' Shows Its Strength." *Xinhuanet*, May 30, 2018. http://www.xinhuanet.com/english/2018-05/30/c_137217942.htm.

Yang, Xiangfeng. 2021. "US-China Crossroads Ahead: Perils and Opportunities for Biden." *Washington Quarterly* 44 (1): 129–53.

Yeo, Andrew I. 2019. *The State of Asian Regionalism and Current Developments in the Context of China's Rise*. Unpublished manuscript prepared for the workshop on "China and Asian Regionalism," Rajaratnam School of International Studies, Nanyang Technological University, Singapore, Aug. 7, 2019, 22.

Yeung, Benjamin. 2008. "China in the Era of Globalization: The Emergence of the Discourse on Economic Security." *Pacific Review* 21 (5): 635–60.

Yilmaz, Serafettina, and Wang Xiangyu. 2019. "Power Transition Theory Revisited." *China Quarterly of International Strategic Studies* 5 (3): 317–41.

Yong, Charissa. 2022. "The Geopolitical Realities of Ream Naval Base." *Straits Times*, June 27, 2022, A17.

———. 2023. "Pushback in the U.S. Against Engagement with China." *Straits Times*, July 31, 2023. https://www.straitstimes.com/opinion/pushback-in-the-us-against-engagement-with-china.

Yong, Hee Kong. 2016. "China's infrastructure financing diplomacy." *New Straits Times*, Aug. 2, 2016. https://www.nst.com.my/news/2016/08/162345/chinas-infrastructure-financing-diplomacy.

York, Geoffrey. 2013. "Why China Is Making a Big Play to Control Africa's Media." *Toronto Globe and Mail*, Sept. 11, 2013. https://www.theglobeandmail.com/news/world/media-agenda-china-buys-newsrooms-influence-in-africa/article14269323/.

Yu, Kien-Hong Peter. 2003. "The Chinese (Broken) U-Shaped Line in the South China Sea: Points, Lines, and Zones." *Contemporary Southeast Asia* 25 (3): 405–30.

Yu, Yongding. 2009. "China's Policy Responses to the Global Financial Crisis." Richard Snape Lecture, Productivity Commission, Melbourne, Nov. 25, 2009. https://www.pc.gov.au/news-media/speeches/yongding/2009-yongding.pdf.

Yuen, Yee William. 2021. "Explaining China's Relationship with Indonesia, Its Gateway to Southeast Asia." *SupChina*, Dec. 2, 2021. https://supchina.com/2021/12/02/explaining-chinas-relationship-with-indonesia-its-gateway-to-southeast-asia/.

Zaini, Khairulanwar. 2021. "China's Vaccine Diplomacy in Southeast Asia: A Mixed Record." *ISEAS Perspective*, June 24, 2021. https://www.iseas.edu.sg/articles-commentaries/iseas-perspective/2021-86-chinas-vaccine-diplomacy-in-southeast-asia-a-mixed-record-by-khairulanwar-zaini/.

Zhang, Pepe. 2019. "Belt and Road in Latin America: A Regional Game Changer?" *Atlantic Council*, Oct. 8, 2019. https://www.atlanticcouncil.org/in-depth-research-reports/issue-brief/belt-and-road-in-latin-america-a-regional-game-changer/.

Zhang, Phoebe. 2020. "TCM Can't Stop People Getting Covid, Expert Says." *South China Morning Post*, Aug. 21, 2020, A6.

Zhang, Rachel. 2021. "China Looks to Central Asia on Security to Create 'Safe Silk Road.'" *South China Morning Post*, May 14, 2021. https://www.scmp.com/news/china/diplomacy/article/3133520/china-looks-central-asia-security-create-safe-silk-road.

Zhang, Zhexin. 2019. "The Belt-and-Road Initiative: China's New Geopolitical Strategy?" *China Quarterly of International Strategic Studies* 4 (3): 327–43.

Zheng, Sarah. 2021. "China Offers Vaccines, Projects in Bid to Shore Up Relations with Central Asian Neighbours." *South China Morning Post*, May 13, 2021. https://www.scmp.com/news/china/diplomacy/article/3133319/china-holds-infrastructure-goodies-bid-shore-relations-central.

Zheng, Shuwen, and Ying Xia. 2021. *Private Security in Kenya and the Impact of Chinese Actors*. Working Paper No. 2021/44. China Africa Research Initiative, School of Advanced International Studies, Johns Hopkins University, Washington, DC. http://www.sais-cari.org/publications.

References

Zhou, Laura. 2019. "Ethiopia in Talks with China to Ease 'Serious Debt Pressure' Tied to New Silk Road Rail Link, Envoy Says." *South China Morning Post*, Mar. 24, 2019. https://www.scmp.com/news/china/diplomacy/article/3002957/ethiopia-talks-china-ease-serious-debt-pressure-tied-new-silk.

———. 2021. "China and US Go Dose to Dose in Covid-19 Vaccine Donations to El Salvador." *South China Morning Post*, July 4, 2021. https://www.scmp.com/news/china/diplomacy/article/3139703/china-and-us-go-dose-dose-covid-19-vaccine-donations-el.

Zhou, Viola. 2016. "Belt and Road Set to Deliver Significant Boost to China Railway." *South China Morning Post*, Aug. 14, 2016. https://www.scmp.com/business/companies/article/2003669/belt-and-road-set-deliver-significant-boost-china-railway.

Zhou, Xiaochuan. 2009. "Reform the International Monetary System." People's Bank of China. https://www.bis.org/review/r090402c.pdf.

Ziromwatela, Raphael, and Changfeng Zhao. 2016. "Africa in China's One Belt, One Road Initiative: A Critical Analysis." *ISOR Journal of Humanities and Social Sciences* 21, 21–34.

Zweig, David, and Kang Siqin. 2020. "America Challenges China's National Talent Programs." Center for Strategic & International Studies (CSIS). https://www.csis.org/analysis/america-challenges-chinas-national-talent-programs.

References in Chinese

21st Century Economic Times (Beijing). 2015. "Ping jishu ping jiage Zhong-Ri jiaozu chao 10 wanyi Riyuan Yindu tielu shichang" [Competing on skills and prices China and Japan lock horns on more than 10 thousand million Yen worth of India's railway market]. Dec. 21, 2015. http://epaper.21jingji.com/html/2015-12/24/content_28230.htm.

Channel News Asia (Singapore). 2015. "Zhong-Yin IT canye yuanqu luojiao Guizhou" [China-India IT industrial park set foot on Guizhou]. May 25, 2015. http://www.worldjournal.com/3262166/article-%E4%B8%AD%E5%8D%B0it%E7%94%A2%E6%A5%AD%E5%9C%92%E5%8D%80-%E8%90%BD%E8%85%B3%E8%B2%B4%E5%B7%9E/?ref=%E4%B8%AD%E5%9B%BD.

China Times (Taipei). 2014. "Lu za 50 yi Meiyuan Yindu gai gongye yuanqu" [Mainland spends 5 billion American dollars in India to build industrial park]. Sept. 7, 2014. http://www.chinatimes.com/newspapers/20140907000080-260203.

Hu, Zhengyuan. 2017. " 'Yidai yilu' zhanlue, Zhonggong zhongyang dangxiao chubanshe" [The "One Belt One Road" Strategy]. Beijing: Chinese Communist Party Central Party School.

Lianhe Zaobao (Singapore). 2015. "Yindu Zhongguo wenti zhuanjia Xiegang: Zhongguo dui Yazhou zhanlue yijing couxiao [Indian China affairs expert

Srikanth: China's Asia strategy already operates]. Oct. 5, 2015. http://www.zaobao.com/news/china/story20161005-674063.

Lin, Xujia. 2020. "FangOu shoucuo dao Dongnanya qunuan Wangyi mengda yimiao waijing maopai lalong" [Frustrated in his visit to Europe, warming up in Southeast Asia, Wang Yi hard sells the vaccination diplomatic trade card]. *NewTalk News*, Oct. 15, 2020. https://newtalk.tw/news/view/2020-10-15/479960.

Phoenix Television (Hong Kong). 2017. "Bajisitan ren weihe dui Zhongguo xiangmu ruci xin'gan qingyuan datouru" [Why Pakistanis are so willing to get greatly involved in Chinese projects]. May 8, 2017. http://news.ifeng.com/a/20170508/51058023_0.shtml.

Sina (Hong Kong). 2015. "ZhongRi Yindu tielu shichang jingzheng riqu bairi Zhngguo youxing jiabi youshi" [Rivalry between China and Japan for India's railway market growths white-hot China intends to compete on price advantage]. Dec. 2, 2015. http://sina.com.hk/news/article/20151224/0/2/2/%E4%B8%AD%E6%97%A5%E5%8D%B0%E5%BA%A6%E9%90%B5%E8%B7%AF%E5%B8%82%E5%A0%B4%E7%AB%B6%E7%88%AD%E6%97%A5%E8%B6%A8%E7%99%BD%E7%86%B1-%E4%B8%AD%E5%9C%8B%E6%9C%89%E6%80%A7%E5%83%B9%E6%AF%94%E5%84%AA%E5%8B%A2-1647964.html.

Wang, Hao, Shiban Mingfu, and Cheng Xiaonong. 2023. "Zhongguo jingji can, shenxian ye nanjiu!" [China's Economy Terrible, Hard Even for Saints and Fairies to Help!] Sanguo Yanyi Program. China Television (Taiwan), July 22, 2023. https://www.youtube.com/watch?v=Noo71y3u3-8.

Xinhua News Agency. 2017. "Gòng jiàn "yīdài yīlù": Lǐniàn, shíjiàn yǔ zhōngguó de gòngxiàn" [Together Build "One-Belt-One Road": Concept, Practice and China's Contribution]. May 10, 2017. http://www.xinhuanet.com/politics/2017-05/10/c%5f1120951928.htm.

Xinhuanet. 2017. "Mei meijie cheng Zhongguo chaoyue MeiYing chang Feizhou xuesheng zhuyao liuxuedi: Zhangxian Zhongguo ruanzhili" [US media claims that China has surpassed the US and UK to become the main destination for African students to study abroad: demonstrating China's soft power]. July 3, 2017. http://big5.xinhuanet.com/gate/big5/us.xinhuanet.com/2017-07/03/c_129646085.htm.

Zhou, Yongjie. 2015. "Yinni zhuanjia: Yidai yilu keneng you junsi dongji" [Indonesian expert: One Belt One Road may contain military motivations]. Central News Agency, June 3, 2015. http://www.msn.com/zh-tw/news/other/%E5%8D%B0%E5%B0%BC%E5%B0%88%E5%AE%B6%E4%B8%80%E5%B8%B6%E4%B8%80%E8%B7%AF%E5%8F%AF%E8%83%BD%E6%9C%89%E8%BB%8D%E4%BA%8B%E5%8B%95%E6%A9%9F/ar-BBkCunY.

Index

Abe, Shinzo, 25, 33
Abuja–Kaduna railway (Nigeria), 137
Addis Ababa city light-rail transit
    system (Ethiopia), 109
Addis Ababa-Djibouti railway
    (Djibouti), 109
Aden Gulf, 108
ADIZ. *See* air defense identification
    zone
Advisory Council of the Belt and Road
    Forum, 170n3
Afghanistan, 46–47, 128–129
Africa
    Asia-Africa Growth Corridor, 155
    Confucius Institutes in, 114
    Forum on China-Africa
        Cooperation, 107
    HSR COVID-19 diplomacy to, 125
    Rwanda, 113
    Senegal, 137–138, 156
    Seychelles, 102–103
    West, 137–138, 156
    Zambia, 157–158
Africa, East, 107
    Ethiopia, 108, 109–110, 148
    Kenya, 108, 110–111, 115, 116,
        125
    MSR projects in, 108–116
African Union, 121, 137
Afrobarometer, 116

agricultural cooperation agreements, 13
Ahmed, Abiy, 109
AIIB. *See* Asian Infrastructure
    Investment Bank
air defense identification zone (ADIZ),
    25
Alaska (US), 152
Alibaba, 144, 148–149
Amazon Waterway Project, 142
"America's Pacific Century" *(Foreign
    Policy)*, 30
Android, 147
anti-Chinese sentiment
    among Central Asian population, 55
    for Filipinos, 85
    in Kyrgyzstan, 56
    in Pakistan, 69
    in Vietnam, 77, 83
Aquino, Benigno, III, 37
the Arctic, 150–152
ARF. *See* ASEAN Regional Forum
Argentina, 141
Armitage, Richard, 24–25
arms, Southeast Asian countries
    purchasing, 83
ASEAN. *See* Association of Southeast
    Asian Nations
ASEAN Defense Ministers' Meeting,
    Pivot to Asia involvement with,
    35

214 | Index

ASEAN Regional Forum (ARF), 26, 27, 28, 34
Asia-Africa Growth Corridor, 155
Asian Development Bank, 134
Asian Forum for Polar Sciences, 152
Asian Infrastructure Investment Bank (AIIB), 8, 9, 42, 48, 97, 129, 156, 157
Asia-Pacific, 30–31, 125
Association of Southeast Asian Nations (ASEAN), 169nn1–2. *See also* Southeast Asia
   Biden's infrastructure pledge to, 157
   Bush, George W., presidency disengagement with, 30, 31
   CAFTA, 21, 31, 34, 73
   China-ASEAN Maritime Cooperation Fund, 75
   Defense Ministers' Meeting, 35
   HSR influencing, 122
   MSR impacting, 72, 88–89
   RCEP of, 40
   on South China Sea disputes, 26, 27, 28
   Treaty of Amity and Cooperation, 32, 34–35
Australia, 11, 140, 148, 154, 158–159
authoritarianism, of China's internet model, 146

Bagamoyo port (Tanzania), 112, 116
Bajwa, Asim Saleem, 69
Baloch Raaji Aajoi Sangar, 68
Baltic states, 62, 148
Bangladesh, 97–99, 105
Bangladesh-China-India-Myanmar initiative (BCIM), 97, 105
Beidou Navigation Satellite System, 144
Belarus, 58, 156
Belt and Road: A Chinese World Order (Maçães), 16

Belt and Road High Level Meeting on Health Cooperation towards Health Silk Road, 119
The Belt and Road Initiative: Law, Economics, and Politics (Chaisse and Górski), 15
The Belt and Road Initiative: The Threat of an Economic Cold War with China (Rosenberg), 16
Belt-and-Road Initiative (BRI). *See specific topics*
Biden, Joe, 36, 52, 150, 153, 154, 155, 157, 164, 165
Biden administration, 149–150, 152, 156, 157
BioNTech COVID-19 vaccines, 128, 129
Bishkek Power Plant (Kyrgyzstan), 49, 55–56
Blinken, Anthony, 152, 165
Bolivia, 141
Brazil, 125, 141
BRI. *See* Belt-and-Road Initiative
Bridge Consulting, 125
bridge development projects, BRI
   Foundiougne Bridge, 137–138
   Friendship Bridge, 96
   Nyerere Bridge, 111–112, 116
   Yavuz Sultan Selim Bridge, 57
Brunei, MSR support of, 77
Budapest-Belgrade railway (Hungary), 61
Buddhism, 85, 95, 100
Build Back Better World, xiii, 155, 156–157
Bush, George W., 30, 31, 34

CAFTA. *See* China-ASEAN Free Trade Area
Cambodia, 33, 76, 78, 79, 82–83, 135, 160
Campbell, Kurt, 36
Canada, 148

Index | 215

Caribbean, 140–142
Castillo, Pedro, 142
CCP. *See* Chinese Communist Party
Central Asia
China's forum with, 55
Kazakhstan, 7, 11, 48, 49, 55
Kyrgyzstan, 48, 49, 55–56
Sino-Russian rivalry over, 54
Uzbekistan, 46, 48, 56, 118
Chabahar port (Iran), 103
Chaisse, Julien, 15
Chan, Gerald, 16
Chancay Port Terminal (Peru), 142
Chile, 142
China. *See specific topics*
China Academy of Sciences, 143
China Bridge and Road Corp, 137
China Communications Construction
Company, 92
China Daily, 114
China Development Bank, 8, 9, 48,
84, 121, 145, 151
The China Dream (Liu Mingfu), 42
China Export-Import Bank. *See* Exim
Bank
China Harbor Engineering Company,
92, 93
China International Development
Cooperation Agency, 162
China Merchants Holdings Company,
92, 109, 112
China Merchants Port Holdings, 93
China Ocean Shipping Company
Shipping Ports Limited
(COSCO), 141–142, 150
China Power International Holding, 55
China Railway International, 79
China seas
East China Sea, 22, 23–25
South China Sea, 22, 26–29, 34,
77–78, 87, 159
US-China rivalry in, 21–29, 159

China Southern Power Grid, 82
China-Arab Health Cooperation
Forum, 120
China-ASEAN Free Trade Area
(CAFTA), 21, 31, 34, 73
China-ASEAN Maritime Cooperation
Fund, 75
China-Central and Eastern European
Countries (China-CEEC), 43–
44, 58, 59, 60–61, 62–63, 64,
123
China-Pacific Islands Forum summit,
140
China-Pakistan Economic Corridor
(CPEC), xi, 44, 64, 65
Gwadar port of, 66–67, 90, 102
India's opposition to, 102
security challenges of, 68–69, 158
China's Asian Dream (Miller), 15
China's Digital Silk Road (Chan), 16
Chinese Communist Party (CCP), xi,
7, 11, 19, 160, 163, 166
chips, computer, 149–150, 157, 165
Chittagong-Kunming highway
(Bangladesh), 98
Chung, Chien-peng, 88
CICA. *See* Conference on Interaction
and Confidence Building in Asia
Clinton, Hillary, 35, 36, 41
ARF statements of, 27, 28, 34
on Asia-Pacific strategy, 30–31
on Diaoyu/Senkaku Islands, 24, 25
Vietnam visit of, 26, 27
Coca Codo Sinclair hydroelectric dam
(Ecuador), 141
Collective Security Treaty Organization,
49
Colombo (Sri Lanka), 91, 92, 94–95
Commission on the Limits of the
Continental Shelf, UN, 21
common prosperity *(gong fu)*, 149
complex interdependence, 13, 14

216 | Index

Comprehensive and Progressive Trans-Pacific Partnership (CPTPP), 40
Conference on Interaction and Confidence Building in Asia (CICA), 8, 40, 75
Confucius Institutes, 86–87, 114, 160
Connectivity and Standards Action Plan, BRI, 146
constitution, CCP, 11
Conte, Giuseppe, 121
corruption, in Central Asia, 49
COSCO. *See* China Ocean Shipping Company
Covax Facility, 123
COVID-19 pandemic, 4, 11, 89, 170n1
  China's border closure due to, 55
  CPEC impacted by, 68
  Delta variant of, 124, 128, 129, 161
  HSR diplomacy for, 60, 117–118, 120–130
  ICT promoted during, 144
  lockdowns, 149, 161, 166
  Maldive's tourism industry impacted by, 97
  Omicron variant of, 129, 161, 166
  origin inquiry into, 154
  Suez Canal economic zone impacted by, 116
  vaccines, 61, 121–123, 124, 125–126, 128, 129, 130, 142, 159
  Xi's social distancing for, 50
CPEC. *See* China-Pakistan Economic Corridor
CPTPP. *See* Comprehensive and Progressive Trans-Pacific Partnership
crude oil, 111, 159
cultural-education exchanges, SCO, 50–51
currencies, global, 39, 40, 50, 164, 169n2

Dar es Salaam (Tanzania), 111–112
DBAR. *See* Digital Belt and Road
debt
  to Exim Bank, 61–62, 161
  of Kyrgyzstan, 56
  of Sri Lanka, 93
  trap diplomacy, 12, 114, 135, 155, 158
Delta variant, COVID-19, 124, 128, 129, 161
Denmark, 151
DeWe Security Service, 116
Diamer-Basha Dam (Pakistan), 68
Diaoyu/Senkaku Islands (East China Sea), 22, 23–25
diaspora, Chinese, 86
Didi, 148–149
difang rongzi pingtai gongsi (local investment platform companies), 18
Digital Belt and Road (DBAR), 143
Digital Silk Road (DSR), xii, 2, 5, 142–143, 144–145, 146–150, 157
Djibouti, MSR projects in, 108–109
dollar, US, 39, 40
Donilon, Tom, 32
DSR. *See* Digital Silk Road
Dubai (UAE), 145
Duterte, Rodrigo, 78, 85

East Asia Summit (EAS), 27, 34–35, 169n2
East China Sea, Diaoyu/Senkaku Islands in, 22, 23–25
Ecuador, Coca Codo Sinclair hydroelectric dam in, 141
EEZ. *See* exclusive economic zone
Egypt, MSR projects in, 113, 116
eHub, 144
El Espino–Boyuibe Highway Project (Bolivia), 141
El Salvador, COVID-19 vaccines in, 130

electric vehicles, from China, 165
Electricite du Laos, 82
The Emperor's New Roads (Hillman), 15–16
energy security, MSR strategy of, 77
Erdogan, Recep Tayyip, 57
Estonia, 62, 148
Ethics and Anti-Corruption Commission (Kenya), 115
Ethiopia, 108, 109–110, 148
EU. *See* European Union
Eurasian Economic Union, 49
Europe, Western, 63, 64, 127, 147, 148, 155, 156, 159
European financial crisis, 58
European Parliament, 62, 64
European Union (EU), 61, 62, 64, 123, 127
Europe-China Railway Express. *See* Iron Silk Road
exclusive economic zone (EEZ), 23–24, 26
Exim Bank, 9, 48, 56, 93, 96, 112, 121, 145, 151
   Addis Ababa-Djibouti railway funded by, 109
   Coca Codo Sinclair hydroelectric dam financed by, 141
   concessional loans from, 138
   debt owed to, 61–62, 161
   Gabon BRI project financing from, 137
   Mombasa-Nairobi Standard Gauge Railway underwritten by, 110
   Philippines funding from, 80
   South Sudan's crude oil export to, 111
Export-Import Bank of China, 8, 59
ExxonMobil, 151

Fanell, James, 22
FDI. *See* foreign direct investment

Federated States of Micronesia, 158
5G telecommunication systems, Huawei developing, 145, 147, 148
Five-Year Plan (PRC), 14, 132, 143
food security, 57–58, 82
foreign direct investment (FDI), 14, 48, 60, 64, 66, 99, 127
foreign policy
   PRC, 43, 44
   US, 21, 24–25, 153–154
Foreign Policy, 30
Forty Knights (Kyrgyz-Chorolor), 56
Forum on China-Africa Cooperation, 107
Fourth China-India Strategic and Economic Dialogue, 104
Foxconn, 149, 161
France, 155, 156
Freymann, Eyck, 15
Friendship Bridge (Maldives), 96

Gabon, Exim Bank financing for, 137
gas pipelines, 47–48, 50, 51
gas routes, 77
Gates, Robert, 26, 35
GDI. *See* global development initiative
GDP. *See* gross domestic product
General Agreement on Tariffs and Trade, 38
Germany, 147, 148, 159
GFC. *See* global financial crisis
Ghani, Ashraf, 47
Gilpin, Robert, 31, 35
global development initiative (GDI), 161–162
global financial crisis (GFC), xi, 17, 18, 19–21, 73, 132
Global Positioning System (GPS), 144
global security initiative (GSI), 161–162
Global Times, 99, 106

218 | Index

globalism, 5–6
gong fu (common prosperity), 149
Google, 147
Górski, Jędrzej, 15
GPS. *See* Global Positioning System
great recession. *See* global financial
  crisis
Greater Male Connectivity Project,
  96–97
Greece, 60
Greenland, 151–152
Griffith, Richard T., 16
gross domestic product (GDP), 18,
  88, 164
Group 42, 126
G7, xiii, 155, 156
GSI. *See* global security initiative
G20, 17
Guangxi Beibu Gulf International Port
  Group, 79–80
Guinea, 138
Gwadar CPEC port (Pakistan), 66–67,
  90, 102

Hadley, Stephen, 24–25
Hagel, Robert, 35
The Hague, South China Sea territorial
  dispute ruling of, 77–78
Hambantota port (Sri Lanka), 91, 92,
  93–94, 95
Health China 2030 program, 119
Health Silk Road (HSR), xii, 2, 5, 119
  China-Arab Health Cooperation
    Forum, 120
  COVID-19 pandemic diplomacy of,
    60, 117–118, 120–130
  faulty medical equipment from, 127
  Serbia assistance received from,
    60–61, 123–124, 128
Hiebert, Murray, 16
highway development projects, BRI,
  97–98, 138, 141
Hikvision, 147

Hillman, Jonathan E., 15–16, 156–157
Hishamuddin Hussein, 76
History of The Peloponnesian War
  (Thucydides), 169n1
Ho, Selina, 16
Hong Kong International Arbitration
  Centre, 136
How China Loses (Patey), 15
HSR. *See* Health Silk Road
Hu Jintao, 47
Hu Zhengyuan, 16
Huawei, 56, 62, 138, 145, 147, 148
Hulhule (Maldives), 96
human rights, 134, 154, 163, 164
human trafficking, 84
Hundred Year Marathon (Pillsbury),
  15, 42
Hungary, 61, 62, 124, 128

Ibrahim Nasir International Airport
  (Maldives), 96
ICT. *See* information and
  communication technology
IMF. *See* International Monetary Fund
Impeccable, USNS, 26
In the Dragon's Shadow (Strangio), 16
India, 33, 48
  BCIM, 97, 105
  China's relationship with, 101–107
  COVID-19 vaccines from, 130
  Global Times editorial on, 99
  joint naval exercises with, 102–103
  Kashmir administered by, 51, 52,
    102
  MSR impacting, 89, 91, 100–106,
    107
  Pakistan's encirclement policy
    against, 67–68
  SCO membership of, 51, 52–53
  Sri Lanka influenced by, 102–103,
    158
  string of pearls strategy against,
    90–91, 101

territorial disputes with, 51, 52, 87, 104

Indian Ocean, 89, 90–91, 101, 106

Indonesia, 11, 83
  Jakarta–Bandung high-speed rail project in, 84
  MSR initiative in, 73, 76
  Sinovac COVID-19 vaccines accepted in, 124
  Weda Bay Industrial Park's projects in, 80

Indo-Pacific Strategy, 52, 139

information and communication technology (ICT), 59, 75, 112, 144–145

Interior Ministry of Kyrgyzstan, 56

International Development Finance Corporation, 155

International Monetary Fund (IMF), 10, 39, 68

Internet Data Centre (Dar es Salaam, Tanzania), 112, 116

Iran, 50
  Chabahar port of, 103
  HSR diplomacy to, 128
  PRC bilateral partnership agreement with, 56–57
  SCO membership of, 53

Iron Silk Road, 55, 60, 62

Islamic State, 97

IT Security Law 2.0 (Germany), 147

Italy, 63–64, 123, 127, 148

Jack Ma, 122

Jaishankar, Subrahmanyam, 101–102

Jaish-e-Mohammed group (JeM), 52

Jakarta–Bandung high-speed rail project (Indonesia), 84

Japan, 80, 159
  Asian Forum for Polar Sciences initiated by, 152
  Bangladesh FDI from, 99
  chip manufacturing tools from, 149
  Diaoyu/Senkaku Island claim of, 23–25
  territorial disputes with, 87

Japan-Guam-Australia fiber-optic submarine cable system project, 148

JeM. See Jaish-e-Mohammed group

Jiang Zemin, 45

Johnson, Christopher, 41

Kamuzora, Faustin, 112

Karot Hydropower Project (Pakistan), 66, 68

Kashgar, China, 47

Kashmir
  Indian-administered, 51, 52, 102
  Pakistan-held, 51, 52, 102

Kazakhstan, 7, 11, 48, 49, 55

Kenya, 108, 110–111, 115, 116, 125

Keohane, Robert O., 15

Kerry, John, 25, 28–29, 37, 165

Khan, Imran, 68, 69

Khorgas, China, 47

Khyber-Pakhtunkhwa (KPK) (Pakistan), 68, 69

Kiribati, 139

Kondapalli, Srikanth, 101

KPK. See Khyber-Pakhtunkhwa

Kuik, Cheng-chwee, 16

Kyrgyz-Chorolor (Forty Knights), 56

Kyrgyzstan, 48, 49, 55–56

Lagos–Kano standard metrics Nigeria Railway Modernization Project (Nigeria), 137

Lampton, David, 16

Laos, 76–77, 78–79, 82, 83

Larson, Deborah Welch, 3

Latin America, 125, 130, 140–142

Latvia, 62, 148

Lee Kuan Yew, 1, 166

Li Keqiang, 65–66

220 | Index

Liaoning Health Silk Road Action Adolescents Eye Health Comprehensive Project, 118
Liow Tiong Lai, 86
LIPCs. *See* local investment platform companies
Lithuania, China-CEEC withdrawal of, 62
Liu Mingfu, 42
loans
  from China Development Bank, 145
  Exim Bank's concessional, 138
  Russo-Ukrainian war impacting, 156
  Zambia defaulting on, 157–158
local investment platform companies (LIPCs), 18
lockdowns, COVID-19 pandemic, 149, 161, 166
Lotus Tower (Colombo, Sri Lanka), 95
Lukashenko, Alexander, 62
Lumbini (Nepal), 100

Maçães, Bruno, 16
Macclesfield Bank *(Zhongsha)* (South China Sea), 28
Macron, Emmanuel, 163
Made in China 2025 initiative, 20, 132–133, 143
Magufuli, John, 112
Mahathir Mohammed, 82, 85
Maina, Kariuki, 115
Malaysia, 73, 76, 79–80, 82, 85, 144
Maldives, 96–97, 102–103
Maritime Silk Road (MSR), xi, 7, 42, *42*
  ASEAN impacted by, 72, 88–89
  in East Africa, 108–116
  in Latin America, 140
  Pan-Asian railway of, 78–79
  PLAN's geostrategic intentions with, 87

political mistrust against, 75–76, 80–81
  in South Asia, 89–100, 105–107
  in Southeast Asia, 72–107
  sovereignty concerns regarding, 81–83
  US-China rivalry over, 71, 73–74, 75, 81–82
  Xi's involvement with, 73, 96, 140
The Maritime Silk Road (Griffith), 16
Mauritius, 102–103
Meituan, 148–149
memorandums of understanding (MOUs), 98
Mexico, 141
military
  Chinese, 20, 40, 67, 72, 160
  junta, 32, 85
  US, 32, 36, 46–47, 158, 167
Millennium Challenge Corp., Nepal's ratification of, 100
Miller, Tom, 15
Ming dynasty, 74
Ministry of Defense (China), 25
Ministry of Foreign Affairs (China), 8, 157
Mischief Reef (South China Sea), 26
Moderna COVID-19 vaccines, 122, 129, 130
Modi, Narendra, 51, 102, 103
Mohamand Dam (Pakistan), 68
Mombasa-Nairobi Standard Gauge Railway (Kenya), 110–111, 115, 116
Monroe Doctrine, 29
Montenegro, 61–62
MOUs. *See* memorandums of understanding
MSR. *See* Maritime Silk Road
Murray, Michelle, 3
Musharraf, Pervez, 67

Mwalimu Julius Nyerere Leadership
School (Tanzania), 114
Myanmar, 135
BCIM through, 97, 105
Kyaukpyu port in, 84
military junta of, 32, 85
Myitsone Dam protests in, 84–85
oil and natural gas corridor of, 77
Pan-Asian railway in, 78

Najib Razak, 76, 82
Nansha. See Spratly Islands
National Defense Authorization Act,
US (2013), 25
National Defense Transportation Law
(China), 72
National Development and Reform
Commission (China), 7, 8
National Intelligence Law (China), 146
NATO. *See* North Atlantic Treaty
Organization
Nepal, 99–100
New York Convention on the
Recognition and Enforcement of
Arbitral Awards (1958), 136
Nigeria, railway development projects
in, 137
North Atlantic Treaty Organization
(NATO), 53
nuclear icebreakers, 151
Nuclear Non-Proliferation Treaty, 107
Nuclear Suppliers Group, 107
Nye, Joseph S., 15, 24–25
Nyerere Bridge (Tanzania), 111–112,
116

Obama, Barack, 17, 41
ASEAN Treaty of Amity and
Cooperation signed by, 32, 34–35
on defense spending cuts, 36
on Diaoyu/Senkaku Islands, 24, 25

on Pivot to Asia, 27, 30, 40
on South China Sea disputes, 27–28
Obama administration, 24, 27, 30–42,
42
Office of the Leading Group on
Promoting the Implementation of
Belt and Road Initiatives, 7
oil pipelines, 47–48
oil routes, to China, 64–65, 67, 77
oil supply, Russo-Ukrainian war
disrupting, 54
Okinawa Archipelago, Diaoyu/Senkaku
Islands within, 23–24
Olympics, Beijing, 17, 54
Omicron variant, COVID-19, 129,
161, 166
"One Belt, One Road" (Belt-and-Road
Initiative), 7
One Belt One Road (Freymann), 15
"open-door" reforms, 18
Orban, Viktor, 61
organized crime, 84

Pacific Island nations, 140, 158
Pakistan, 48, 135. *See also* China-
Pakistan Economic Corridor
anti-Chinese sentiment in, 69
Gwadar port in, 66–67, 90, 102
HSR in, 118
India encirclement policy of, 67–68
Kashmir held by, 51, 52, 102
SCO membership of, 51, 52
terrorism in, 158
Pan-Asian railway, 78–79
Panetta, Leon, 32, 33
Papua New Guinea (PNG), 139, 158
Paracel Islands *(Xisha)* (South China
Sea), 22, 26, 28, 77–78, 87
Partnership for Global Infrastructure
and Investment, of G7, xiii, 156
Patey, Luke, 15

222 | Index

Peloponnesian War, 169n1
Penh, Phnom, 76, 82–83
People's Liberation Army (PLA), 23
People's Liberation Army Navy
(PLAN), 76, 87, 94, 108
People's Republic of China (PRC). *See specific topics*
Permanent Court of Arbitration, 37
Peru, 141–142
Pew Research Center, 164
Pfizer COVID-19 vaccines, 122, 123, 129
Philippines, 37, 84, 157
COVID-19 vaccines in, 124, 130
Exim Bank funding in, 80
leadership changes in, 85
MSR participation of, 77–78
Visiting Forces Agreement in, 81
Pillsbury, Michael, 15, 42
Pivot to Asia
alliance strengthening and
intra-Asian security network
encouragement in, 32–33
ARF in, 34
ASEAN Defense Ministers' Meeting
involvement of, 35
China's response to, 37–42, *42*
East Asia Summit involvement of, 34–35
Obama administration initiative of, 27, 30–42, *42*
Trans-Pacific Partnership of, 33–34, 40, 73
US military force repositioning in, 32, 36
PLA. *See* People's Liberation Army
PLAN. *See* People's Liberation Army Navy
PNG. *See* Papua New Guinea
Polar Silk Road, xii, 2, 5, 150–152, 159
Port City Project (Colombo, Sri Lanka), 91, 92

ports
Bagamoyo, 112, 116
Chabahar, 103
Chancay Port Terminal, 142
China constructing, 72, 90–91
in Djibouti, 109
in Gwadar, 66–67, 90, 102
of Hambantota, 91, 92, 93–94, 95
in Indian Ocean littoral, 90–91
in Kyaukpyu, 84
Power and Interdependence (Keohane and Nye), 15
Power of Siberia natural gas pipeline, 50
power transition. *See specific topics*
power transition theory, xiii, 2, 3–4, 5, 37–38, 163–164, 167
Prayut Chan-o-cha, 124, 125
PRC. *See* People's Republic of China
PRC National Health and Family Planning Commission, 118
propaganda, of China, 134
protests, 84–85, 94
Putin, Vladimir, Xi's relationship with, 50, 54, 163

Qian Gang, 19
Qwant, 147

rail projects
Abuja–Kaduna railway, 137
Addis Ababa-Djibouti railway, 109
Budapest-Belgrade railway, 61
Iron Silk Road, 55, 60, 62
Jakarta–Bandung high-speed, 84
Mombasa-Nairobi Standard Gauge Railway, 110–111, 115, 116
Pan-Asian railway, 78–79
Tanzanian Standard Gauge Railway, 112–113
Rajapaksa, Gotabaya, 95–96
Rajapaksa, Mahinda, 91–92, 93, 94, 95–96

RATS. *See* Regional Anti-Terrorist Structure
RCEP. *See* Regional Comprehensive Economic Partnership
realpolitik, 13, 64
Ream naval base (Cambodia), 160
Red Sea, 107–116
Regional Anti-Terrorist Structure (RATS), 45–46
Regional Comprehensive Economic Partnership (RCEP), 40
renewable energy, 55, 56, 82, 104
Rimpac exercise, 37
Rio Tinto, 138
Rivers of Iron (Lampton, Ho, and Kuik), 16
Rosenberg, Jerry M., 16
Russia, 49–50, 53–54, 152, 159, 163
Russo-Ukrainian war, 6, 54, 57, 62–63, 156, 159
Ruto, William, 115
Rwanda, 113

sanctions, 56, 64, 131
Sansha City (Three-sha City) (PRC), 28
Saudi Arabia, 145, 159
Scarborough Shoal (South China Sea), 22, 28
SCO. *See* Shanghai Cooperation Organization
sea, control and denial of, 20
second track dialogue mechanism, 12–13
secretariat, SCO, 45
security, 135
  between China and India, 101–103
  CPEC challenges, 68–69, 158
  from DeWe Security Service, 116
  energy, 77
  global security initiative, 161–162
  in Indian Ocean, 106
  intra-Asian relations on, 32–33, 34, 88
  SCO, 46–47

self-driving vehicles, 144
Semiconductor Manufacturing International Corp., 148
Senegal, 137–138, 156
SenseTime, 144, 145
Serbia, 60–61, 62, 123–124, 128, 146
Seychelles, 102–103
al-Shabab terrorist group, 115
Shambaugh, David, 16
Shanghai Cooperation Organization (SCO), 54–56, 63
  cultural-education exchanges, 50–51
  economics, 47–49, 57
  external and Sino-Russian cooperation, 49–50
  membership of, 44–45, 51, 52–53
  security, 46–47
  SREB developing from, 43–44, 58
Shanghai Cooperation Organization Interbank Consortium, 47–48
Shanghai spirit, 44
Sharif, Nawaz, 65–66
Shevchenko, Alexei, 3
shi (strategic configuration of forces), 39
Siberia, 151, 152
Silk Road, 7, 10, 41, 95
Silk Road Economic Belt (SREB), xi, 7, 42, *42*, 43–44, 45, 58, 159
Silk Road Fund, 8, 42, 48, 66, 97, 145, 151, 161
Silk Road International Bank, 109
Singapore, 1, 77, 82, 129, 156
Sino-CEE Fund, 59
Sinohydro Corp., 61, 93, 141, 142
Sino-Indian rivalry, in Indian Ocean, 90–91, 101, 106
Sinopec, 159
Sinopharm COVID-19 vaccines, 123, 125–126, 128, 129, 142
Sino-Russian relations, 49–50, 53–54
Sinovac COVID-19 vaccines, 123, 124, 125, 129
Sirisena, Maithripala, 92, 93, 95

224 | Index

Sogavare, Manasseh, 139
Solih, Ibrahim Mohamed, 96
Solomon Islands, 139–140, 145
Somalia, al-Shabab terrorist group in, 115
South Asia, 89–100, 102–103, 105–107, 118, 124, 158, 160
South China Sea
  Paracel Islands in, 22, 26, 28, 77–78, 87
  Spratly Islands in, 22, 28, 34, 77–78, 87
  US-China rivalry in, 26–29, 159
South Korea, Asian Forum for Polar Sciences initiated by, 152
South Pacific, 138–140
South Sudan, 108, 111, 116
Southeast Asia. *See also* Association of Southeast Asian Nations
  arms purchase diversification in, 83
  Cambodia in, 33, 76, 78, 79, 82–83, 135, 160
  ethnic Chinese populations in, 86
  Malaysia, 73, 76, 79–80, 82, 85, 144
  MSR initiative in, 72–107
  Myanmar, 32, 77, 78, 84–85, 97, 105, 135
  security cooperation in, 88
  Singapore, 1, 77, 82, 129, 156
  Sinovac COVID-19 vaccines accepted in, 124
  South Korea in, 152
  Thailand, 77, 79, 83–84, 124, 129, 160
  Vietnam, 26–27, 77, 78, 81, 83, 148
South-South cooperation, 14, 118, 138, 162
sovereignty, 13, 81–83, 94, 142
SPFS, 50
Spratly Islands *(Nansha)* (South China Sea), 22, 28, 34, 77–78, 87
SREB. *See* Silk Road Economic Belt

Sri Lanka, 124
  Hambantota port in, 91, 92, 93–94, 95
  HSR in, 118
  India influencing, 102–103, 158
  joint naval exercises with, 102–103
  Lotus Tower in, 95
  MSR and, 91–96
  national debt of, 93
Sri Maha Bodhi Temple (Anuradhapura, Sri Lanka), 95
State Administration for Market Regulation (China), 149
State Grid Corp., Chilean energy companies purchased by, 142
Steinberg, James, 24–25
Strait of Hormuz, 67
Strait of Malacca, 77
Strangio, Sebastian, 16
strategic configuration of forces *(shi)*, 39
The Strategy of "One Belt One Road" (Zhengyuan), 16
string of pearls, around Indian Ocean, 90–91, 101
Suez Canal economic zone (Egypt), 113, 116
Supreme Court, China's, 136
surveillance, by PRC government, 126
Swazuri, Muhammad, 115
Sweden, 151
SWIFT international financial managing system, 50

Taiwan, 13, 139, 140, 149
Tajikistan, 48
Taliban regime, 47, 128–129
Tanzania, 108, 111–113, 114, 116
tariffs, 38, 131, 133, 154
territorial disputes
  with India, 51, 52, 87, 104
  South China Sea, 22, 26–29, 34, 77–78, 87, 159

terrorism
China and India impacted by, 107
in Pakistan, 158
RATS against, 45–46
SCO security against, 46–47
of al-Shabab, 115
Thailand, 83–84
Chinese military Falcon Strike
exercise with, 160
HSR COVID-19 diplomacy to, 124,
129
MSR participation of, 77, 79
Pan-Asian railway in, 79
Thiès–Touba Toll Expressway (Senegal),
138
Thousand Talents Program, 19–20,
132–133, 143
Three-sha City (Sansha City) (PRC),
28
"Three-Year Implementation Plan
for Advancing Belt-and-Road
Initiative Health Cooperation
(2015–2017)" (PRC National
Health and Family Planning
Commission), 118
Thucydides, 169n1
Tillerson, Rex, 114
Tonga, 139
tourism, 97, 100
Trans-Pacific Partnership (TPP), 33–
34, 40, 73
Treaty of Amity and Cooperation,
ASEAN, 32, 34–35
Trump, Donald, 34, 39, 40, 52, 153,
154, 155
Trump administration, 92, 121, 131,
133, 154
Turkey, 53, 57, 125

UAE. *See* United Arab Emirates
Uganda, 113
UN. *See* United Nations
Under Beijing's Shadow (Hiebert), 16

United Arab Emirates (UAE), 125–
126, 145
United Nations (UN), 13, 60, 119
Commission on the Limits of the
Continental Shelf, 21
Convention on the Law of the Sea,
23–24, 27
Security Council, 56, 162
on South China Sea territorial
disputes, 77–78
United States (US), xi, 1–2
Alaska, 152
Build Back Better World of, xiii,
155, 156–157
defense spending cuts of, 36
dollar, 39, 40
East Asia ship visits from, 22
foreign policy, 21, 24–25, 153–154
Huawei banned by, 147
India's military coordination with,
103
Iran and Turkey's SCO membership
status antagonizing, 53
medical equipment manufacturing
in, 127
military, 32, 36, 46–47, 158, 167
Pivot to Asia, 27, 30–42, *42*, 73
2024 elections, 165, 166
University of Shanghai Cooperation
Organization, 51
US. *See* United States
US Coast Guard, 158
US Department of Defense, 90
US Innovation and Competition Act
(2021), 150, 157
US National Security Strategy report,
1–2
US State Department, 26
US-China rivalry, 2, 4, 14, 132, 162–
166, 167
in China seas, 21–29, 159
Chinese peoples public opinion on,
17, 19

226 | Index

US-China rivalry *(continued)*
  over MSR, 71, 73–74, 75, 81–82
  over tech, 148, 149
  over trade war, 131, 133, 154
  around Philippines, 81
  Pivot to Asia contestation of, 27,
    30–42, *42*
US-Japan Treaty of Mutual
  Cooperation and Security, 23, 25
Uyghur Muslim minority, China's
  alleged human rights violations
  against, 134, 154, 164
Uzbekistan, 46, 48, 56, 118

vaccines, COVID-19, 61, 121, 159
  BioNTech, 128, 129
  Moderna, 122, 129, 130
  Pfizer, 122, 123, 129
  Sinopharm, 123, 125–126, 128,
    129, 142
  Sinovac, 123, 124, 125, 129
Vanuatu, 139
Venezuela, 141
Vesterbacka, Peter, 62
Vietnam
  anti-Chinese sentiment in, 77, 83
  Cam Ranh Bay naval base of, 26–27
  5G in, 148
  MSR participation of, 77, 78, 81
  South China Sea islands disputes
    of, 26
  sovereignty concerns of, 81, 83
"Vision and Actions on Jointly
    Building Silk Road Economic Belt
    and 21st-Century Maritime Silk
    Road" (National Development
    and Reform Commission,
    Ministry of Foreign Affairs, and
    Ministry of Commerce), 8
Visiting Forces Agreement, in
    Philippines, 81
Voon, Thomas J., 88

Vucic, Aleksandar, 61, 123

Wang Jisi, 19
Wang Yi, 29, 121, 124, 140, 152,
    158, 160
war, 3, 5
  Peloponnesian War, 169n1
  Russo-Ukrainian, 6, 54, 57, 62–63,
    156, 159
  US-China trade, 131, 133, 154
"war on drugs," in Philippines, 78
Wen Jiabao, 17
Where Great Powers Meet (Shambaugh),
    16
White House, 40
WHO. *See* World Health Organization
Widodo, Joko, 76, 124
wind farm, in Kazakhstan, 55
World Bank, 10
World Health Organization (WHO),
    119, 120, 121, 123, 129, 170n1
World Trade Organization (WTO), 14,
    39, 153

Xi Jinping, 14, 41, 43, 74, 92, 129,
    164, 166, 167
  Bagamoyo port approved by, 112
  Bangladesh visit of, 98, 99
  Biden on, 153
  on Chinese military, 40
  common prosperity pushed by, 149
  on Diaoyu/Senkaku Islands, 24, 25
  GDI launched by, 161, 162
  on HSR, 118, 121
  leadership of, xi, 2, 4, 6, 7, 10, 17,
    37, 56, 90, 160, 163
  Made in China 2025 initiative of,
    20, 132–133, 143
  MSR involvement of, 73, 96, 140
  Putin's relationship with, 50, 54,
    163
Xinjiang, China, 47

Index | 227

Xinjiang (Uygur) Autonomous Region (China), 65, 154
Xisha. See Paracel Islands

Yamal liquefied natural gas project (Siberia), 151
Yameen, Abdulla, 96
Yan Xuetong, 40, 131
Yang Jiechi, 27, 152
Yangtze Memory Technologies, 149
Yanzhong, Huang, 122

Yavuz Sultan Selim Bridge (Turkey), 57
Yellen, Janet, 165
yidai yilu (Belt-and-Road Initiative), 7
Yin Weidong, 123
Yuan Wang 5, 158

Zambia, 157–158
Zelensky, Volodymyr, 62–63
Zheng He, 74
Zhongsha. See Macclesfield Bank
ZTE, 145, 146, 147, 148

www.ingramcontent.com/pod-product-compliance
Ingram Content Group UK Ltd.
Pitfield, Milton Keynes, MK11 3LW, UK
UKHW041832030225
454357UK00010B/12